TEACHING CHALLENGED AND CHALLENGING TOPICS IN DIVERSE AND INCLUSIVE LITERATURE

This groundbreaking text provides practical, contextualized methods for teaching and discussing topics that are considered "taboo" in the classroom in ways that support students' lived experiences. In times when teachers are scapegoated for adopting culturally sustaining teaching practices and are pressured to "whitewash" the curriculum, it becomes more challenging to create an environment where students and teachers can have conversations about complex, uncomfortable topics in the classroom. With contributions from scholars and K-12 teachers who have used young adult literature to engage with their students, chapters confront this issue and focus on themes such as multilingualism, culturally responsive teaching, dis/ability, racism, linguicism, and gender identity. Using approaches grounded in socioemotional learning, trauma-informed practices, and historical and racial literacy, this text explores the ways in which books with complicated themes can interact positively with students' own lives and perspectives.

Ideal for courses on ELA and literature instruction, this book provides a fresh set of perspectives and methods for approaching and engaging with difficult topics. As young adult literature that addresses difficult subjects is more liable to be considered "controversial" to teach, teachers will benefit from the additional guidance this volume provides, so that they can effectively reach the very students these themes address.

Rachelle S. Savitz is Associate Professor of Reading/Literacy at East Carolina University, USA.

Leslie D. Roberts is Assistant Professor of Reading at Georgia Southern University, USA.

Jason DeHart received his Ph.D. from the University of Tennessee, Knoxville, USA.

TEACHING CHALLENGED AND CHALLENGING TOPICS IN DIVERSE AND INCLUSIVE LITERATURE

Addressing the Taboo in the English Classroom

Edited by Rachelle S. Savitz, Leslie D. Roberts, and Jason DeHart

Routledge
Taylor & Francis Group

NEW YORK AND LONDON

Cover image: © Getty Images

First published 2023
by Routledge
605 Third Avenue, New York, NY 10158

and by Routledge
4 Park Square, Milton Park, Abingdon, Oxon, OX14 4RN

Routledge is an imprint of the Taylor & Francis Group, an informa business

© 2023 Taylor & Francis

The right of Rachelle S. Savitz, Leslie D. Roberts, and Jason DeHart to
be identified as the authors of the editorial material, and of the authors
for their individual chapters, has been asserted in accordance with
sections 77 and 78 of the Copyright, Designs and Patents Act 1988.

ISBN: 978-1-032-29821-4 (hbk)
ISBN: 978-1-032-28302-9 (pbk)
ISBN: 978-1-003-30221-6 (ebk)

DOI: 10.4324/9781003302216

Typeset in Bembo
by Apex CoVantage, LLC

CONTENTS

FOREWORD
The Necessity of Teaching Taboo Topics

Stergios Botzakis

My introduction to teaching middle school was a rude awakening. I was in my early twenties, had moved to a new city without a job, and finally found what I felt was my dream gig, teaching reading. Things were lining up for me, and when I got my first paycheck I went out and celebrated with my friends. I had a little bit too much to drink, closed down one establishment, and was walking to another with my friends when I saw a couple of figures walking toward us on a dark street. One of my friends made an off-color joke to them, and I then realized that one of them was a student in my homeroom, a sixth grader. The other, I later learned, was a fifth grader who also attended the K-8 school where I taught. Panicked, and in an altered state, I yelled at my friend, "You dumb duck!" (not the actual word I used) "I teach those kids!" I immediately realized what I had just done, looked straight ahead and walked away as fast as I could, hoping against hope that the kid had not recognized me. That hope was quickly dashed on Monday morning, as the student walked into class smiling a huge, Cheshire cat grin.

"I saw you Friday night. You cussed at your friend!" the student gushed, then immediately began to spread the gossip with neighbors. I cut in, said I knew that they were going to talk about it, but asked that they please do it outside of my presence. The student was respectful and catered to my request, and I saved a little face, at least in that moment.

That event colored my perceptions of my students for the entire year and still sticks with me to this day, hence my relating this anecdote to you. I was shocked that with all that transpired what made an impression was that I dropped an F-bomb. But more so I was gobsmacked that a couple of kids, 11- and 12-year-olds, were walking down a dark, urban street late at night, unattended. That was not the reality where I was raised, and I wondered what kinds of things these students observed on a regular basis.

Over the next few years teaching these students and living in the neighborhood where I taught, I learned a lot about these adolescents. They were worldly beyond what I was at their ages. Some of them drank alcohol, and some of them saw me when I was drinking alcohol. They had questions for me, and I answered them as honestly as I could. I felt that dodging their queries was not an option when they came from a sincere place, and I also knew that if I could do something to help demystify drinking, it may have a positive impact on some of them. I tried to impress on them that I was of an age where it was legal for me to do so, and that they were still young and growing and needed to take better care of their brains and bodies. I always made sure to tell them that I was talking about my own personal views and that I was not telling them what to do, that I was not their parent, just an older person trying to share my version of wisdom. It was my introduction to teaching taboo topics. I also did not know it then, but it was my introduction to dialogic teaching (Fecho & Botzakis, 2007), a way of interacting with students in a way that valued their input in co-constructing knowledge.

I tried to make my classroom a safe space for multiple topics, for students to ask genuine questions that they had about the world, a place where they were valued and could get an adult's honest opinion on a topic. I even pitched in for some of my colleagues, a pair of sisters who taught a self-contained 6–8 grade classroom, when it came time for "the talk." I assembled half of their class, the boys, while they talked with the girls about sex. I read to them from a dated picture book and then had them write down questions they had for me to answer, so they could be anonymous. Their questions ranged from innocent ones like "How do you tell a girl you like her?" to more detailed ones about sexually transmitted diseases and specific acts and whether they could result in pregnancy, making me realize that some of them were pretty active, if in need of some knowledge. Needless to say, conversations sometimes pushed my comfort zone farther than I would have liked. I realize now that it is not in every teacher's purview to delve into these discussions as I did, and that some of these areas could seriously jeopardize one's employment, but I do not regret having them.

Today's Taboo Topics and Taboo Texts

What is considered taboo can change over time. Books that were once considered scandalous because they tackled issues like divorce or bullying might seem more quaint or acceptable today. Some topics, however remain forbidden, including, not surprisingly, sex. Consulting the American Library Association's (2022) most recent list of frequently challenged books, I found that nine out of the ten titles were included because of what some have called inappropriate sexual content. However, taboos do not just entail topics that some find discomfiting. After perusing multiple definitions of taboo, I found that most point to it as something prohibited, forbidden, or avoided due to societal or religious customs. One thing that is apparent from these definitions is that what is considered taboo comes from places of privilege and authority, and that taboo topics are those largely marginalized and at the short end of societal power relations. Just as I had come from a place of privilege as a middle school teacher, not being able to relate to the freewheeling ways some of my students were allowed to roam the streets, something I had to actively tell myself not to judge, so too does privilege affect what else is considered taboo.

An example of how taboo is enacted via social categories lies in the second most prevalent reason why books were challenged in 2021, according to the ALA: depictions of LGBTQIA+ (their designation) characters and issues. I will describe what I mean here by reference to a YA graphic novel I have recently read, Mike Curato's (2020) Lambda Literary Award-winning *Flamer*.

"This book will save lives," wrote Jarrett J. Krosoczka for a cover blurb for *Flamer*. Such a statement might seem hyperbolic, a huge import placed on a single text, but I feel it is apt, a testament to what happens when people engage with taboo topics. This book, set in the 1990s and about an adolescent named Aiden who attends summer camp just before entering into high school, explores his inner turmoil about his sexuality. He knows that being gay is bad, because of what he has learned from his religious upbringing. He also does not much like boys because many of them bully him. Still, he finds solace in some friendships, and one in particular with a kind boy named Elias, whom he cannot stop thinking about. Isolation and his inner monologue drive him to question his feelings to the point where he starts contemplating doing violence against himself.

Flamer is a deeply personal book, based on Curato's own experiences, and it brings to light an experience that is often regarded as taboo and kept hidden. Such frank discussions of sexual orientation are largely considered taboo in contemporary US culture, and just like Aiden from *Flamer*, at this point in time, LGBTQ youth get messages from social and religious authorities that they are inferior, unnatural, and even undesirable and that books about them do not belong in schools. The taboo concerning LGBTQ youth has palpable effects, as the Center for Disease Control and Prevention (CDC, 2016) reported that "gay, bisexual, and other men who have sex with men are at even greater risk for suicide attempts, especially before the age of 25," and also that "a study of youth in grades 7–12 found that lesbian, gay, and bisexual youth were more than twice as likely to have attempted suicide as their heterosexual peers" (para. 2). The Trevor Project (2019) reported from their most recent survey that "42% of LGBTQ youth seriously considered attempting suicide in the past year, including more than half of transgender and nonbinary youth" (para. 4).

This situation is amplified by anti-LGBTQ laws about education in several states, including some like Texas and Alabama that specifically state that "students must be taught that being gay 'is not a lifestyle acceptable to the general public'" (Lambda Legal, 2022, para. 3). Other states bar teachers even discussing LGBTQ people, such as South Carolina, which by law "forbids discussing 'homosexual relationships' in comprehensive health education, except to discuss sexually transmitted diseases" (para. 3). So, in these contexts LGBTQ youth receive explicit messages that they are deviant and potentially diseased. One extension of this mindset also puts LGBTQ youth in harm's way, with almost 40% of LGBTQ high school youth reporting being bullied at school (CDC, 2019, para. 14), making them vulnerable to verbal and physical trauma.

Thus, what Curato has detailed in fictionalized fashion has a basis in reality and is often something suffered in silence and seclusion. Having a fairly high-profile text like this available to students for instruction or in a library might help someone realize that they are not alone in what they are experiencing, others have felt the same way, and they may have found a kindred spirit in Aiden. This book might help these individuals find a way to keep going.

Other Taboo Texts

Flamer is an example of one book that I have recently read that places a spotlight on an individual who gets marginalized due to their involvement with a societal taboo. Although LGBTQ issues are the reason why half of the top ten most challenged books were targeted, it was not the sole taboo represented on the list, and not the only category that focuses on marginalized youth. Two of the titles most targeted for challenges, Ashley Hope Perez's *Out of Darkness* and Toni Morrison's *The Bluest Eye* were singled out for their depictions of sexual abuse, even though such instances occur with alarming frequency. According to the Rape, Abuse & Incest National Network (2022), "one in 9 girls and 1 in 53 boys under the age of 18 experience sexual abuse or assault at the hands of an adult" (para. 2), with the victim being acquainted with the abuser a shocking 93% of the time. It seems to me that challenging these books does an extreme disservice to young people who might have experienced such violence, and who often do not report the crime.

Another book that features prominently on the ALA challenged book list is Angie Thomas's *The Hate U Give*, for being anti-police and a piece of social indoctrination. This situation persists amid a time of social turmoil, where there have been multiple, prominent instances of police violence against Black people. According to statistics quoted by the Brookings Institute (Schindler & Kittredge, 2020), such violence is a phenomenon, considering "of all Black people killed by police, Black emerging adults [ages 20–24] accounted for 31 percent, despite representing only 12 percent of the Black population and just one percent of the entire U.S. population" (para. 6). Such a statistic should be alarming, and a book that reflects this reality could do a great service to all young people, but perhaps especially those who would be such casualties.

Legislation That Enforces Taboos

The battle over who and what are considered taboo topics does not just occur in classrooms and libraries, it also exists in state legislatures, with increasing amounts of laws being passed that target specific identity categories and even languages. Such political action takes place even when, according to the Office of Population Affairs (2022), in 2019 nearly half of US adolescents identified as a racial or ethnic minority (para. 5). Laws banning teachers from engaging in speaking about controversial topics like Critical Race Theory have been prominent in news stories, but there are other subtler ways that legislation has been enacted to marginalize students by making their literacy practices taboo.

For instance, many states are by law "English-only," with several even going so far as to dictate that all instruction and assessment must be in English. Such a move marginalizes those whose first language is not English, which could affect "about 23% of school-age children [who] spoke a language other than English at home, and 4% of school-age children [who] both spoke a language other than English at home and had difficulty speaking English" (Federal Interagency Forum on Child and Family Statistics, 2021, para. 3). Such action seems cruel, cutting off young people from their home languages and ham-stringing them in terms of potential learning opportunities. They run the risk of being marginalized even more by not being given access to language necessary for learning.

Such laws also smack of the persistent anti-immigrant stance taken by the United States, dating back to colonial times and affecting all sorts of ethnic groups, including the Chinese, the Irish, Italians, Jews, and Latinos, who were blamed for usurping people's jobs, violent crime, and other social ills. Recent statistics indicate that "22% of young people ages 14 to 24 were foreign-born or lived with at least one foreign-born parent in 2015–2019" (Annie E. Casey Foundation, 2021, para. 18), so young people from immigrant families may account for almost a quarter of all school-aged students. It is harmful to have so many deemed "illegal," and be considered taboo just for existing.

The Necessity for This Book

Looking at learning as a dialogic process, I contend that meaning is so dependent on context that it remains forever in process, at the intersection of centripetal tensions—those forces that usually represent collective authority and seek to stabilize and center—and centrifugal tensions—those forces that usually represent individual interpretation and seek to diversify and pull outward. It's not an either/or proposition. Language is constantly being tugged in opposite directions (Fecho & Botzakis, 2007, p. 551). So is language learning constantly being tugged in opposite directions.

Considering the maelstrom of the contemporary educational milieu, there are multiple ways that taboo topics can be operationalized to constrict and/or expand learning. By refusing to acknowledge particular realities, by excluding so-called deviants, and by depriving them of opportunities to use their home languages, there are those who would deny students access to specific texts and ideas, attempting to keep these taboo topics on the margins and, by extension, to rob them of opportunities to gain any social power. However, the converse is also in play. There are those who would provide potentially marginalized students with the texts, the activities, and occasions to engage with taboo topics, to recognize the power in various types of representation and instances where they can exercise their own agency. They can see themselves as powerful authors of their own lives and important contributors to society. That is the power of this book. Taking these chapters as a whole, readers will find texts, practices, and pedagogy that will save lives.

— Stergios Botzakis

References

American Library Association. (2022). *Top 10 most challenged book lists*. www.ala.org/advocacy/bbooks/frequentlychallengedbooks/top10

Annie E. Casey Foundation. (2021, October 21). *Who are children in immigrant families?* www.aecf.org/blog/who-are-the-children-in-immigrant-families

Center for Disease Control and Prevention. (2016). *Suicide and violence prevention*. www.cdc.gov/msmhealth/suicide-violence-prevention.htm

Center for Disease Control and Prevention. (2020). *Interpersonal violence victimization among high school students—Youth risk behavior survey, United States, 2019*. www.cdc.gov/mmwr/volumes/69/su/su6901a4.htm?s_cid=su6901a4_w

Curato, M. (2020). *Flamer*. Henry Holt and Co. BYR.

Fecho, B., & Botzakis, S. (2007). Feasts of becoming: Imagining a literacy classroom based on dialogic beliefs. *Journal of Adolescent & Adult Literacy, 50*(7), 548–558.

Federal Interagency Forum on Child and Family Statistics. (2021). *America's children: Key national indicators of well-being*. www.childstats.gov/americaschildren/family5.asp

Lambda Legal. (2022). *#DontEraseUs: FAQ about anti-LGBT curriculum laws*. www.lambdalegal.org/dont-erase-us/faq

Office of Population Affairs. (2022). *America's diverse adolescents*. https://opa.hhs.gov/adolescent-health/adolescent-health-facts/americas-diverse-adolescents

Rape, Abuse & Incest National Network. (2022). *Children and teens: Statistics*. www.rainn.org/statistics/children-and-teens

Schindler, M., & Kittredge, J. (2020, December 2). *A crisis within a crisis: Police killings of Black emerging adults*. www.brookings.edu/blog/how-we-rise/2020/12/02/a-crisis-within-a-crisis-police-killings-of-black-emerging-adults/

The Trevor Project. (2019). *National survey on LGBTQ mental health*. www.thetrevorproject.org/wp-content/uploads/2019/06/The-Trevor-Project-National-Survey-Results-2019.pdf

INTRODUCTION

*Rachelle S. Savitz, Leslie D. Roberts,
and Jason DeHart*

Over the past few years, like many of you, we have heard how we are teaching in strange times right now. Indeed, times keep getting stranger and, for many, more volatile as legislature and administrators force teachers to "agree" to new mandates and initiatives. Teachers are getting removed from classrooms for teaching true history inclusive of all perspectives, and books are being culled from shelves because the content is inappropriate. Educators and students are forced into new silos and told that there is only one "right" or "correct" way to teach their students.

At the time of our writing this introduction, 28 states have introduced anti-CRT laws and book banning/culling that push school districts to create new policies that prohibit and prevent teachers from incorporating an inclusive and diverse curriculum. As teachers, we know the importance of implementing an inclusive and diverse curriculum because it promotes a safe space for students to ask questions, learn about diverse perspectives, and share personal lived experiences related to these crucial topics. Unfortunately, these new policies and restrictions resulting from anti-CRT laws often whitewash curriculum and instruction (Compton-Lilly et al., 2022), perpetuating disruptive and harmful mindsets. As Anyon (2005) and others have suggested, implemented curricula often reify, rather than challenge, social barriers. There is an intentional push to continue silencing all voices within and among those in the classroom.

This type of teaching and required instruction is problematic for many reasons, including how dominant narratives and curricula repeatedly silence historically marginalized voices and perspectives—which typically means people of color, speakers of languages other than English, and those living in poverty (Giroux & Penna, 1979; Muhammad & Haddix, 2016; Tatum & Muhammad, 2012). Focusing solely or predominantly on dominant cultural norms further marginalizes students from diverse racial and ethnic backgrounds (Madrigal-Garcia & Acevedo-Gil, 2016; Milner, 2020). And while some teachers from the dominant culture may not realize the impact, students see and feel it when instruction does not include or value them and their diversity (Picower, 2021).

While this may not be a complete surprise to the readers of this book, knowing and understanding the changing demographics of US schools is crucial as students are more culturally, linguistically, and economically diverse. Diverse students are the fastest growing and most heterogeneous group in US classrooms (Herrera et al., 2020). According to the National Center for Education Statistics (2020), the percentage of White and Black students is decreasing, to some degree, while the percentage of Hispanic students is notably increasing. Krogstad (2019) noted that the Latinx population made up 18% of the United States' total population and projected that Latinx children would soon account for 52.9% of public students in K–12 education. Additionally, the percentage of first- and second-generation immigrants has increased (NCES, 2020; Zong et al., 2020).

This is particularly important because the demographics of teachers remain overwhelmingly White, monolingual, and female, despite changes in students' demographics (NCES, 2020). The discrepancies between the stagnant changes in the teacher population and the rapidly changing student demographics could often lead to teacher misconceptions and assumptions about students and their behaviors. These misconceptions often influence classroom issues, from increased student behavior referrals to the inappropriate use of texts and materials (Au, 2012; Matias, 2013).

As an editorial team, we continue to witness educators standing up for themselves and their students, using hashtags such as #diversebooks, #BlackLivesMatter, #TransLivesMatter, and #untilallcanread. And we wanted to be part of taking a stand by uplifting teachers' voices and teaching practices that value culturally, linguistically, racially, and economically diverse students and their lived experiences. This project has come to fruition based on how many teachers tackle challenges and silencing instead of using and embedding culturally sustaining practices. Our background and experiences are not only related to affirming and cherishing the unique backgrounds and experiences of those we work with but also the beauty and power of children's literature, voices in middle-grade literature, and the transformative and affirming nature of young adult novels (Borsheim-Black & Sarigianides, 2019; Ivey & Johnston, 2015, 2018; Nikolajeva, 2016).

Why Do We Need to Know About Diversity?

More than likely, as you read the title of this next section, you had a dozen answers and responses. Like us, you chose to read this book because you value diversity and want to learn new ways to embed asset-based approaches within your instruction. However, it is essential for us to gently remind readers that many factors impact our students when they walk through the classroom door. And these factors all influence students' academic success and willingness to engage with others to learn and grow. For instance, some students may be experiencing a traumatic experience, such as divorce or the loss of a parent. Other students may be dealing with bullying because they are not "from America," while other students could be dealing with racist comments from friends, community members, and even teachers.

But other connections need to be made and often are not explicitly discussed in classrooms and across schools. Thinking deeper, consider your student demographics regarding the impact and connection between historically marginalized communities and poverty (Fisher et al., 2020; Bethell et al., 2017). For example, in 2018, 18% of children, 13 million, had family incomes below the poverty line, while 32% of African American children and 26% of Latinx children lived in families with total incomes below the poverty line (Anne E. Casey Foundation, 2020). Another consideration is the connection between poverty and trauma. According to the 2017–2018 National Survey of Children's Health (2019), one of every three children between birth and age 17 had at least one Adverse Childhood Experience, and 14.1% had two or more ACEs in the past year. This survey also notes the inequitable distribution of trauma based on poverty and demographics. Twenty-two percent of children whose family income falls below the federal poverty level experienced two or more ACEs, whereas only 7.3% of children whose family income is four times the federal poverty level experienced two or more ACEs. A more significant percentage of non-Hispanic Black children experience two or more ACEs than non-Hispanic White children (21.3% vs. 12.9%). As Craig (2017) states, "those marginalized by race, sexual orientation, disability, poverty, or immigration status" are especially vulnerable (p. 5). Sadly, these statistics highlight the pervasiveness of trauma in children's and adolescents' lives.

At this point, you may be wondering why this isn't discussed more often during professional learning opportunities. Trust us, we also wonder this, especially when knowing the importance and cruciality of including all students' voices and input within instruction. Research has shown that there is much uncertainty regarding the implementation of inclusive education and various reasons teachers are hesitant to do so. At times, teachers fear not being "politically correct" (Coleman-King & Groenke, 2019; Tatum, 2000) during classroom lessons, including diverse perspectives and critical dialogue, and using inclusive "controversial" texts, all of which could result in community members or parents protesting their instructional practices. Another fear or concern is that teachers do not necessarily understand their biases or racial and cultural identities (Howard, 2010; Michael, 2015; Sue, 2015), leading them to unintentionally hold and teach from dominant cultural assumptions without being aware (Howard, 2016). This is common, as many people resist examining long-held racial beliefs, privileges, and biases (Borsheim-Black & Sarigianides, 2019; Sleeter, 2008; Tatum, 2015). And even then, many educators want to introduce dialogue, texts, and instruction that is more inclusive and exploratory of people who do not look or identify as they do. Still, they are unsure how and feel uncomfortable engaging with students without being more prepared.

Another prominent issue is teachers' choice to self-censor or not incorporate inclusive materials and pedagogy which is crucial because even if unconscious, convictions of educators influence their teaching and learning as a whole as these underlying, subtle beliefs produce a "silent curriculum" (Hosford, 1980). These underlying beliefs influence curricula, materials, pedagogy, and teacher attitudes toward students (Butler, 2017; Thomas, 2015). More importantly, race and other social constructs are crucial to understanding students' lived experiences and the inequitable practices they endure because of the dominant perspectives that impact learning, involvement inside and outside the classroom, and enjoyment in their educational learning.

As educators, we can intentionally select these experiences and situations within our instruction if we choose to evaluate what we ask of our students. We can step away from the whitewashed curriculum, instructional practices, and texts that center on dominant privileged perspectives (Giroux & Penna, 1979; Gutierrez et al., 2009; Muhammad, 2020; Muhammad & Haddix, 2016) that cause many of our historically marginalized students to feel shame, invisible, and left out of the conversation and instruction. If we allow that to continue in our classrooms, students and families will not feel like a welcomed part of the school system, souring their academic experience (Love, 2019; Muhammad, 2020) and perpetuating harmful ideologies and narratives.

You may be asking right now, "But what can we do? How do we push ourselves to be uncomfortable using instruction that focuses on critical dialogue and promotes a safe space to investigate race, ethnicity, sexual orientation and identity, socioeconomic status, and linguistic differences?" This type of questioning is pivotal to moving toward identity-affirming work that acknowledges and appreciates students' values, cultural identities, and lived experiences. And the authors of this book share many answers to these questions, often engaging in what we and others call "taboo" teaching.

What Is "Taboo"?

As an editorial team, when we discussed the term "taboo" and its meaning, we realized that many practices are considered "taboo" depending on many variables. For instance, taboo for teachers working in a conservative school or district may look like instruction or learning anything outside of the privileged dominant perspective or use of anything outside of the district-chosen textbook. For other educators, the instruction may be able to address oppression as it relates to race and ethnicity but not only on a surface level. This list of what is "allowed" to be discussed in classrooms and what is banned either by district officials, the community, or self-censorship is quite long and rarely changing.

While this list is not exhaustive, instruction and teaching that requires students to learn about and confront issues such as racism, linguicism, sexism/genderism, classism, ableism, heterosexism, ethnocentrism, religious oppression, Anti-Semitism, colorism, and ageism are crucial in classrooms, but often considered taboo if a school or district is against this necessary work. And unfortunately, the topics are not the only pieces being questioned in various states as politicians and community leaders are asking for critical school support such as social and emotional learning, trauma-sensitive practices, and culturally responsive-sustaining pedagogy.

We understand the "taboo" nature of these topics. Critical school support's potential restriction likely influences teachers' instruction and current teaching practices, prompting teachers to shy away from discussing these topics in the classroom. However, we posit that teachers must confront *and* disrupt the standard and current practices by creating more reflective and culturally appropriate educational experiences for students (Gorski, 2018). While confrontation might not seem like the most positive word, we advocate for a new understanding of the word "confront." In this text, we position the word "confront" as taking action to address the disparities in our world through our instruction, classroom practices, and interactions with students. Likewise, the chapters within our text show the multitude of ways educators can confront *and* disrupt the standard.

When we created our call for chapters, we expected to see a wide variety of how current teachers interpreted this word as we intentionally left our definition and request relatively broad. We cannot determine what "taboo" looks like for teachers across the United States. If we did, then we would essentially be saying that teachers' realities were not authentic or accurate, which goes against the intent of this book. We were surprised how teachers' instruction was framed differently across all chapters. While most chapters paid their respects to the revered Sims Bishop for her work on mirrors, windows, and sliding glass doors (1990), authors made connections to many other frameworks. Interestingly, when we initially proposed this chapter, we saw the relationships across frameworks and the theories that guided each author team's writing and instruction.

Theories That Can Relate to "Taboo" Instruction

There are quite a few ways research and literature frame "taboo" teaching, primarily through lenses that value culturally, linguistically, ethnically, racially, and socioeconomically different students. Across the chapters that follow, authors use frameworks that intentionally address inequitable instruction through curricula (Ladson-Billings, 2014, 2017; Muhammad, 2020; Paris, 2012) and frame their teaching practice as subversive teaching (Dyches et al., 2020), with many emphasizing the need for teachers and students to develop an awareness of historical, social, political, and economic impacts experienced by racially marginalized groups (Kinloch et al., 2020; Love, 2019; Muhammad, 2020; Tatum, 2009). Our authors attempt to address social inequities and critical perspectives through authentic practices (Ladson-Billings, 1995; Moje, 2007) by acknowledging and valuing the many assets and cultural backgrounds that all people possess (Gonzales, 2005; Moll et al., 1992).

These varying approaches and frames are understandable because, over the past few decades, much research has attempted to understand equitable and asset-based teaching practices and pedagogies (e.g., Ladson-Billings, 2014, 2017; Muhammad, 2020; Paris, 2012). For instance, culturally relevant pedagogy is an ideology that considers a student's cultural identity while focusing on critical perspectives to challenge inequalities perpetuated by schools and society (Ladson-Billings, 1995), ultimately resulting in students' success. It conceptualizes the varied, cultural ways of being, speaking, and knowing that students bring with them to the classroom as assets capable of supporting students' "access to the opportunities afforded by proficiency in the dominant academic and social" ways of being, speaking, and knowing (Paris, 2012, p. 94).

In the same vein, culturally responsive teaching promotes the use of a student's cultural knowledge, prior experiences, and performance styles of diverse students to make learning more appropriate and effective for them; it teaches to and through the strengths of these students (Gay, 2018). The overall aim of culturally responsive teachers is to identify, respect, and support diverse students by recognizing the importance of including students' culture and funds of knowledge in all aspects of learning (Ladson-Billings, 2014, 2017).

While chapter authors frame their instructional practice in different ways, many emphasize the importance of valuing our students and engaging them in what many call critical literacy. Bishop (2014) defined critical literacy as:

> (a) mobilizing learners as social actors with knowledge and skills to disrupt the commonplace; (b) conducting research, analysis, and interrogation of multiple viewpoints on an issue; (c) identifying issues focused on socio-political realities in the context of the lives of the learners; (d) designing and undertaking actions focused on social justice outside of the classroom; and (e) reflecting upon actions taken and creating vision(s) for future project(s).
>
> *(p. 55)*

Through critical analysis and examination of texts, students learn that constructs such as race are socially constructed, meaning that the concept is a "product of social thought and relations" (Delgado & Stefancic, 2017, p. 9). The intent with critical literacy is that students become agentic.

We understand this change is needed, including how educators and educational systems frame instruction to address social inequities. Critical perspectives can be honored analytically and in authentic practice. One significant understanding that readers will take away after reading each chapter is that while there are "no shortcuts for true equity" (Dugan, 2021, p. 35), there are many ways to begin this pivotal and needed work.

What Does Literature Have to Do With It?

As teacher educators and former classroom teachers, we advocate for a rich, diverse, and inclusive approach to instruction that provides mirrors, windows, and sliding glass doors for students (Sims Bishop, 1990). We believe that classroom instruction should be focused on more than scripts and monolithic approaches that center on a narrow range of experiences (Muhammad, 2020; Love, 2019). We know that connecting with students, embracing moments of empathy, and exploring tough questions is about more than "teaching to the test," and we know that the texts used with students are rich and have the potential to engage and transform. As Mentor and Sealy-Ruiz (2021) suggest, part of this work is personal and involves the interrogation of self.

Therefore, we believe that classrooms should be full of books written by authors of all demographics, genders, and sexual orientations so that students can read books that call to them, teach them, help them problem-solve solutions to relatable problems, and learn about others who may be a little different from them (Fisher et al., 2020). Reading should be inclusive of opportunities to showcase and discuss a range of experiences and identities. Students can explore their own identities and build a sense of agency through literature. Students read to understand themselves and understand others' lives (Sims Bishop, 1990; Bishop, 2014), witnessing how characters deal with hardships, empowering students with the ability to peek into lives or situations that may not directly apply to them (Rodríguez, 2019). This type of learning promotes civically engaged (Lent & Voigt, 2019) students who take ownership through participation in relevant and authentic instruction that connects real-world relationships (Ladson-Billings, 2014; Lent & Voigt, 2019). This type of instruction promotes the development of empathy (Mirra, 2019) and student understanding of their pre-existing beliefs and assumptions while simultaneously encouraging their learning from others' perspectives (Fisher et al., 2020; Ivey & Johnston, 2018; Mirra & Garcia, 2020; Turner & Reed, 2018).

Unfortunately, since we began work on this project, the pushback on voices in young adult literature in the classroom has only increased and, arguably, has become even more overt and heated. In late September 2021, one school district in Texas canceled a virtual author visit with Jerry Craft, the Newbery-winning author/artist of the book *New Kid*. The district pulled the book for review. A few months later, in January 2022, a school district in Tennessee voted to remove *Maus* by Art Spiegelman, a Pulitzer Award-winning graphic novel about the Holocaust. *The New York Times* reported that minutes from the Tennessee school board meeting indicated that swear words contained in the text were the focus of this pushback (Gross, 2022). *The New York Times* stated that Maia Kobabe's graphic novel, *Gender Queer*, was another frequent challenge target. Meanwhile, Forbes reported that the Maus controversy led to a 753% increase in book sales in January 2022. In one of his courses on adolescent literacy, Jason had a student express interest in reading the book—the first mention of the title as a text of interest in his work with university students.

The New York Times reported in April 2022 that "Attempts to ban books in the United States surged in 2021 to the highest level since the American Library Association began tracking book challenges 20 years ago" (Harris & Alter, 2022, n.p.). *The New York Times* and a similar story in *The Washington Post* (Natanson, 2022) drew on the American Library Association's annual report on censorship, a document which notes that there were 729 attempts to remove books from public libraries, schools, and universities in 2022 and 1,597 challenges on books and/or removals of books. The report also noted that hate crimes surged in 2022, noting that San Francisco State University "tracked more than 10,000 incidents of hate from March 2020 through September 2021" (ALA, 2022, p. 13). The most often targeted titles for banning included *The Hate U Give* by Angie Thomas, *All Boys Aren't Blue* by George M. Johnson, and *The Bluest Eye* by Toni Morrison, among others.

The bans include a range of texts, including graphic novels which depict people of color and members of the LGBTQ+ community, among other intersections of identity. The striking pattern of book bans aimed at titles written by and featuring people of color and members of the LGBTQ+ community is difficult to ignore. The state of Florida, for example, introduced legislation popularly referred to as the "Don't Say Gay" bill, an action stipulating "Classroom instruction by school personnel or third parties on sexual orientation or gender identity may not occur in kindergarten through grade 3 or in a manner that is not age-appropriate or developmentally appropriate for students per state standards" (CS/CS/HB 1557, Section 1, 1001.42, 2022, n.p.).

We had no idea that the discussion around book banning would reach such a fever pitch in the months following our beginning work on this edited collection. We saw the necessity to speak up and take action is needed now more than it was before, as there is an immense amount of work to advocate for a range of voices and experiences. As students learn and grow throughout the years, having characters in their books to whom they connect is essential. The contents of a classroom bookshelf and our choices as educators send a clear message to students—what is centered and silenced. Amid controversy and heated debates occurring in society and among families, teachers provide a calm voice of reason and hope in classrooms within instruction and use texts that represent their lives and questions. We hope that children receive the message that they matter and that the materials they read and write matter. Books are welcoming and affirming places where difficult conversations are met in community with other students, teachers, and the authors themselves.

Although many topics centered in some books tend to be considered "taboo," and teachers may self-censor which books get used with students, literature provides a great way to address controversial issues (Heron-Hruby et al., 2015; Ivey & Johnston, 2018; Malo-Juvera & Greathouse, 2020) that students may be experiencing. Reading is far from a lonely practice; in fact, it is a collection of history across time and space. Students bring their lives, backgrounds, and experiences into their readings and use them when creating meaning with and from their texts (Wilhelm, 2016). Students' comprehension is influenced by their ability to "make sense of their own and others' lives through the storylines that tell them what to expect in social situations" (Buehler, 2016, p. 12). These texts often further a student's understanding of historical and political impacts (Vasquez et al., 2019).

Reading about characters going through similar experiences can minimize students' feelings of loneliness, belonging, and grief. Students learn additional ways to cope with stress, heartbreak, and the myriad other emotions they experience day-to-day. Identifying characters from the same culture empowers students to accept their culture, while reading about different cultures teaches them to embrace and celebrate diversity. Gomez-Najarro (2020) suggest that children need experiences reading texts with relatable characters that extend beyond stereotypical representations and that these texts lead to more motivation and engagement. Otherwise, children experience "the amputation of their identities" (Gomez-Najarro, 2020, p. 405), or the erasure of the complexities or even the existence of their experiences due to barriers placed around books in the classroom or curriculum.

From picture books to chapter books, verse novels to graphic novels, middle grades literature to young adult literature, and all other forms of text, books are part of the movement in connecting readers, helping children feel seen and heard, and crafting classrooms as places of compassion. Literature allows students to see the world through other people's perspectives related to race and culture (Ginsberg & Glenn, 2019; Hughes-Hassell, 2013; Rodríguez, 2019), gender and sexual identity (Batchelor et al., 2018), and social perceptions of (dis)abled populations (Curwood, 2013).

As author and advocate Phil Bildner (2021) shared in the context of the 2021 Banned Books Week, "It is not a badge of honor to have any of my books on a banned books list. It's awful. It's denying kids access to books" (n.p.). Books take us to places of student inquiry. They help us meet challenging questions and answer them. They also prompt all to include voices heard in the classroom that might not otherwise be considered. Access is powerful.

As educators, we stand in solidarity with Ryan Law (2021), who wrote, "children's literature exists as one important tool for increasing representations in classrooms" (p. 145). Literature promotes students to become engaged with relevant storylines and characters who experience many of the same moral dilemmas they encounter in their everyday lives (Ivey & Johnston, 2018).

As an editorial team, we appreciate the beauty of sharing texts and engaging in conversation that prompts students to learn and question complex and controversial societal issues. Students actively engage with others as they read to negotiate and problem-solve characters' situations and experiences. Such changes call for intentional action on the part of education systems, including the need to promote literature and curriculum that is authentic and that reflects the changing nature of society. Literature that represents the lived experiences of all students should be treasured, honored, and centered—not viewed as too controversial for the classroom and, as a result, neglected.

As Ryan Law (2021) suggests, teachers need support in this transformative work, and we hope this book helps the reader share ideas and creates new pathways for students through an open, critical dialogue. We recognize that books alone cannot make the change, which is why teachers like you are so important. Along with ALA's (2022) *State of America's Libraries*, we note educators' essential and critical role in this work. As such, each chapter in this book features the voice of a practicing teacher.

It may bear repeating: You are not alone. As a teacher, we know that you are facing a plethora of uphill battles related to implementing inclusive and diverse texts among the myriad of other things, such as standardized assessments and required standards. Luckily, many others also want to strengthen their instruction, classroom library, and texts used with students. We hope you travel through these chapters, collect ideas, and find inspiration from the wonderful educators who have taken steps to confront the "taboo" and share ways to begin your "taboo" journey within your classrooms and pedagogy. As former classroom teachers and current teacher educators, we recognize that teaching at any time is not an easy task, and we thank you for the profound and impactful work that you do.

Introducing Our Road Map

Throughout the writing of this book, we often heard a reverberating phrase— how timely this book is and how much educators of all levels: teacher educators, teacher leaders, and so on need a safe space to discuss the ways they can provide a supportive, equitable, and inclusive learning environment for all students. This is exceptionally crucial as teachers strengthen their ability to actively promote student empowerment and uplift the voices of all students, including students of color, students whose primary language is not English, students from low socioeconomic backgrounds, and LGTBQ students. And the reality is that teachers must understand the -isms and intersectionalities related to culture, social class, race, gender, sexuality, ethnicity, and language (Compton-Lilly et al., 2022; Ladson-Billings & Dixson, 2022; Milner, 2019) to fully provide spaces that support students' empathy and agency. When political ideologies are so closely intertwined with the goings-on in classrooms, many teachers may feel restricted by curricular mandates, scripted curricula, and, in some cases, state laws prohibiting the use of any literature that might seem political or controversial. We want this book to serve as a haven for those who approach their teaching with trepidation.

At all stages of our personal and professional development, there is a need for learning and unlearning in a supportive environment that encourages us to become even better educators. This need is why we want to stress the importance of employing equity across all social constructs. While there may be some chapters in this book that you are not readily willing to implement in your class-room, it is essential to note that we cannot "cherry-pick" whichever aspects of life we want to be equitable to in our classrooms. Students come to our classrooms from varying cultures, races, socioeconomic statuses, gender identities and preferences, and (dis)abilities. Because of this, we need to be the teacher that creates a space for them. Just as we differentiate instruction for our learners of varying academic needs, we should also differentiate our students' learning experiences to encompass the beautiful variety of backgrounds in our classrooms.

Therefore, this volume offers teachers support and guidance to do this critical work, shifting and mitigating their mindsets and ideologies to learn how to be agentive and equitable educators. Some of this support can arrive in the form of the stories and strategies that colleagues offer in practice and research. If nothing else, those striving to make positive changes in society can take heart and draw professional knowledge from others who are allies and supporters in this work. While this collection of voices is hardly a one-stop solution, teachers' ideas might help others know they are not alone in this struggle and might be generative for including more texts and approaches in K–12 classrooms.

We believe that this work must occur in classrooms throughout early child-hood and to graduation; therefore, our chapters will provide representation across all grade levels. Each chapter spotlights how teachers incorporate "taboo" topics and instructional practices within their classrooms to confront the inequitable practice or social constructs while simultaneously teaching required standards and content. Chapter authors provide you with their teaching practices, portraits of their classrooms, specific applications, and approaches to particular texts that have been impactful in practice or use.

To that end, the organization of the chapters in this book falls into three sections: creating a space and environment to welcome the discussion of taboo topics; traversing the difficulty of censorship within the classroom, including how teachers find themselves in a position of vulnerability as they attempt to celebrate and highlight a range of social and cultural identities through reading; and the importance of instilling empathy and agency with students.

Setting the Stage: Creating a Space and Environment for Taboo Topics

In our first section, we discuss the importance of creating a space where the discussion of taboo topics can occur. Too often, students are not invited to share their thoughts, ask questions, or learn from others, even through the eyes of characters in the books they read. Instead, teachers use texts to teach skills and strategies, not intentionally chosen to represent and include all students' identities. Theses texts do not allow students to create a world where they can live, breathe, and belong. Yet, students need the space and invitation to explore themselves and ways of being in a safe space and with others. They must feel a sense of safety and belonging to participate and thrive academically. Therefore, this section focuses on teachers creating a welcoming environment and understanding that everyone belongs; students are more apt to share and learn with and from others.

In our opening chapter, "*Un Maravilloso*, Dual-Language Read Aloud: Making Families Visible Through Testimony in the Primary Classroom," Beth A. Buchholz and Jean Carlos Garcia Reyes share their belief on how the picture books selected for classroom read alouds play a significant role in cultivating the inclusive classroom environment. These picture books can communicate explicit and implicit messages to children about who counts as a family and whose family experiences and stories are worthy of inclusion in this space and, consequently, as (re)sources for school literacy engagements. This chapter explores the experiences of a beginning teacher and his students during a read aloud and shares how discussion and reflection allow particular children and their family stories, experiences, and languages to become (more) visible in the classroom as they understand *their* family as a (re)source for talking, reading, and writing.

In the next chapter in this section, "What Makes You Unique?: Valuing Classroom Diversity Within Writing Instruction," authors Kate Bentley, Amy Broemmel, and M. Chris Douglass narrate the experiences of two classroom teachers who advocate for and articulate how the use of integrated writing instruction can serve as a mechanism for including diverse literature in elementary classrooms. Built around the idea of "unique," students discuss the character traits and the overarching development of characters found in picture book biographies. Students share and compare their own experiences with those of the characters, building understandings of cultures, addressing potential misconceptions often embedded within single-story narratives, and revisiting their autobiographies to elaborate on their own stories. This type of instruction highlights the importance of intentionally selected representative literature as an impetus for students to articulate their uniqueness through the development of autobiographies.

In the final chapter of this section entitled, "Sliding the Glass Door: Making Time and Space for Difficult Conversations With Youth Through Multivoiced Young Adult Literature," contributors Heather Waymouth, Keith Newvine, Sarah Fleming, Pamela Margolis, Sarah Mellon, and Tina Middaugh extend Sims Bishop's (1990) metaphor of texts as sliding glass doors by illustrating how two teachers used multivoiced young adult literature centered around taboo topics to reposition the perspective of students' understanding that although singular characters, perceptions, or realities in a predominantly white high school classroom may be the dominant narrative, there is often more to the story.

Traversing the Difficulty of Censorship Within the Classroom

In our second section of the book, we have collected voices that speak to dimensions of censorship. As we have suggested in this introduction, this book has arrived at a time when pushback on books and authors from minoritized communities is occurring at a historical level. School districts and libraries are censoring the voices present in classrooms as teachers navigate self-censorship questions and subsequent vulnerability. What is a teacher safe to say? What is a teacher safe to talk about? Teachers find themselves in a unique and potentially stressful position as they navigate the political spectrum and attempt to consider their values, the needs of students, and the voices of stakeholders. In this section of the book, the authors share both high-quality literature and practical steps for engaging in conversations that might otherwise seem unapproachable. And while some chapters emphasize vulnerability or confronting the many -isms such as racism, we understand that each geographic and school setting has unique circumstances. These chapters consider ways teachers can take steps into the uncomfortable to support all students. While the titles in this section relate to secondary education, we see much potential in the thinking of these authors across grade levels.

In the first chapter of this section titled, "Exploring Gender Identity and Equity Through *Lily and Dunkin*," contributors Jennifer S. Dail, Julie M. Koch, Shelbie Witte, and Lauren Vandever feature a text that opens up opportunities to discuss adolescent identities, including gender identity. Furthermore, this author team speaks to the ways in which schools and school districts attempt to silence or even change students who do not conform to expectations of gender expression. The authors provide ideas for creating a safe environment for students through the young adult text, *Lily and Dunkin*, by Donna Gephart and offer a toolkit for navigating the challenges and censorship.

Brooke Bianchi-Pennington and Arianna Banack co-author the next chapter in this section, "Remixing for Relevance: Talking Gentrification in Pride." The authors consider the intersections of identity explored in the classical work *Pride and Prejudice* by Jane Austen and the contemporary young adult novel *Pride: A Pride and Prejudice Remix* by Ibi Zoboi. The chapter includes a focus on the laws currently in play to censor classroom voices and how classic and contemporary texts can speak to identities as paired texts. This work is a testament to the need to include voices from literature in schools to reach deeper levels of reflection and discussion.

Then, in the chapter entitled "Layering Discourse: Encouraging Diverse Perspectives in a High School Literature Class," authors Renee Stites Kruep and Lauren Popov explore the need for constructing spaces for confronting bias. The authors share an approach that includes independent, small-group, and whole-class readings and encourage teachers to be constant readers. In the context of a high school course that centers on global voices, the authors advocate for including, rather than erasing, a range of authors and experiences, including Sandra Cisneros, Wes Moore, and Trevor Noah.

In the final chapter of this section, "Curating Socially Just Classroom Libraries for Middle Grade Readers" contributors Kristie W. Smith and Erica Adela Warren address the importance of locating and sharing intentional curricula and reading materials to speak to topics of social justice and influence social change in middle grades. The authors make the case that reading should be a critical exercise and that teachers have a vital role to play as curators of voices and creators of classroom environments to foster diverse perspectives. Smith and Adela include steps in the process and recommended resources and titles.

The Importance of Instilling Empathy and Agency With Students

While the previous section focused on teachers being agentive and vulnerable, teachers must also traverse topics and conversations with students that are sometimes uncomfortable from our day-to-day experiences. This type of teaching involves inviting students to be active participants through a dialogic discussion in which both teachers and students are active contributors to the knowledge shared. Therefore, this book's final section closes with chapters that reiterate the importance of promoting student agency and empathy within instruction by employing teaching strategies and considerations that promote relevant learning activities and exploration of students' identities. Importantly, we, and the authors of these chapters, know that literature and literacy is not only a skill for students to learn or read to pass a test, but literacy and literature can be tools to support students' development of empathy and agency, to stand up for themselves and their needs (Muhammad, 2020).

The first three chapters of this section stress the importance of intentionality while selecting books for use in the classroom. By including diverse literature in the school and through the idea of books serving as windows, mirrors, and sliding glass doors, educators help to support and expand students' identity development. Moving beyond student agency and identity, the final two chapters of this section involve action—how students can lean into their experiences in the classroom to help transform their communities and worlds.

We invite you to explore these chapters and note the opportunities teachers provide for students to expand their thinking by immersing themselves in the realities of others unlike themselves. Through this immersion, it is our hope that teachers can find opportunities to expand students' learning by taking action and becoming agents of change. By exploring texts and centering student voices, contributors in this section explore the implications linking to social and emotional learning to build empathy both across linguistic practices and diverse abilities. The authors in both chapters use children's literature as a primary vehicle for building empathy.

The first chapter of this section entitled "'I Don't Understand, I Don't Speak Spanish': Exploring Linguistic and Cultural Differences Through Picture Books," co-authors Dr. Julia López-Robertson and Maria del Rocio Herron share the important role that multicultural picture books play in helping develop a positive view of those who represent linguistic and cultural backgrounds that may be unfamiliar to students. They describe the intentionality of engaging young students with these picture books in order to build on the knowledge and experiences that students bring with them to school to prepare them for life in our global society. This chapter explores how teachers can use read alouds, songs, and artistic engagements, with Latinx children's literature, to talk with young children about issues like the right to one's language, what it means to be bilingual, why people move, the right to be safe, and what it means to have pride in one's linguistic and cultural heritage.

In the second chapter of this section, co-authors Emily Poynter and Rachelle S. Savitz emphasize the importance of books to instill empathy with students in their chapter "Combating Ableism With Classroom Literature." Because "general education classrooms" housing "typical students" are often anything but general and its students are anything but typical, children's literature has evolved over decades to include characters with disabilities, both invisible and visible. In addition to the academic and personal growth among students with disabilities, studies have also shown the benefits for their classroom peers regarding their academics and empathic development. Therefore, pieces of diverse and inclusive literature that encourage inclusion and teach empathy to students without disabilities are a crucial component of the classroom library to combat ableism and promote inclusion in elementary schools and classrooms.

In their chapter, K. N., H. S., Amanda Carter, and Nayelee Villanueva explore the importance of adopting an inclusive curriculum with their chapter, "Engaging Dynamic Discussions Through Storytelling." Their chapter explores the importance of an inclusive curriculum with the inclusion of texts representing diverse families, specifically those who identify as members of queer communities. This chapter is written for all educators to ponder and push back against the "what if" questions when deciding which books to include and which to not share with students. This chapter defines and details the conceptual framework and vision behind the EDD professional development, presents the implementation of a lesson plan created during the professional development, and includes the success story of one teacher participant who chose to implement a lesson using the picture book *Prince and Knight: Tale of the Shadow King*, a queer-friendly fairy tale by Daniel Haack and illustrated by Stevie Lewis.

In the following chapter, "Cultivating Students' Civic Agency Through Participation in a Social Justice-Themed Book Club as a Subversive Approach to Critical Literacy in Education," Elizabeth E. Schucker provides an overview of a school year through two social-justice themed book club texts, which allowed for open dialogue with students and teachers. Through the use of a critical lens, conversations focused on global competencies with students as they cultivated their civic identity through social justice-themed texts. These conversations served as a foundation based on civic development, justice-oriented citizenship, and culturally responsive pedagogies, which ultimately lead to students taking action in the critical improvement of the students' surrounding communities.

In the final chapter of this section, authors Rebecca Harper and Alicia Stephenson stress the importance of graphic novels as appealing to struggling and unmotivated readers due to the inclusion of both words and images in their chapter: "Scattering Stars: Graphic Novel Book Studies With Middle Grades Students to Explore Refugee Stories." However, this medium still challenges students to think deeply and critically about the elements of storytelling utilized in the visual narrative. For some students, their realities may be different from their peers or may include challenges that they find difficult to openly discuss. With this and the current political climate regarding immigration policies in mind, this middle grade classroom explored the integration of graphic novels that focus on the stories of immigrants and refugees. Through poignant stories and visuals that highlight the struggles of immigrants and refugees, this chapter promotes the idea that students expand their thinking beyond the dominant narrative and then take action to address the complex social issues that define their worlds.

Who Are We?

As noted earlier, as editors, researchers, teacher educators, and collaborators, we wanted to reflect and share who we are and why we feel we are the "right" people to edit this book. Before becoming scholars and teacher educators, we worked in K–12 classrooms for 25 years. We worked in linguistically, culturally, economically, and racially diverse schools, with two of us working predominantly in Title 1 schools. We have also worked in schools across the country. As White cis-educators, we understand that we do not have expertise related to all backgrounds and nuances surrounding potential cultural stigma associated with each taboo topic discussed throughout our book.

Although none of us are licensed mental health or school counselors, nor school psychologists, we all have witnessed, observed, and worked with students deeply influenced by various traumas. We witnessed the silencing of historically marginalized students and active pushback from colleagues and administration against students who did not adhere to dominant gender identity and sexual orientation perspectives. We also have experienced our traumatic situations and experiences. It is essential to be clear about our positionality. The three of us are not only literacy educators but also actively investigate and explore the use of literature to disrupt and confront harmful stereotypes and biases and ways teachers can use literature in their classrooms.

As you listen and learn from the presented teachers' voices, ponder their actions and agency, and consider ways to empower yourself and your students, we want to acknowledge and reiterate our admiration for the many educators who want to investigate their pedagogy and teaching practices. Educators like you, reading this book, and the many educators who have shared in other excellent books using inclusive and diverse texts or the power of subversive teaching, such as *Acts of Resistance* (2020) edited by Jeanne Dyches and colleagues, *Breaking the*

Taboo with Young Adult Literature (2020), edited by Victor Malo-Juvera and Paula Greathouse, *Engaging with Multicultural YA Literature in the Secondary Classrooms* (2019) edited by Ricki Ginsberg and Wendy J. Glenn, *Multicultural Children's Literature: A Critical Issues Approach* (2011) edited by Ambika Gopalakrishnan, and many, many other beautiful texts about inclusive literature!

Based on conversations with teachers in our university programs and professional learning opportunities that we are providing to local schools and teachers, we quickly became aware that teachers thirst for learning from others—how educators are bridging these gaps in what they are required to teach and ways to be more inclusive of all students' perspectives, lived experiences, and identities. Learning from other teachers about how they have authentically welcomed students' stories and encouraged discussion and questioning to create relevant instruction related to real-world situations (Beckelhimer, 2017; Collins, 2017).

References

American Library Association. (2022). *State of America's libraries: Special report: Pandemic year two.* www.ala.org/news/sites/ala.org.news/files/content/state-of-americas-libraries-special-report-pandemic-year-two.pdf

Anne E. Casey Foundation. (2020). *Kids count data book: State trends in child well-being.* Author.

Anyon, J. (2005). *Radical possibilities: Public policy, urban education, and a new social movement.* Routledge.

Au, W. (2012). *Critical curriculum studies: Education, consciousness and the politics of knowing.* Routledge.

Batchelor, K. E. (2018). Using linked text sets to promote advocacy and agency through a critical lens. *Journal of Adolescent & Adult Literacy, 62*(4), 379–386.

Beckelhimer, L. (2017). One teacher's experiences: Responding to death through language. *English Journal, 107*(2), 41–46.

Bethell, C. D., Carle, A., Hudziak, J., Gombojav, N., Powers, K., Wade, R., & Braveman, P. (2017). Methods to assess adverse childhood experiences of children and families: Toward approaches to promote child well-being in policy and practice. *Academic Pediatrics, 17*(7), 1–3.

Bildner, P. (2021, September 26). *Banned books week [Twitter moment].* https://twitter.com/PhilBildner/status/1442191823389315073

Bishop, E. (2014). Critical literacy: Bringing theory to praxis. *Journal of Curriculum Theorizing, 30*(1), 51–63.

Borsheim-Black, C., & Sarigianides, S. T. (2019). *Letting go of literary whiteness: Antiracist literature instruction for white students.* Teachers College Press.

Buehler, J. (2016). *Teaching reading with YA literature.* National Council of Teachers of English.

Butler, T. T. (2017). #Say[ing] HerName as critical demand: English education in the age of erasure. *English Education, 49*(2), 153–178.

Coleman-King, C., & Groenke, S. L. (2019). Teaching #BlackLivesMatter and #SayHerName: Interrogating historical violence against Black women in Copper Sun. In R. Ginsberg & W. Glenn (Eds.), *Engaging with multicultural YA literature in the secondary classrooms: Critical approaches to critical education* (pp. 122–131). Routledge.

Collins, B. R. (2017). Associative mourning: Learning to lose through literature. *English Journal, 107*(2), 47–52.

Compton-Lilly, C., Lewis Ellison, T., Perry, K. H., & Smagorinsky, P. (Eds.). (2022). *Whitewashed critical perspectives: Restoring the edge to edgy ideas.* Routledge.

Craig, S. E. (2017). *Trauma-sensitive schools for the adolescent years: Promoting resiliency and healing.* Teachers College Press.

CS/CS/HB 1557, 2022, Section 1, 1001.42. (2022). www.flsenate.gov/Session/Bill/2022/1557

Curwood, J. S. (2013). Redefining normal: A critical analysis of (dis)ability in young adult literature. *Children's Literature in Education, 44*, 15–28.

Delgado, R., & Stefancic, J. (2017). *Critical race theory* (3rd ed.). New York University Press.

Dugan, J. (2021). Beware of equity traps and tropes. *Educational Leadership, 78*(6), 35–40.

Dyches, J., Sams, B., & Boyd, A. S. (Eds.). (2020). *Acts of resistance: Subversive teaching in the English language arts classroom.* Myers Education Press.

Fisher, D., Frey, N., & Savitz, R. S. (2020). *Teaching hope and resilience for students experiencing trauma: Creating safe and nurturing classrooms for learning.* Teachers College Press.

Gay, G. (2018). *Culturally responsive teaching: Theory, research, and practice* (3rd ed.). Teachers College Press.

Ginsberg, R., & Glenn, W. J. (Eds.). (2019). *Engaging with multicultural YA literature in the secondary classrooms: Critical approaches to critical education.* Routledge.

Giroux, H. A., & Penna, A. N. (1979). Social education in the classroom: The dynamics of the hidden curriculum. *Theory and Research in Social Education, 7*(1), 21–42.

Gomez-Najarro, J. (2020). Children's intersecting identities matter: Beyond rabbits and princesses in the common core book exemplars. *Children's Literature in Education, 51*(3), 392–410.

Gonzales, L. D. (2005). *Comparative research on political and civic engagement: Young Hispanic women as political actors.* ETD Collection for University of Texas, El Paso.

Gopalakrishnan, A. G. (Ed.). (2011). *Multicultural children's literature: A critical issues approach.* SAGE.

Gorski, P. C. (2018). *Reaching and teaching students in poverty: Strategies for erasing the opportunity gap.* Teachers College Press.

Gross, J. (2022, January). School board in Tennessee bans teaching of Holocaust novel 'Maus.' *The New York Times.* www.nytimes.com/2022/01/27/us/maus-banned-holocaust-tennessee.html

Gutierrez, K. D., Zitlali Morales, P., & Martinez, D. C. (2009). Re-mediating literacy: Culture, difference, and learning for students from nondominant communities. *Review of Research in Education, 33*(1), 212–245.

Harris, E. A., & Alter, A. (2022, April). Book banning efforts surged in 2021. *The New York Times.* www.nytimes.com/2022/04/04/books/banned-books-libraries.html

Heron-Hruby, A., Trent, B., Haas, S., & Allen, Z. C. (2015). Using a youth lens to facilitate literary interpretation for "struggling" readers. *English Journal, 104*(3), 54–60.

Herrera, S. G., Murry, K. G., & Cabral, R. M. (2020). *Assessment of culturally and linguistically diverse students.* Pearson Higher Ed.

Hosford, P. L. (1980). Improving the silent curriculum. *Theory into Practice, 19*(1), 45–50.

Howard, G. R. (2016). *We can't teach what we don't know: White teachers, multiracial schools* (3rd ed.). Teachers College Press.

Howard, T. C. (2010). *Why race and culture matter in schools: Closing the achievement gap in America's classrooms.* Teachers College Press.

Hughes-Hassell, S. (2013). Multicultural young adult literature as a form of counter-storytelling. *The Library Quarterly, 83*(3), 212–228.

Ivey, G., & Johnston, P. H. (2015). Engaged reading as a collaborative transformative practice. *Journal of Literacy Research, 47*(3), 297–327.

Ivey, G., & Johnston, P. H. (2018). Engaging disturbing books. *Journal of Adolescent & Adult Literacy, 62*(2), 143–150.

Kinloch, V., Burkhard, T., & Penn, C. (2020). *Race, justice, and activism in literacy instruction*. Teachers College Press.

Krogstad, J. M. (2019). A view of the nation's future through kindergarten demographics. *Pew Research Center*. www.pewresearch.org/fact-tank/2019/07/31/kindergarten-demographics-in-us/

Ladson-Billings, G. (1995). Toward a theory of culturally relevant pedagogy. *American Educational Research Journal, 32*(3), 465–491.

Ladson-Billings, G. (2014). Culturally relevant pedagogy 2.0: A.K.A. the Remix. *Harvard Educational Review, 84*(1), 74–84.

Ladson-Billings, G. (2017). "Makes me wanna holler": Refuting the "culture of poverty" discourse in urban schooling. *The Annals of the American Academy of Political and Social Science, 673*(1), 80–90.

Ladson-Billings, G., & Dixson, A. (2022). Put some respect on the theory: Confronting distortions of culturally relevant pedagogy. In C. Compton-Lilly, T. Lewis Ellison, K. H. Perry, & P. Smagorinsky (Eds.), *Whitewashed critical perspectives: Restoring the edge to edgy ideas* (pp. 122–137). Routledge.

Lent, R. C., & Voigt, M. M. (2019). *Disciplinary literacy in action: How to create and sustain a schoolwide culture of deep reading, writing, and thinking*. Corwin Literacy.

Love, B. L. (2019). *We want to do more than survive: Abolitionist teaching and the pursuit of educational freedom*. Beacon Press.

Madrigal-Garcia, Y. I., & Acevedo-Gil, N. (2016). The New Juan Crow in education: Revealing panoptic measures and inequitable resources that hinder Latina/o postsecondary pathways. *Journal of Hispanic Higher Education, 15*(2), 154–181.

Malo-Juvera, V., & Greathouse, P. (Eds.). (2020). *Breaking the taboo with young adult literature*. Rowman & Littlefield.

Matias, C. E. (2013). Check yo'self before you wreck yo'self and our kids: Counterstories from culturally responsive white teachers? . . . to culturally responsive white teachers! *Interdisciplinary journal of Teaching and Learning, 3*(2), 68–81.

Mentor, M., & Sealy-Ruiz, Y. (2021). Doing the deep work of antiracist pedagogy: Toward self-excavation for equitable classroom teaching. *Language Arts, 99*(1), 19–24.

Michael, A. (2015). *Raising race questions: Whiteness and inquiry in education*. Teachers College Press.

Milner, H. R. (2019). Race to improve teacher education: Building awareness for instructional practice. *American Educator, 43*(3), 13–17.

Milner, H. R. (2020). *Start where you are, but don't stay there: Understanding diversity, opportunity gaps, and teaching in today's classrooms* (2nd ed.). Harvard Education Press.

Mirra, N. (2019). *Education for empathy: Literacy learning and civic engagement*. Teachers College Press.

Mirra, N., & Garcia, A. (2020). "I hesitate but I do have hope": Youth speculative civic literacies for troubled times. *Harvard Educational Review, 90*(2), 295–321.

Moje, E. B. (2007). Developing socially just subject-matter instruction: A review of the literature on disciplinary literacy teaching. *Review of Research in Education, 31*(1), 1–44.

Moll, L. C., Amanti, C., Neff, D., & Gonzalez, N. (1992). Funds of knowledge for teaching: Using a qualitative approach to connect homes and classrooms. *Theory into Practice*, *31*(2), 132–141

Muhammad, G. E. (2020). *Cultivating genius: An equity framework for culturally and historically responsive literacy*. Scholastic.

Muhammad, G. E., & Haddix, M. (2016). Centering Black girls' ways of knowing: A historical review of literature on the multiple literacies of Black girls. *English Education*, *48*(4), 299–336.

Natanson, H. (2022, April). More books are banned than ever before, as Congress takes on the issue. *The Washington Post*. www.washingtonpost.com/education/2022/04/07/book-bans-congress-student-library/

National Center for Education Statistics. (2020). Racial/ethnic enrollment in public schools. *The Condition of Education*. https://nces.ed.gov/programs/coe/pdf/coe_cge.pdf

National Survey of Children's Health. (2019, October). *National survey of children's health: NSCH fact sheet*. https://mchb.hrsa.gov/sites/default/files/mchb/Data/NSCH/NSCH-2018-factsheet.pdf

Nikolajeva, M. (2016). Recent trends in children's literature research: Return to the body. *International Research in Children's Literature*, *9*(2), 132–145.

Paris, D. (2012). Culturally sustaining pedagogies: A needed change in stance, terminology, and practice. *Educational Researcher*, *41*(3), 93–97.

Picower, B. (2021). *Reading, writing, and racism: Disrupting whiteness in teacher education and in the classroom*. Beacon Press.

Rodríguez, R. J. (2019). *Teaching culturally sustaining and inclusive young adult literature: Critical perspectives and conversations*. Routledge.

Ryan, C. L. (2021). Reading the K-8 Rainbow: A virtual, LGBTQ-inclusive children's literature book club for elementary and middle school teachers. *Journal of Children's Literature*, *47*(1), 145–148.

Sims Bishop, R. (1990). Mirrors, windows, and sliding glass doors. *Perspectives*, *6*(3), ix–xi.

Sleeter, C. E. (2008). Preparing white teachers for diverse students. In M. Cochran-Smith, S. Feiman-Nemser, & J. McIntyre (Eds.), *Handbook of research in teacher education: Enduring issues in changing contexts* (pp. 559–582). Routledge.

Sue, D. W. (2015). *Race talk and the conspiracy of silence: Understanding and facilitating difficult dialogues on race*. Wiley.

Tatum, A. W. (2009). *Reading for their life: (Re)building the textual lineages of African American adolescent males*. Heinemann.

Tatum, A. W. (2015). Writing through the labyrinth of fears: The legacy of Walter Dean Myers. *Journal of Adolescent & Adult Literacy*, *58*(7), 536–540.

Tatum, A. W., & Muhammad, G. E. (2012). African American males and literacy development in contexts that are characteristically urban. *Urban Education*, *47*(2), 434–463.

Tatum, B. D. (2000). *Why are all the Black kids sitting together in the cafeteria? And other conversations about race*. Basic Books.

Tatum, B. D. (2000). *Why are all the Black kids sitting together in the cafeteria? And other conversations about race*. Basic Books.

Thomas, E. E. (2015). "We always talk about race": Navigating race talk dilemmas in the teaching of literature. *Research in the Teaching of English*, *50*(2), 154–174.

Turner, K. H., & Reed, D. (2018). Responding to young adult literature through civic engagement. In J. S. Dail, S. Witte, & S. T. Bickmore (Eds.), *Toward a more visual literacy:*

Shifting the paradigm with digital tools and young adult literature (pp. 41–52). Rowman & Littlefield.

Vasquez, V. M., Janks, H., & Comber, B. (2019). Critical literacy as a way of being and doing. *Language Arts*, *96*(5), 300–311.

Wilhelm, J. D. (2016). *"You gotta be the book": Teaching engaged and reflective reading with adolescents.* Teachers College Press.

Zong, J., Blizzard, B., & Bolter, J. (2020). Frequently requested statistics on immigrants and immigration in the US. *Migration Policy Institute.* www.migrationpolicy.org/article/frequently-requested-statistics-immigrants-and-immigration-united-states

SECTION 1

1

UN MARAVILLOSO, DUAL-LANGUAGE READ ALOUD

Making Families Visible Through Testimony in the Primary Classroom

Beth A. Buchholz and Jean Carlos Garcia Reyes

Second graders lounge comfortably on the carpeted area awaiting today's read aloud. Mr. Garcia pulls up a digital version of the picture book on the screen. The colorful book cover features a multiracial family: Mom with blonde hair, blue eyes, and skin-like "crema"; Dad with black hair and eyes and brown skin "like leather"; and a child with dark hair and skin the color of "café con leche." Mr. Garcia reads the title aloud, his bilingualism allowing each word to shine: *Marvelous Maravilloso: Me and My Beautiful Family* by Lara (2018). He wonders how children will respond to the first dual-language picture book of the year. Just last week, Jeremiah expressed surprise, and some discomfort, after hearing Mr. Garcia speak Spanish in the classroom, asking: "What is going on? What is that? What are you saying?"

Families are children's first and most important teachers. Educators understand that building connections between families and schools is an essential part of supporting all children's development. One strand of this work is how teachers frame the way families are discussed inside classroom communities. Classrooms, particularly at the primary level (pK–2), tend to focus heavily on the concept of family as part of instructional engagements and invitations. Although the topic of families may appear to be a fairly uncontroversial, because families in the real world exist in and are produced at the intersection of issues like race and racism, xenophobia, and gender, sexual orientation and sexual identity, discussing families in ways that are fully inclusive in the classroom can be challenging. Recent surveys have found teachers are self-censoring the topics they share in classrooms more than ever, as they worry discussing particular topics, including those listed previously, will land them in trouble with some groups of parents and administrators (Pendharkar, 2022).

Picture books selected for classroom read alouds play a significant role in communicating explicit and implicit messages to children about who counts

DOI:10.4324/9781003302216-2

as a family and whose family experiences and stories are worthy of inclusion in this space, and, consequently, as (re)sources for school literacy engagements. Mainstream discourses are deeply embedded in how families are represented in children's literature. Lo's (2019) critical content analysis of award-winning international children's picture books found that family variation/diversity (e.g., family models, race, class, religion, immigrant status, language, ability) remained uncommon. Cultural products like picture books validate and make particular lived experiences—and families—visible, rendering others invisible. This has significant consequences for how children engage with reading and writing invitations in the classroom and, ultimately, how they construct literate identities.

This chapter explores a beginning teacher's experience sharing the dual-language book *Marvelous Maravilloso: Me and My Beautiful Family* as part of an interactive read aloud in his second-grade classroom. We consider the classroom community's response to the book as forms of testimony and witnessing, allowing particular children—and the family stories/experiences and languages they carried with them—to become (more) visible in the classroom as they understood *their* family as a (re)source of/for talking, reading, and writing.

Co-Authors

This chapter is co-authored by a bilingual second-grade teacher (Mr. Jean Carlos Garcia Reyes) and a monolingual teacher educator (Dr. Beth A. Buchholz). The read aloud and discussion of *Marvelous Maravilloso: Me and My Beautiful Family* (Lara, 2018) was facilitated by Mr. Garcia in mid-September during his first year of teaching. "We" and "our" are used to indicate our collective voice/perspective, while "Mr. Garcia" is used when describing classroom (inter)actions and instructional moves. Additionally, "I" will be used when sharing excerpts from Mr. Garcia's reflective field notes that reveal his retrospective thinking/writing about particular moments in his classroom.

Focal Picture Book

The children's book featured in this chapter is *Marvelous Maravilloso: Me and My Beautiful Family*, written by Carrie Lara and illustrated by Christine Battuz. The book explores the development of cultural identity, including the dynamics of race, ethnicity, and language, through the perspective of a very young child. Throughout the book, the child, who comes from a bi-cultural family, learns to appreciate the differences between her parents' skin colors, cultures, and languages and the unique mix that makes up her own identity. As she explores her identity, she comes to "see the beauty" in how families come in "hundreds and hundreds of colors" as well as different sizes, shapes, and models.

Representations of Families, Culture, and Language

Family is considered "one of the most fundamental units of societies . . . [is] critical in the identity development of children" (Shema, 2016, p. 95). However, long-standing heteronormative narratives narrowly define who and what counts as a family. In America, the "traditional" family has classically been understood as a mother, father, and children who speak English and live together in a single home. Families that do not fit those parameters are considered "non-traditional" (Shema, 2016). Narrow definitions of family limit which children (and teachers) are positioned as having valid expertise/knowledge and stories to share within classroom communities.

Marvelous Maravilloso: Me and My Beautiful Family is an example of a book that disrupts some of the "gentle bias[es]" Lo (2019) identified across picture books. By positioning a bi-cultural, multiracial, multilingual child as the narrator, the book broadly invites young readers to consider the ways parents/caregivers might look and speak differently than their children and the beauty inherent within those differences. Additionally, the young main character's regular use of Spanish and English across the narration in the book foregrounds language as a critical component in cultural and, by extension, family identity. As a dual-language picture book, the running text in *Marvelous Maravilloso* is primarily written in English, with Spanish words and phrases integrated within most sentences. For example: "My skin is another color. Daddy says café con leche or a mezcla—a mixture of both colors. A color all my own" (p. 18). Research on dual-language picture books suggests that they increase and validate children's linguistic and cultural awareness/knowledge and nurture language development by forging cross-linguistic connections (Ma, 2008).

Dual-language picture books offer a diverse range of models for how languages are organized, separated, and positioned on the page, each embedded with implicit messages about a language's importance and power (Przymus & Lindo, 2021). In dual-language books where English is positioned at the left/top of the page(s) and the Spanish translation is positioned at the right/bottom, the message to readers is that Spanish is the "other" or lesser language. However, interlingual books like *Marvelous Maravilloso* that integrate multiple languages within and across sentences/paragraphs model translanguaging as a norm. Translanguaging disrupts assumptions about languages as separated in the mind and practice of multilingual speakers and highlights the complex, fluid language practices of multilingual children, families, and communities (García et al., 2016).

The translanguaging modeled in the text of *Marvelous Maravilloso* includes direct translation, context clues, and/or illustration clues to help readers make sense of unfamiliar words, but, importantly, the author alternates whether Spanish or the English context/translation appears first in the sentence. The text/narration moving back and forth between languages mirrors the notions of linguistic flexibility and fluidity that are at the heart of translanguaging theory. The only visual marker that a word is in Spanish or English in the book is the font color: English is in black, Spanish is in a different color of the rainbow on each page. In interviews, Carrie Lara, the author, indicated she integrated the two languages in the book to help her bi-cultural, bilingual daughter—and other children across the world—see *both* languages spoken at home as important, integral parts of cultural identity.

Dual-language books are often assumed to be strictly for the ELL/ESL classroom, and teachers may find administrators resistant to their inclusion in English-medium classrooms. However, research in translanguaging disrupts these assumptions by asserting that "all language-minoritized students—both bilingual students and those viewed as monolingual, but whose uses of English have been marginalized . . . engage in translanguaging and would benefit from linguistic flexibility in their education" (Seltzer, 2019, p. 6). Language-minoritized children are often excluded from meaningful educational experiences. Consequently, English-medium classroom teachers are challenged to enact pedagogies that acknowledge *all children's* full linguistic repertoires as resources for meaning-making and learning rather than a problem to overcome (Garcia et al., 2016).

Representation as a Form of Testimony and Witnessing

Books invite particular identities, experiences, and issues into classroom spaces in ways that allow children to see themselves and their lives reflected (i.e., a "mirror book") and to peek into worlds that are largely unfamiliar (i.e., a "window" book) (Bishop, 1990). Books shared in classrooms send messages to children about which parts of themselves are valid and welcomed resources for school literacy engagements and what parts of themselves should be left at the classroom door. In Dutro's (2011, 2013, 2019) decades-long sociocultural work around trauma and literacy, rooted in humanities scholarship in trauma studies (e.g., Caruth, 1996; Kaplan, 2005), she argues passionately that too often what we ask children to leave at the classroom door are the challenging life experiences they face due to poverty, racism, xenophobia, and homophobia.

> Supporting children in the midst of challenging circumstances . . . means designing literacy curriculum and instructional practices that value the difficult experiences children face through everyday instruction and interactions in literacy classrooms rather than silencing such experiences as inappropriate for school or *rendering them invisible in the texts and talk of classrooms."*
>
> *(Dutro, 2019, p. 5, emphasis added)*

By inviting hard stories into the classroom, intentionally weaving in opportunities for "testimony" and "witnessing" into classroom literacy routines, children and teachers have opportunities to become more visible to each other while illuminating a world of beauty as well as pain, sadness, and violence. Within Dutro's pedagogical framework, *testimony* is the sharing of hard truths and stories from one's life (e.g., death of a loved one, housing or food insecurity, incarceration of a parent, divorce) while *witnessing* is the deep, compassionate listening engaged in by the larger community, rooted in a "sense of being entwined with others" (Dutro, 2019, p. 31). Positioning the classroom as a site for engaging in testimony and witnessing requires vulnerability and reciprocity for both children and teachers. When teachers find spaces to weave their own testimony into day-to-day established routines of literacy instruction, they create opportunities for children to engage in critical witnessing, learning how to listen, engage with, and respond to a community member sharing something difficult and personal. Within a model of reciprocity, teachers' vulnerable testimonies create opportunities for children to engage in witnessing as well as an invitation to draw on their own deeply felt experiences as "source and resource for school literacies" and healing (Dutro, 2019, p. 24). Thoughtfully selected books/texts can be(come) a critical tool for cultivating a spirit of witnessing in the classroom. Therefore, when it comes to selecting books, educators must critically consider the harm that is inflicted when books—and classroom talk/writing/drawing—do not fully represent the complexity of children's lived experiences, including those connected to families and language(s).

Context and Overview of the Read Aloud

Mr. Garcia works at a K–5 school with a 99% minority-identifying student population and a 100% rate of students receiving free and reduced lunch. In Fall 2021, his second-grade classroom included 15 racially and linguistically diverse students. Seven of these students spoke some degree of both English and Spanish at home. All students were present for the read aloud of *Marvelous Maravilloso,* during which time they sat on the carpet as the digital book was projected on the large screen.

Although this read aloud was not part of a formal research project, Mr. Garcia audio recorded the read aloud and discussion as part of an assignment for graduate school, allowing him to reflect on how children engaged with and responded to this particular book. As part of our work on this chapter, the audio recording was transcribed to make it possible for us to dig deeply into children's talk and identify key instructional moves. We were interested in exploring the following questions: (1) How did children respond to and engage with the dual-language picture book during the reading and afterward? What aspects were salient for them? and (2) What instructional moves did Mr. Garcia use to engage children during the read aloud effectively?

In the following sections, we examine two children's responses to and engagement in/with the read aloud—and related interactions—to better understand how children engaged with/responded to the book as forms of testimony and witnessing. Each section opens with an excerpt from Mr. Garcia's own reflective field notes and then moves back into our shared voice.

Giselle: "De dónde eres tú y tu familia?"

> I continue to reflect on the ways Giselle, a newcomer in our classroom from El Salvador, demonstrated a deep level of engagement during the read aloud of *Marvelous Maravilloso* through facial expressions rather than words. Her face illuminated as she heard me read words in Spanish and, critically, when she noticed how intrigued her classmates were with *her* language. I thought to myself how proud she must be at seeing characters in this book she could relate to and to hear her beloved native language outside of just translation: a language she is used to hearing in both her current and past home(s). I wish I had books like this when I was in school—books I could identify with and authentically see and hear myself in.

Giselle moved to the United States just a few months before school started in Fall 2021. In her first few weeks at her new school in August, it was clear the transition to a new country, new culture, new language, new school, new teachers, and new classmates was, unsurprisingly, difficult for Giselle. However, she and Mr. Garcia quickly built a strong relationship, forged to some degree through their shared ability to communicate using Spanish, but also deeply rooted in the humanizing, asset-oriented stance that he brings to his interactions with all children. As a bilingual educator, Mr. Garcia immediately leveraged multiple strategies for easing Giselle's transition, but even as she grew to be more comfortable at school, Giselle was reluctant to leave the safe space of the classroom for specials each day (Music, Art, STEM, PE, or Media). She explained her feelings to Mr. Garcia: "No quiero ir a otra maestra. Nadie habla español allá adentro y no entiendo nada. No me gusta aquí . . . Todo es diferente." ("I don't want to go to another teacher. Nobody speaks Spanish in there, and I don't understand anything. I don't like it here . . . Everything is different.") Giselle's testimony makes visible just how challenging and shocking the transition can be for newcomers and the vulnerability required to learn a new language in English-dominant American contexts.

Giselle's experiences and testimony as a newcomer were heavy on Mr. Garcia's mind when monolingual classmate Jeremiah asked, "What is going on? What is that? What are you saying?" in response to hearing Spanish spoken in the classroom early in the school year. Mr. Garcia had responded by framing translanguaging as an opportunity for empathy, sharing: "We have a student in our classroom who doesn't understand very much English yet. Some of the ways you're feeling right now are how she feels all day." In this case, Mr. Garcia saw an opportunity to make visible—to testify to—the challenges of being a Spanish speaker in an English-medium classroom. Children's brief feelings of discomfort when hearing an unfamiliar language cracked open space for classroom communities to begin thinking critically together about language practices and policies at work in schools/classrooms and the ways those practices and policies can inflict harm/

violence on multilingual students. When Mr. Garcia shared *Marvelous Maravilloso* with his students in mid–September, it marked the first dual-language picture book he had read aloud that year. The translanguaging in *Marvelous Maravilloso* allowed Mr. Garcia to bring Spanish to life in the classroom. Without prompting, children began repeating the Spanish words and phrases aloud throughout the book while sharing connections (e.g., "I know Spanish!" and "My sister speaks Spanish") and asking questions (e.g., "How do you say ___ in Spanish?" and "Can you say it again?"). Though Giselle did not talk during the read aloud, her illuminated face and shy/bright smile indicated that she was experiencing this instructional context quite differently than other classroom literacy engagements. Mr. Garcia regularly spoke Spanish with Giselle, but during the read aloud of *Marvelous Maravilloso* Giselle's English-speaking peers became the "language learners," hearing words that were unfamiliar but beautiful, yearning to have their stilted attempts match the gentle vibrations of Mr. Garcia's alveolar trill and the musical lilt. Looking back, Mr. Garcia sees this read aloud as a significant turning point for both himself and Giselle, one where Spanish became a sustained area of class-wide inquiry.

After observing children's responses to *Marvelous Maravilloso*, Mr. Garcia knew that it was vital to continue reading aloud books that incorporated both Spanish and English. One dual-language picture book that caught his eye in connection to *Marvelous Maravilloso* was *Dreamers* by Yuyi Morales (2018), featuring the story of a mother and son immigrating to the United States from Mexico and the challenges they faced to speak/understand English and feel like they belonged until discovering the world of books at the public library. During this read aloud, Giselle revealed little verbally or nonverbally, leaving Mr. Garcia to wonder if the story and/or language were too much for her. He was surprised a few minutes later when Giselle initiated a conversation with him as the class waited in line to use the bathrooms: "de dónde eres tú y tu familia?" This question, imbued with a level of trust and connection with Mr. Garcia, and the vulnerability that followed revealed the ways Giselle had deeply connected to these dual-language books featuring characters/families, language(s), and experiences that mirrored her own and her teacher's:

Giselle:	"¿De dónde eres tú y tu familia?" (Where are you and your family from?)
Mr. Garcia:	"De Ecuador. Queda a lado de Colombia en Sur America" (From Ecuador. It is next to Colombia in South America.)
Giselle:	"Ah. Yo sé donde queda." (Oh. I know where that is.)
Mr. Garcia:	"Y tu familia es de El Salvador, ¿verdad?" (And your family is from El Salvador, correct?)
Giselle:	"Si. Bueno. Pero ahora vivimos aquí." (Yes. But, now we live here.)
Mr. Garcia:	"Y vives con tu mama, verdad?" (And you live with your mom, right?)
Giselle:	"Si. ¿Has conocido a mi mamá?" (Yes. Have you met my mom?)
Mr. García:	"No todavía. Solo conozco a tu tía que vino para Open House." (Not yet. I only know your aunt that came to Open House.)

This conversation continued for another few minutes, with Giselle sharing intimate details about her family's difficult journey to the United States and revealing how much she missed her father, who was still living in El Salvador for the time being. This was the first time Giselle had openly initiated sharing stories—let alone hard stories—from her own life with Mr. Garcia or her classmates.

We view this impromptu interaction as a powerful moment of testimony and witnessing. Feeling unprepared for a conversation of this magnitude, Mr. Garcia remained present in the moment, bearing witness to Giselle's difficult life experiences. While he had known that Giselle's transition from a Spanish- to English-medium school/classroom was understandably onerous, he had not fully understood the sadness and heartache that permeated her family life. In the United States, both Giselle's mother and aunt worked in close partnership to care for Giselle. However, in Giselle's testimony, it was clear that she was experiencing a deep sense of longing—and even grief—for family like her father, who remained in El Salvador. Moreover, it was through this act of witnessing that Mr. Garcia began to better understand how deeply Giselle had been engaged with the recent dual-language read alouds. Her testimony was a kind of response to the testimonies offered by characters in the books—speaking directly to hard, complex stories around families, culture, and language practices.

Jonathan: "When I was one or two . . ."

> I was—and still am—learning what vulnerability looks like in the classroom. When reading aloud *Marvelous Maravilloso*, I felt nervous when a student pointed out an illustration of a family with a single caregiver; I knew my own life could offer students a real life example of this. In a brief moment before deciding to share my own story, I thought back to the numerous reasons I wanted to become a teacher. I didn't have many teachers I could identify with growing up. Although my parents were together when I was a child, in early high school, they formally separated. This was hard. All of it. I wanted my students who have single caregivers to see that they weren't alone, that their teacher was also a product of a hard, strong, and independent single mother. This was my chance to offer what I needed in the classroom growing up: representation of the hard (and triumphant) stories I was and still am living.

While the translanguaging was children's focus across the early pages of the *Marvelous Maravilloso*, the conversation turned more explicitly to families in the final pages. The spread that elicited particularly rich interaction featured an illustration with fourteen ornate picture frames (see Figure 1.1). Inside each frame, families of different sizes (including those that are childless) and structures/models are included, representing diversity across race, age, gender, and sexual orientation. After reading the short text accompanying this illustration, Mr. Garcia asked children, "What do you notice?" Initially, children focused on the various skin colors of the members of each family: "They're all white and . . . their baby is like kind

The world is full of hundreds of colors and hundreds and hundreds and hundreds of beautiful families.

FIGURE 1.1   Spread from *Marvelous Maravilloso: Me and My Beautiful Family*

of black."; "All three of these people look the same." Each observation was a chance for Mr. Garcia to reiterate the book's theme that *all* families are beautiful. His simple and repeated invitations to "notice" allowed children to pull from their own lived experiences and identities to dig into the layered meanings within the illustration.

After a few minutes of discussing observations around race, the second graders' conversation took a turn when Kenzie, pointing to a frame of an adult holding up a baby in blue pajamas noticed, "[That] one doesn't have a husband."

Mr. Garcia: "Kenzie, can you repeat what you said?"
Kenzie: "I noticed that she doesn't have a husband. She only has a kid . . . and herself."
Mr. Garcia: "Okay . . . So we may have a single mom . . . or maybe her aunt or her grandmother. Right, sometimes we have families that may have just one mom or one dad." [cross talk amongst children]

We noted the ways here that Mr. Garcia extended the language used by Kenzie in her observation, opening up an even wider range of interpretations by suggesting that the adult pictured in the frame might be a single mom or a grandmother, or an aunt. Moments like this serve to disrupt assumptions about who can enact caretaking roles with children.

Up until this point, children's "noticings" on the spread remained fairly impersonal. There was some informal crosstalk indicating children were seeing their own lives mirrored in pages of the book, but it was Mr. Garcia's impromptu decision to share his own story that changed the tenor of the discussion. Unsure whether to move on or dig into Kenzie's observation, Mr. Garcia leaned into his own vulnerability, bringing his own testimony to his teaching in ways that positioned his students as witnesses to his life beyond the walls of the classroom.

Mr. Garcia: "Like Mr. Garcia at home really only has his mom. I don't really talk to my dad anymore, so it's cool that we can also see that there are also single parent households."

Furthermore, his testimony did not end there. Children wanted to know more; they wanted to better understand their teacher whom they were growing to care for and trust.

Kenzie: "Wait, Mr. Garcia. Why you don't talk to your dad anymore?"

Mr. Garcia: "He did some not great things, so I don't really talk to him anymore . . . I only talk to my mom. I live with my mom right now. But he's okay though. And I am okay. He's doing his own thing. But thank you for asking."

Mr. Garcia's testimony positioned children/students as trusted witnesses. In response, and as evidence of the reciprocal relationship between testimony and witnessing, Jonathan, a bilingual seven-year-old, spoke up and testified in response to his teacher's testimony:

Jonathan: "When I was one or two my dad broke up with my mom and I haven't . . . I'm going with him today . . . 'cause I haven't seen him. The last time I seen my dad was on my birthday."

Mr. Garcia: "Jonathan, I really appreciate you sharing that. Thank you for sharing that. It's okay to have only one parent. It's ok if our parents aren't together, or if we go see Mom one weekend and Dad another—or if we only see them on special days like birthdays . . . So we have different family types."

While Jonathan had previously mentioned "visiting dad" in private conversations with Mr. Garcia, this was the first time Jonathan had shared these details from his life publicly with the larger classroom community. This interactional moment speaks to the "possibilities of pedagogies that tangibly attempt to show that the sharing of hard stories is a risk that can be taken" in classrooms and, critically, that this risk will "not be taken alone" (Dutro, 2019, p. 56). Mr. Garcia's in-the-moment decision to lean into his own vulnerabilities initiated a cycle of testimony and witness in that classroom that would continue to emerge and develop over their year together.

A Reflective Coda

Children's interactions during and after reading a dual-language book like *Marvelous Maravilloso* highlight how classroom discussions about family are bound up with discussions and school-based policies around language(s) and culture. Which children get to count their family as a (re)source for school-based literacy instruction depends not only on teachers critically selecting picture books that are inclusive of different family structures/models but in selecting books that also make visible diverse language and cultural practices within and across families. When primary level teachers shy away from books that address issues like race and racism, (language-based) xenophobia, and gender, sexual orientation and sexual identity, particular families are rendered invisible in the classroom.

Mr. Garcia's impromptu testimony about his own father opened up space for children, particularly those who were multilingual, to share some of their own hard family stories. Looking back, he notes how the book helped nudge him into sharing his own testimony. Earlier in the year, he introduced himself to children by sharing photographs of his life but was unsure how to respond when one child asked why his dad was not pictured in any family photos. Mr. Garcia shared that he did not talk to his dad anymore but moved quickly to the next photograph, intentionally removing any space/time for more discussion. As a beginning teacher, he was not sure how much he wanted or should share with children. Nearly a month later, it was the text and illustrations in *Marvelous Maravilloso* that acted as their own kind of testimony—making visible bi-cultural, bilingual families as well as families of different shapes, sizes, and forms. Even as an adult, seeing his own family (and language) represented on the pages, made him feel more comfortable, more willing to be vulnerable as he shared about his own hard stories.

Thoughtfully selected picture books, when shared in trusted communities, open up new pathways for witnessing and positioning vulnerability as a strength. Teachers interested in taking the first steps toward doing similar work in their own classrooms, whether monolingual or multilingual, might begin by exploring a range of dual-language picture books. Beyond those discussed in this chapter, a list of additional recommended titles and resources, with a particular focus on families, is included as part of the references. When bringing these books into the classroom for read alouds, teachers will want to take time to practice any unfamiliar language(s). Then, taking Mr. Gracia's lead, try exploring the power of focusing on *noticing* and *wondering* as ways to open up conversations— and potential space for testimony and witnessing—rooted in children's lived experiences.

Ultimately, the read aloud of *Marvelous Maravilloso* (re)ignited Mr. Garcia's commitment to creating more space/time for all children to explore critical issues and translanguaging in the classroom, including reading aloud additional dual-language texts, implementing a Spanish word of the day, and various other invitations for all children to explore writing, speaking, and listening (to) multiple languages across the day. What emerged over time was a shared classroom curiosity around Spanish. Although this chapter featured the testimony of two multilingual class members, Mr. Garcia was equally surprised by the impact of critical witnessing by/on monolingual classmates. The surprise and discomfort once raised when classmates heard Spanish in the classroom were replaced with monolingual classmates like Cameron choosing to explore Spanish at school *and* at home. Working to compose a multilingual written note that he gave to his bilingual teacher Mr. Garcia, Cameron demonstrated an understanding that caring for others includes learning/using the language(s) that they use with their families: "Te quiero/I Love you" (see Figure 1.2). Cameron positioned (learning) Spanish as a (re)source for deeply knowing and connecting with his teacher

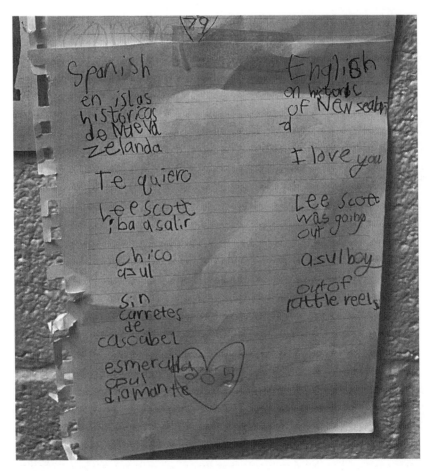

FIGURE 1.2 Second Grader Cameron's "At Home" Writing (Gifted to Mr. Garcia)

Mr. Garcia, his classmates, and the wider world, sharing his own dual-language writing with Mr. Garcia. We see this as a form of critical witnessing, described by Dutro (2019) as being rooted in action and advocacy, serving to challenge the deficit-framing of which children are identified as "language learners" and which families are "othered" in our schools and communities.

We share this final story not to suggest that it was the result of reading a single dual-language book, but rather that *Marvelous Maravilloso: Me and My Beautiful Family*, and the testimonies it made visible, ignited a new way forward for this beginning teacher and his students. By bringing his own testimony—connected to family and language—to his teaching in ways that positioned his students as witnesses to his life, space was opened up for children's families to be(come) more visible, humanizing (re)sources for classroom literacy learning.

References

Bishop, R. S. (1990). Windows and mirrors: Children's books and parallel cultures. In K. Holmes (Ed.), *Perspectives on teaching and assessing language arts* (pp. 83–92). Association of Teachers of English.

Caruth, C. (1996). *Unclaimed experience: Trauma, narrative, and history.* Johns Hopkins University Press.

Dutro, E. (2011). Writing wounded: Trauma, testimony, and critical witness in literacy classrooms. *English Education, 43*(2), 193–211.

Dutro, E. (2013). Towards a pedagogy of the incomprehensible: Trauma and the imperative of critical witness in literacy classrooms. *Pedagogies: An International Journal, 8*(4), 301–315.

Dutro, E. (2019). *The vulnerable heart of literacy: Centering trauma as powerful pedagogy.* Teachers College Press.

García, O., Johnson, S., & Seltzer, K. (2016). *The translanguaging classroom: Leveraging student bilingualism for learning.* Caslon.

Kaplan, A. E. (2005). *Trauma culture: The politics of terror and loss in media and literature.* Rutgers University Press.

Lo, R. S. (2019). Resisting gentle bias: A critical content analysis of family diversity in picturebooks. *Journal of Children's Literature, 45*(2), 16–30.

Ma, J. (2008). 'Reading the word and the world': How mind and culture are mediated through the use of dual-language storybooks. *Education 3–13, 36*(3), 237–251.

Pendharkar, E. (2022, January 27). Efforts to ban Critical Race Theory could restrict teaching for a third of America's kids. *Education Week.* www.edweek.org/leadership/efforts-to-ban-critical-race-theory-now-restrict-teaching-for-a-third-of-americas-kids/2022/01

Przymus, S. D., & Lindo, E. J. (2021). Dual-language books as a red herring: Exposing language use and ideologies. *The Reading Teacher, 75*(3), 317–327

Seltzer, K. (2019). Reconceptualizing "home" and "school" language: Taking a critical translingual approach in the English classroom. *TESOL Quarterly, 53*(4), 986–1007.

Shema, A. (2016). Families. In N. M. Rodriguez, W. J. Martino, J. C. Ingrey, & E. Brockenbrough (Eds.), *Critical concepts in queer studies and education* (pp. 95–104). Palgrave Macmillan.

Children's Literature Referenced

Lara, C. (2018). *Marvelous Maravilloso: Me and my beautiful family*. Magination Press.
Morales, Y. (2018). *Dreamers*. Holiday House.

Additional Dual-Language Read Aloud Recommendations With a Focus on Families

Anand, S. (2021). *Laxmi's mooch*. Kokila. [English/Hindi]
Lara, C. (2020). *The heart of mi familia*. Magination Press. [English/Spanish]
Lê, M. (2018). *Drawn together*. Little, Brown Books for Young Readers. [English/Thai]
Perskin, M. (2019). *Between us and Abuela: A family story from the border*. Farrar, Straus and Giroux. [English/Spanish]
Tonatiuh, D. (2010). *Dear primo: A letter to my cousin*. Harry N. Abrams. [English/Spanish]
Yang, K. K. (2020). *The most beautiful thing*. Carolrhoda Books. [English/Hmong]

Recommended Resource for Locating Additional Dual-Language Texts

Burns, M., & Enriquez, G. (2022, February 1). Books. *Libros for Language*. https://libros-forlanguage.org/books

2

WHAT MAKES YOU UNIQUE?

Valuing Classroom Diversity Within Writing Instruction

Kate Bentley, Amy Broemmel, and M. Chris Douglass

Introduction

In 1990, Rudine Sims Bishop advocated that children needed to be engaged with literature that metaphorically presented both *windows* and *mirrors*. Mirrors, in this case, referred to books that allowed children from historically marginalized populations to see themselves reflected in the pages of books. In contrast, windows allowed children from the majority population to see and familiarize themselves with cultures different from their own. Now, just over 30 years later, many classroom teachers feel restricted by curricular mandates, scripted curricula, and, in some cases, state laws prohibiting any use of literature that might be considered controversial or political. Yet, we still have children in our elementary classrooms who do not see themselves, their stories, and their cultures reflected in the books and materials they engage with. This chapter describes how two elementary teachers use integrated writing instruction as a mechanism for using diverse literature in their classrooms.

Sally and Don are both considered master teachers. They both have held leadership positions in their schools and districts, have advanced degrees, and have taught for 11 and 14 years, respectively. Sally, a white third-grade teacher in an urban elementary school, has a classroom comprised primarily of Black and Brown children whose families live in poverty. She has been in her current position for two years, though she has taught kindergarten through fifth grade in three states. Don is a Black male who currently teaches first grade in a school that has, over the past decade, moved from serving a primarily White population to serving one that includes a significant number of Black and Brown children, many of whom come from impoverished backgrounds. Teaching is his second career, but he has taught for 14 years in kindergarten through fifth grade in three

DOI:10.4324/9781003302216-3

schools in the same district. Both are committed to integrating diverse literature into their classrooms despite restrictive curricular mandates. Writing instruction is one area that remains somewhat flexible, although both Don and Sally have to be creative in finding time to dedicate to it. In this little bit of time intentionally carved out by each teacher, they have led their students through a unit of instruction on what makes them unique.

We begin by founding our unit in a theoretical framework and established research on using picture book biographies as mentor texts to support writing. We then address the role of literature in helping open students' minds to the worthiness of all types of people, especially themselves. Next, we describe the unit of instruction focusing on character and theme, first through reading and then through the writing of their autobiography. Finally, we discuss students' responses and the implications of this type of writing unit.

Theoretical Frame

This unit is situated in an understanding that literacy learning occurs in socially situated spaces (Vygotsky, 1978). When classrooms include literacy-rich opportunities in which students explore, discuss, and respond to texts as a community of learners, students can develop community-based literacy beliefs and practices that guide them as readers, writers, and conversationalists (Gee, 1990).

A sociohistorical orientation also recognizes the importance of the text as a model of intellectual and personal growth. Text selection allows teachers to reach beyond the traditional cognitive goals of learning to inspire students to "become, act, or think differently because of what they have read" (Tatum, 2009, p. 37). Text selection, in this view, becomes vitally important for nurturing students toward thoughtful consumption of stories during their formative elementary years. Establishing these opportunities in elementary school allows students to develop a vast repertoire of characters, stories, and experiences to draw from as they grow into the person they will become (Tatum, 2018).

Picture Book Biographies

> *"I like reading biographies because I get to see how famous people are like all the rest of us. I get to see that even though they had accomplished great things, they had struggles along the way. That seems like me."*
>
> —*Third-Grade Student*

Picture book biographies are multimodal presentations of content that can both inform and delight, capturing readers' attention with powerful language and illustrations (Dorfman et al., 2017). Over the past several years, there has been a much-needed increase in the number and variety of picture book biographies available. This increase in supply and demand has led publishers to push the envelope and develop books about a wide variety of people who more accurately represent the diversity of the population (Dawes et al., 2019). Teachers have an opportunity to capitalize on this change by bringing these books into their classroom instruction, allowing them to open the door for representation while introducing a variety of people, professions, and backgrounds (Niland, 2021). Students may also find their own challenges—unsupportive teachers, mean bullies, unjust laws, poverty, and so forth—in the pages, where they can also see themselves in the successes. As a result, they often become highly interested in a unique subject or a seemingly out-of-reach occupation. Sometimes, they also begin to identify with the traits displayed by those depicted in the biographies, giving students ideas for helping determine how to define themselves and find the good in who they are becoming (Dore et al., 2017).

Sharing picture book biographies presents an opportunity for the voices of people throughout history and around the world to be heard. Sharing their experiences through texts raises awareness of historical issues that have a lasting impact on the current socio-political environment. For all students, both those who experience great diversity and support in their communities and those who do not, seeing examples of success from across the human experience validates their experience and expands their understanding of the world (Garces-Bacsal, 2021).

Instruction Overview

Laying the Foundation

From kicking off the unit with a study of the etymology of "unique" to distinguishing the differences between biography and autobiography, the first part of the unit uses picture book biographies such as *The Girl Who Thought in Pictures*, *Manji Moves a Mountain*, and *Pride: The Story of Harvey Milk* (see Table 2.1). Each story generates meaningful discussion around the character traits of the real people highlighted in each book. Guided by state ELA standards such as, "Describe characters in a story (e.g., their traits, motivations, or feelings) and explain how their actions contribute to the sequence of events," and "Ask and answer questions to demonstrate understanding of a text, referring explicitly to the text as the basis for the answers," Sally and Don use intentionally selected read alouds to engage their students in discussion, charting, and quick writes about the characteristics of the real people depicted in the books. Then, these master teachers scaffold their learners through comparing and contrasting themselves with the people they've been learning about, resulting in each student writing an autobiography based on their own identified character traits.

Daily literacy instruction was divided into two different time periods in Sally's and Don's classrooms. Due to state and district mandates, the first block of time was devoted to instruction programs with particular curricular materials that limited teacher discretion. The second block of instructional time was dedicated to a

TABLE 2.1 Picture Book Biographies

Picture Book Biographies Book List

Brave Girl: Clara and the Shirtwaist Makers Strike of 1909 (Markel, 2013)

The Cat Man of Aleppo (Shamsi-Basha & Latham, 2020)

Dancing Hands: How Teresa Carreno Played the Piano for President Lincoln (Engle, 2019)

Dinosaur Lady: The Daring Discoveries of Mary Anning, the First Paleontologist (Skeers, 2020)

Emmanuel's Dream: The True Story of Emmanuel Ofosu Yeboah (Thompson & Qualls, 2015)

Evelyn the Adventurous Entomologist: The True Story of a World Traveling Bug Hunter (Evans, 2019)

Farmer Will Allen and the Growing Table (Martin, 2013)

The Girl Who Thought in Pictures: The Story of Dr. Temple Grandin (Mosca, 2017)

I Am Jazz (Herthel, 2014)

Mae Among the Stars (Ahmed, 2018)

Magic Ramen: The Story of Momofuku Ando (Wang, 2019)

Malala's Magic Pencil (Yousafzai, 2017)

Manji Moves a Mountain (Churnin, 2017)

The Oldest Student: How Mary Walker Learned to Read (Hubbard, 2020)

Pride: The Story of Harvey Milk and the Rainbow Flag (Sanders, 2018)

Shark Lady: The True Story of How Eugenie Clark Became the Ocean's Most Fearless Scientist (Keating, 2017)

Wilma Unlimited: How Wilma Rudolf Became the World's Fastest Woman (Krull, 2000)

limited time for writing instruction. The instruction detailed in this chapter took place during that more flexible writing period. The time restrictions often meant that instruction was divided over a few days rather than taught in larger chunks of time. With this in mind, both teachers devoted the first day of teaching to the picture book biography read aloud and discussion and then moved into connecting the students' learning to the writing process on the second day. Throughout the unit of study, which took up to six weeks, the teachers continued this model—introduce a text, read it aloud and discuss it, then tie it to the writing process—to establish the biographies as mentor texts for writing. This model recognizes the connection between reading and writing as mutually beneficial in that as students become more aware of the writing process, they also become more detailed readers. Students' writing improves as they become more attuned to the authors' craft (Dawes et al., 2019).

During the first lesson, both teachers focused on the word "unique." Students brainstormed all the ways they had heard the word unique used. The teacher charted responses on the board and then directed the class to the meaning of the prefix uni- as one. Using this as a clue, they developed the working definition of unique—one of a kind. They then revisited the brainstorming and circled places where the definition applied as a class. Research suggests that this process of identifying the need to define a word further, looking for known or possible morphemes, hypothesizing the definition, and checking its application in context is successful in helping students understand vocabulary terms and apply that learning to their reading (Kieffer & Lesaux, 2007). Before ending the discussion, the teacher asked students to turn and tell their partners something that made them unique. When students returned to their desks, they completed a quick check to define the word unique and recorded something that made them special. Following this introduction, the teachers described the difference between an autobiography and a biography to students. To anchor the unit learning, teachers began a tree map graphic wall organizer to build upon throughout the unit. It was set up to allow space to add each text beneath the guiding question, "What makes you unique?" As seen in Figure 2.1, as the number of texts grew, students could easily compare and contrast the individuals and texts studied.

Students engaged in critical discourse over the following few lessons while the picture book biographies were read aloud. Beginning with the book *Shark Lady*, they learned what made Eugenie Clark unique. Together as a class, they charted her

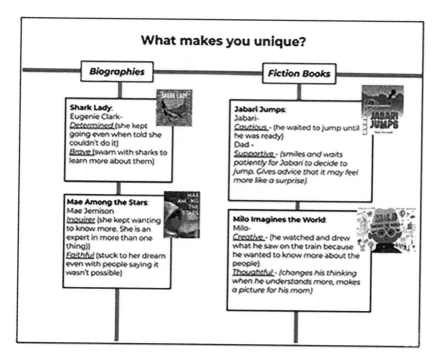

FIGURE 2.1 Example of the tree map graphic organizer. The graphic organizer was made out of painters tape, and the chart was co-created with the class and then added to the wall. At the end of the unit, all books shared were displayed for students to reference and discuss.

character traits, referencing the text for evidence. They noted both her successes, the challenges she faced, and how the author and illustrator moved the story forward. Doing this work during the read aloud is time-consuming but vital to the unit's success, as it allows the students to deepen their understanding of the individual depicted in the biography and establish respect and understanding for their lives (Floyd & Hébert, 2010). Thus, allocating so much time spent engrossed in these picture book biographies allows the reader to experience a closeness with the individual and use both imagination and empathy to immerse themselves in the story (Niland, 2021). By meeting these standards for engagement, the opportunities for students to act or think differently because of what they have read increase. Time spent by students analyzing and understanding a text also allows the student to "savor the impact" of the writing and stimulate a desire to create their own (Laminack, 2017, p. 754).

As students moved into the instructional writing days, they used their writing journals to complete a personal anchor chart comparing and contrasting their lives to that of the focus individual from the previous day. Writing as a craft demands that we help students establish tools to share their own stories (Leung & Hicks, 2014). Therefore, students attempted small elements from the previous day's story on the back of their compare and contrast journal entries. For example, students may have chosen to find a repeated phrase like "hold, aim, swing" from *Manji Moves a Mountain* or "she dove" from *Shark Lady*. They might have chosen a supporting character like Mae's parents in *Mae Among the Stars* or Gilbert Baker in *Pride: The Story of Harvey Milk and the Rainbow Flag*, or they may focus on adversaries like the teacher in *Mae Among the Stars* or *Shark Lady*. The expectations associated with this portion of the unit can vary depending on the grade level. For example, third-grade students looked at the author's craft with words and mimicked them in their model, whereas first-grade students looked in-depth at how the illustrator used art to tell the significant events. Mentor text analysis allows for differentiation depending on the students' standards, objectives, and needs (Dollins, 2016).

As students moved through several chosen texts and writing activities, teachers added to the anchor charts posted on the board. Students added to their writing journals, completing quick writes and trying out different aspects of their craft. Writing instruction then shifted to focus on the writing process for autobiographies. Using the collected models as a guide, students first mapped their autobiography, focusing on the sequential nature of the writing. In this stage, first graders used pictures to show first, next, then, and last, whereas third graders chose to sketch and write the events in order. After students completed their prewrite, they moved to their draft. Teachers modeled and used the mentor texts to provide guidance and instruction to students throughout this time. This writing stage often feels chaotic, but students are highly motivated and engaged in telling their own stories. Teachers can add varying levels of support as needed, such as those depicted in Figure 2.2.

Students finally participated in a gallery walk viewing their peers' autobiography drafts and offering peer-to-peer feedback to culminate the first section of

FIGURE 2.2   Students sequence a mentor text and apply the strategy to their autobiography.

the unit. The framework of notice and wonder guides this feedback. Teachers prompted students to notice two ways the author used the mentor texts to guide their writing and provide one wonder or question for the author to answer. Following the gallery walk, the teacher led a whole-class discussion of the word unique as students recalled the mentor text examples and drew from their autobiography. Culminating this portion of the unit, the teachers asked students to identify how they were unique or one of a kind and add it to the back of their story with a sticky note.

Tatum's *Vital Signs of Literacy Instruction* (2009) proposes that text selection has the potential to help students think critically about what they read and bring it into their own lives. Guided by standards such as, "Describe characters in a story (e.g., their traits, motivations, or feelings) and explain how their actions contribute to the sequence of events," and "Ask and answer questions to demonstrate understanding of a text, referring explicitly to the text as the basis for the answers," these master teachers introduced students to diverse individuals from around the world. Incorporating texts about a diverse range of successful individuals opened the door for students to have windows and mirrors into life outside the classroom. At the end of the first section, students were heard discussing the texts with friends, connecting the biographies to concepts and ideas in other subject areas, and reporting home to their families about the "cool" individuals they encountered in the books. As Tatum suggests, these students' minds were opened by reading, sharing, and celebrating diverse books. This was nowhere more evident than in the joy with which they shared their own lives through their autobiographies.

Building Character Through Culture

The second phase of the unit delves into character development, using literary characters as models for moving beyond character traits and into character development through culture (see Table 2.2). Using models like *Jabari Jumps*, *The Invisible Boy*, and *Milo Imagines the World*, the teachers guide students in discussing the challenges and changes of each protagonist, the impact of the characters' culture and context, and the emotions and feelings depicted throughout (Harper & Brand, 2010). Students are encouraged to share and compare their own experiences with those of the characters, building understandings of cultures and addressing potential misconceptions often embedded within single-story narratives. Children then return to their autobiographies to elaborate on their own stories, ultimately "publishing" them in the classroom.

Beginning with the book *Jabari Jumps*, the teachers started a new anchor chart to track students' learning across several texts. During the read aloud of *Jabari Jumps*, students engaged in turn and talk to first discuss the character of Jabari. In particular, they analyzed why he let the other kids go first and why he said he needed to rest or stretch. Students quickly identified with the emotion of nervousness, acknowledging the desire to hide it by making excuses. Several students reported trying the strategy out when trying something new, just like Jabari.

After finishing the read aloud, where Jabari finally jumps off the diving board, the class revisited the book via the illustrations and discussed Jabari's dad and baby sister. Students concluded during a turn and talk that Jabari's dad knew Jabari was nervous and that his patience and understanding supported Jabari eventually jumping. The discussion ended with a written entry in their writing journal linking both Jabari and his dad to character traits with evidence from the text and a

TABLE 2.2 Character Development Book List

Character Development Texts
A Chair for My Mother (Williams, 1983)
Jabari Jumps (Cornwall, 2017)
Julian Is a Mermaid (Love, 2018)
Julian at the Wedding (Love, 2020)
Last Stop on Market Street (de la Pena, 2015)
Milo Imagines the World (de la Pena, 2021)
My Shadow Is Pink (Stuart, 2020)
Say Something (Reynolds, 2019)
The Invisible Boy (Ludwig, 2013)
The Paper Kingdom (Rhee, 2020)

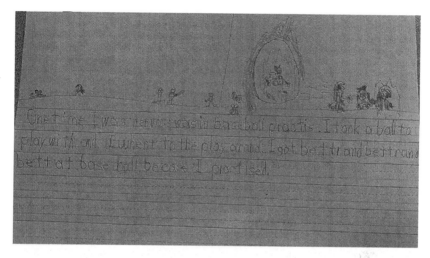

FIGURE 2.3   A first-grade student's reflection on a time they felt nervous and the action they took to feel better.

quick write about a time when they were nervous and how they could continue to try like Jabari. In their writing, the class focused on ideas like the shared life experience of making excuses, feeling nervous, finding strength from others, or a supportive dad, sister, or other relatives.

Using Sharma and Christ's (2017) Cultural Relevance Text Evaluation Rubric, the teachers had carefully selected *Jabari Jumps* as their first text. This story centers around a dad taking his son and daughter to the pool. His son Jabari spies the diving board and runs to join the line. The story follows Jabari through various relatable excuses until, after a conversation with his dad, he "stops feeling scared and more like a surprise" and jumps off the board in front of his cheering dad and sister. While the main characters in the book are Black, the book does not discuss race and offers simply a snapshot into a day at the pool.

In Don's classroom, one student began his reflection by saying that he wasn't surprised that Jabari was nervous because, in his family, they don't swim. He discussed how he and his family stay in the shallow end where they can touch the bottom whenever he goes to the pool. Another student reflected that the dad reminded her of her friend's dad. She shared how he takes them to the park or other fun places. In her case, she currently lives with her grandmother and aunts, and her friend's dad is the steadiest male influence she sees regularly. All students benefit by having a greater understanding of why Jabari and his dad going to the pool might be meaningful and why the supporting character of the dad can be both unexpected and relatable.

The teachers allowed students to connect deeply to the characters and apply the themes to their own lives. Rudine Sims Bishop (1990) suggests that offering texts like this one can help students see themselves in a story or more completely see others, allowing them to better understand the story, themselves, and their community. Throughout this portion of the unit, the teachers were careful to consider both what texts best fit their specific students and the academic objectives of the lesson.

Teachers read *Milo Imagines the World* and *The Invisible Boy* to complete this portion of the unit on character development. In *Milo Imagines the World*, students of an incarcerated parent, same-sex parents, and those judged based on their skin color or appearance found particular connections. Students related to Milo's surprise when the sharp-dressed little boy joined the line for the metal detector; they, too, had imagined differently.

The conversation opened the door to why we might imagine specific images when looking at others and how best to change our habits. As the class moved on to *The Invisible Boy*, the conversation shifted to wanting to be accepted for who you are, feeling left out, enjoying special foods from home, and the power of reaching out. Students instantly related to hiding parts of themselves or feeling like people didn't see them. The book's illustrations vibrantly portray this emotional change in the character by beginning the story with Brian, the main character, in black and white, while slowly moving him to full color by the end. After identifying the emotions depicted in the book, students analyzed each one in-depth, as shown in Figure 2.4. The ongoing conversation and associated

FIGURE 2.4 Students analyze the shades of meaning of words that describe Brian's feeling in *The Invisible Boy*.

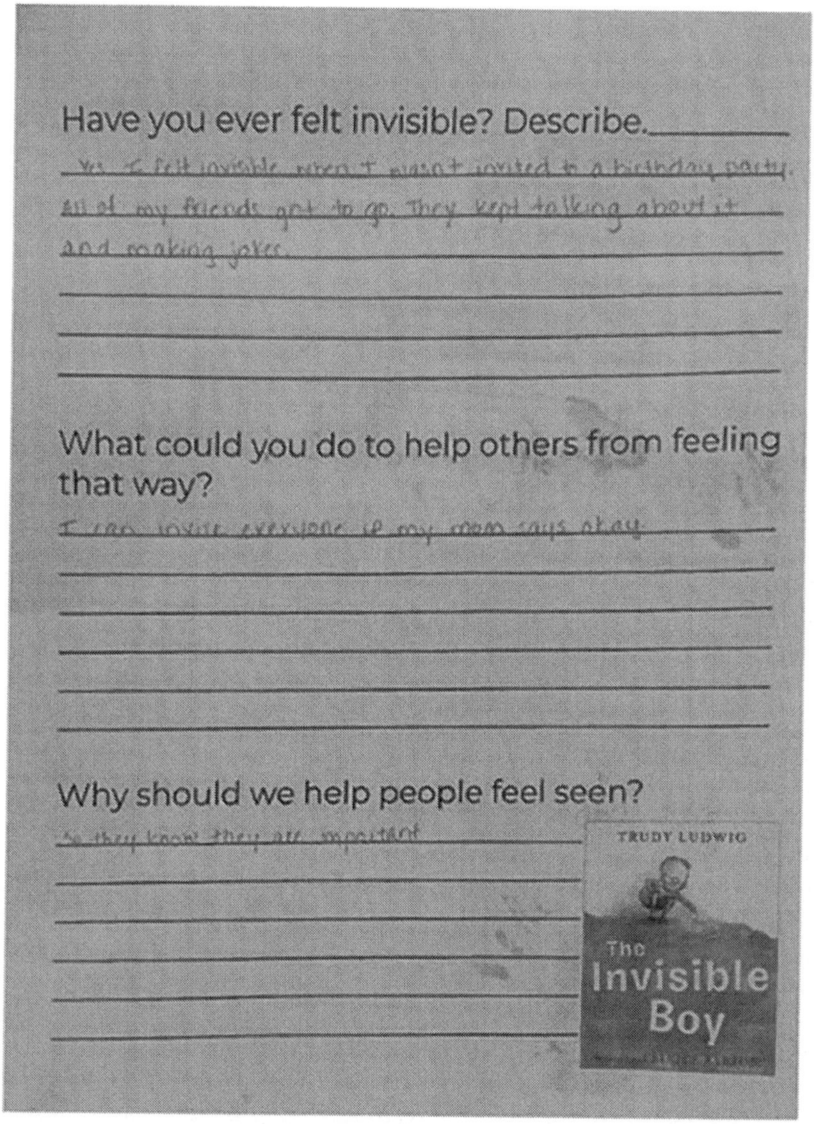

Have you ever felt invisible? Describe._____

Yes I felt invisible when I wasn't invited to a birthday party.
all of my friends got to go. They kept talking about it
and making jokes.

What could you do to help others from feeling that way?

I can invite everyone if my mom says okay.

Why should we help people feel seen?

So they know they are important

TRUDY LUDWIG

The
Invisible
Boy

FIGURE 2.5   Third-grade student's journal reflection on a time they felt invisible.

writing activities allowed students to examine times when they feel this way and what they can do to help keep others from experiencing the feelings of invisibility as shown in Figure 2.5. All of these books provided students with windows and mirrors (Sims Bishop, 1990), but in addition, they pushed students to recognize how to take action in their own lives to help themselves and those around them.

After sharing and writing about the chosen texts, students returned to their autobiography to reread in light of the characters, stories, and illustrations they had read and analyzed. The students made adjustments to their writing, with some choosing to highlight a more specific event in their life like *Jabari Jumps*, some sharing more deeply about their family like *Milo Imagines the World*, and some highlighting their uniqueness as demonstrated in *The Invisible Boy*. After several days spent revisiting, revising, and finalizing their stories, they were ready to share. In a culminating event, students showcased their books to the class through either a read aloud or classroom library display. All students chose to share their work and reported enjoying learning more about each other and what makes them unique.

Implications

"Are you ready to say something?"

—Peter Hamilton Reynolds

The individuals and characters students met throughout the unit guided them in honing their craft of how to "say something" with their lives and stories. The exploration and investigation of purposeful picture book biographies and character development texts served to open students' minds to the profound diversity of our world and our experiences and provided quality mentor text support for their autobiographies.

Throughout the unit of study, students came to know the texts, individuals, and characters well. The tracking of learning through anchor charts on the wall provided scaffolding for students, reminding them of each step in the process and encouraging reflection on prior learning throughout the unit. As Laminack (2017) suggests, this repeated interaction with the texts allowed the teachers to effectively mentor the students' writing. Their final autobiographies demonstrated students' mastery of author moves and wording and the illustrators' use of pictures to move the story along or highlight character emotions. Student work showed that the time spent building background around characters' traits and motives was beneficial; these first- and third-grade readers and writers were moved by and connected with the story. But, most importantly, the final autobiographies made it evident that the students were willing and eager to own their stories and highlight their uniqueness. The tracking of mentor texts built confidence in the class that their voices and stories were exceptional and worthy of sharing.

Teachers historically struggle to implement opportunities for students to engage in critical literacy and culturally relevant texts. They are often unsure where to start or how to guide students to meaningful engagement with the text (Christ & Sharma, 2018; Clarke & Whitney, 2009). We propose that an essential piece is to start. However, it is important to note that this can be intimidating, especially in light of the politicization of curriculum in public schools. This unit was taught face to face before the pandemic and before the scrutiny that many schools and teachers across the United States are experiencing. The students participating in the unit were comfortable answering the difficult questions about power and perspective in the biographies. They connected and responded to the stories about character development, and both Sally and Don received nothing but positive feedback from colleagues, parents, and students. Today, Sally still feels very comfortable with this unit and text selection. However, the rhetoric and increased scrutiny around book selection have made Don more cautious. He still plans to teach the unit but is taking even greater care to select mentor texts and is prepared with a clear rationale for why each is appropriate for use with his students.

We believe that the framework of the unit could be applied in even the most stringent settings, providing students with solid role models and examples across the human experience. Guided by Tatum's (2018) proposition that text selection is the vehicle for meaning-making for students, Tables 2.1 and 2.2 offer a list of texts we believe to be solid examples for students. In addition, many picture books are specifically recommended by national professional organizations such as the National Council for the Social Studies (NCSS), the National Association for the Education of Young Children (NAEYC), and the International Literacy Association (ILA). These organizations can be helpful for educators as they annually publish annotated book lists for teachers.

Conclusion

In an era where teachers and students alike feel bombarded with standardized tests and scripted curricula, it can be challenging to make space for any kind of individualization. And, in an environment where current attacks on diversity make it feel as though it is divisive and shameful—a so-called taboo topic—it can be challenging to effectively discuss the impact of race, gender, poverty, and many other aspects of humanity that speak to the lived experiences of our students. However, Sally and Don were committed to providing opportunities for their students to see both themselves and aspirational role models represented in the picture books used in their classrooms. They designed a two-part unit of literacy instruction using picture book biographies to engage students in identifying unique character traits and then used carefully curated picture books representative of their classroom profile to deepen students' understanding of character development. This unit ultimately culminated in the publication and sharing of student-written autobiographies. Not only did this unit of instruction meet both reading and writing standards, but it also helped to cultivate a classroom community based on an understanding of and respect for the unique traits and lives of each student, thus meeting both the instructional and social-emotional needs of the students through the windows and mirrors provided by the mentor texts.

References

Christ, T., & Sharma, S. A. (2018). Searching for mirrors: Preservice teachers' journey toward more culturally relevant pedagogy. *Reading Horizons: A Journal of Literacy and Language Arts, 57*(1). https://scholarworks.wmich.edu/reading_horizons/vol57/iss1/5

Clarke, L. W., & Whitney, E. (2009). Walking in their shoes: Using multiple-perspectives texts as a bridge to critical literacy. *The Reading Teacher, 62*(6), 530–534. https://doi.org/10.1598/RT.62.6.7

Dawes, E. T., Cappiello, M. A., Magee, L., Bryant, J., & Sweet, M. (2019). Portraits of perseverance: Creating picturebook biographies with third graders. *Language Arts, 96*(3).

Dollins, C. A. (2016). Crafting creative nonfiction: From close reading to close writing. *The Reading Teacher, 70*(1), 49–58.

Dore, R. A., Smith, E. D., & Lillard, A. S. (2017). Children adopt the traits of characters in a narrative. *Child Development Research, 2017.* https://doi.org/10.1155/2017/6838079

Dorfman, L. R., Cappelli, R., & Hoyt, L. (2017). *Mentor texts: Teaching writing through children's literature, K-6.* Stenhouse Publishers.

Floyd, E. F., & Hébert, T. P. (2010). Using picture book biographies to nurture the talents of young gifted African American students. *Gifted Child Today, 33*(2), 38–46. https://doi.org/10.1177/107621751003300211

Garces-Bacsal, R. M. (2021). Of grit and gumption, sass and verve: What gifted students can learn from multicultural picture book biographies. In S. R. Smith (Ed.), *Handbook of giftedness and talent development in the Asia-Pacific* (pp. 431–453). Springer. https://doi.org/10.1007/978-981-13-3041-4_18

Gee, J. P. (1990). *Social linguistics and literacies: Ideology in discourses.* Falmer Press.

Harper, L. J., & Brand, S. T. (2010). More alike than different: Promoting respect through multicultural books and literacy strategies. *Childhood Education, 86*(4), 224–233. https://doi.org/10.1080/00094056.2010.10523153

Kieffer, M. J., & Lesaux, N. K. (2007). Breaking down words to build meaning: Morphology, vocabulary, and reading comprehension in the urban classroom. *The Reading Teacher, 61*(2), 134–144. https://doi.org/10.1598/RT.61.2.3

Laminack, L. (2017). Mentors and mentor texts: What, why, and how? *The Reading Teacher, 70,* 753–755.

Leung, C. B., & Hicks, J. (2014). Writer identity and writing workshop. *Writing & Pedagogy, 6*(3).

Niland, A. (2021). Picture books and young learners' reading identities. *The Reading Teacher, 74*(5), 649–654. https://doi.org/10.1002/trtr.1994

Sharma, S. A., & Christ, T. (2017). Five steps toward successful culturally relevant text selection and integration. *The Reading Teacher, 71*(3), 295–307. https://doi.org/10.1002/trtr.1623

Tatum, A. W. (2009). *Reading for their life:(Re) building the textual lineages of African American adolescent males.* Heinemann.

Tatum, A. W. (2018). Toward a more anatomically complete model of literacy development: A focus on black males students and texts. In D. E. Alvermann, N. J. Unrau, & R. B. Ruddell (Eds.), *Theoretical models and processes of literacy* (7th ed., pp. 281–300). Routledge.

Vygotsky, L. S. (1978). Socio-cultural theory. *Mind in Society, 6*(3), 23–43.

Children's Literature Cited

Ahmed, R. (2018). *Mae among the stars*. Harper-Collins.

Churnin, N. (2017). *Manji moves a mountain*. Creston Books.

Cornwall, G. (2017). *Jabari jumps*. Candlewick.

De la Pena, M. (2015). *Last stop on market street* (1st ed.). G.P. Putnam's Sons Books for Young Readers.

De la Pena, M. (2021). *Milo imagines the world*. G.P. Putnam's Sons Books for Young Readers.

Engle, M. (2019). *Dancing hands: How Teresa Carreno played the piano for President Lincoln*. Simon and Schuster.

Evans, C. (2019). *Evelyn the adventurous entomologist: The true story of a world traveling bug hunter*. The Innovation Press.

Herthel, J. (2014). *I am jazz*. Dial Books.

Hubbard, R. (2020). *The oldest student: How Mary Walker learned to read*. Anne Schwartz Books.

Keating, J. (2017). *Shark lady: The true story of how Eugenie Clark became the ocean's most fearless scientist*. Sourcebooks Explore.

Krull, K. (2000). *Wilma unlimited: How Wilma Rudolph became the world's fastest woman*. Piper.

Love, J. (2018). *Julian is a mermaid*. Penguin Random House.

Love, J. (2020). *Julian at the wedding*. Penguin Random House.

Ludwig, T. (2013). *The invisible boy*. Knopf Books for Young Readers.

Markel, M. (2013). *Brave girl: Clara and the shirtwaist makers strike of 1909*. Balzer + Bray.

Martin, J. (2013). *Farmer will Allen and the growing table*. Readers to Eaters.

Mosca, J. (2017). *The girl who thought in pictures: The story of Dr. Temple Grandin*. The Innovation Press.

Reynolds, P. (2019). *Say something*. Orchard Books.

Rhee, H. (2020). *The paper kingdom*. Penguin Random House.

Sanders, R. (2018). *Pride the story of Harvey Milk and the rainbow flag*. Random House Books for Young Readers.

Shamsi-Basha, K., & Latham, I. (2020). *The cat man of Aleppo*. Penguin Random House.

Sims Bishop, R. (1990). Mirrors, windows, and sliding glass doors. *Perspectives, 6*(3), ix–xi.

Skeers, L. (2020). *Dinosaur lady: The daring discoveries of Mary Anning, the first paleontologist*. Sourcebooks Explore.

Stuart, S. (2020). *My shadow is pink*. Larrikin House.

Wang, A. (2019). *Magic ramen: The story of Momofuku Ando*. Little Bee Books.

Williams, V. (1983). *A chair for my mother*. HarperCollins.

Yousafzai, M. (2017). *Malala's magic pencil*. Little, Brown Books for Young Readers.

3

SLIDING THE GLASS DOOR

Making Time and Space for Difficult Conversations With Youth Through Multivoiced Young Adult Literature

Heather Waymouth, Keith Newvine, Sarah Fleming, Pamela Margolis, Sarah Mellon, and Tina Middaugh

> *Books are sometimes windows, offering views of worlds that may be real or imagined, familiar or strange. These windows are also sliding glass doors, and readers have only to walk through in imagination to become a part of whatever world has been created or recreated by the author.*
>
> *(Sims Bishop, 1990, p. 9)*

Sims Bishop's metaphor has a haunting "othering" to it—potential colonization (Bhattacharya, 2009) that could occur when students read texts by and about people's lives from cultures different from their own. Thomas (2015) and Borsheim-Black (2015) noted that white[1] students were quick to feel discomfort and choose silence over participation in discussions on race. Recent legislation in a growing number of states, such as Florida, prohibits any act in which "an individual should feel discomfort, guilt, anguish, or any other form of psychological distress on account of his or her race, color, sex, or national origin" (Florida Senate, 2022). Such legislation limits how and how often students engage with texts that allow them to learn about experiences different from their own and highlights the urgency for pedagogy to open textual sliding glass doors.

When textual sliding glass doors are "opened" improperly in classrooms, they become tools of voyeurism—mere windows to gawk through into "strange" worlds (Sims Bishop, 1990, p. 9). Yet, students can step through these doors when teachers intentionally navigate the distance between their students' lived experiences and individuals from marginalized communities, allowing texts to become tools for productive conversations, understanding, empathy, and allyship. In this chapter, we will build on Sims Bishop's (1990) metaphor by discussing how two teachers made deliberate and intentional pedagogical moves with three multivoiced young adult sliding glass door texts to (re)move barriers and structure space for youth to explore and explain issues of race and racism.

DOI:10.4324/9781003302216-4

Authors' Positionality

We believe it is vital to note our respective positionalities because they shape our work and influence our interpretation, understanding, and belief in the validity of the research we cite herein. Heather, Keith, and Sarah Fleming are literacy education professors and former high school teachers. Heather was a literacy specialist; Keith was a ninth- and eleventh-grade English teacher; and Sarah was a tenth-grade English teacher in white suburban high schools in New York State. These authors all identify as white and middle class. The next two authors are graduate students enrolled in literacy education programs. Pam is a Doctoral student whose research interests include equity and representation and civic engagement for students of color and the LGBTQIA+ communities. She identifies as Black and middle class. Sarah Mellon is a Master's student who has previously conducted research in inclusive literature and identifies as Black and middle class. Tina is an eleventh- and twelfth-grade English teacher in a white suburban school in Central New York. While the vignettes included in this chapter took place in Keith's and Sarah Fleming's classrooms, all authors have contributed to our analysis and discussion.

Theoretical Framework

Critical Race English Education

Critical theories work to dismantle the ways power hierarchies have privileged some and oppressed many. Those who examine education critically, such as through critical literacy and/or pedagogy, seek to reconstruct education as a tool for equity and liberation (Parker, 2022; Vasquez et al., 2019). Drawing upon the work of foundational critical scholars in education (e.g., Freire, 1970/2000; Moll et al., 1992), Critical Race English Education (CREE) is a necessary framework when building an anti-racist ELA curriculum in white spaces. By an anti-racist ELA curriculum, we mean a curriculum that actively takes up racial themes and identities rather than "omitting critical conversations from the curriculum that explore the intersections of race, gender, religion, language, sexuality, etc." (Johnson, 2021, p. 43) or otherwise preventing students from considering the impact of race on the experiences of characters as well as on their own (Kendi, 2019). Johnson (2021) proposes four central tenets of a Critical Race English Education which:

1. challenges concerns such as antiblack racism, whiteness, white supremacy, patriarchy, and violence that unfolds in school contexts and out-of-school spaces;
2. examines the historical and present-day relationship between language, literacy, race, and education by extending the concept of literacies to include activist contexts and social movements such as slave rebellions, Reconstruction, Black Freedom Movement, Civil Rights Movement, #BlackLivesMatter, and #SayHerName, etc.;

3. aims to work against dominant and canonical texts that exclude the knowledge of Black people and the racial and ethnic experiences of Black people across the Diaspora; and
4. stands on the Black literacy that Black people have created over time and continue to form

(Johnson, 2021, p. 57)

CREE positions English classrooms as places where youth can unpack race through critical dialogue, self-reflection, and opportunities for (re)imagining a more inclusive and just society (Baker-Bell et al., 2017). By bringing this from the periphery to the center of classroom conversations, teachers and students can engage in deconstructing oppressive regimes of power and reconstruct liberatory worlds.

Making time and space for racial conversations starts with a teacher's critical text selection. CREE's third tenet requires teachers to select texts which decenter whiteness (e.g., Borsheim-Black & Sarigianides, 2019) by including equitable access to narratives reflecting the experiences of characters of color. However, a text is a tool, not an end goal, which can facilitate students' grasp of many intersectional identities of individuals within and across cultures. Which narratives are centered and which critical literacy practices are privileged in our classrooms with youth matter (Botelho & Rudman, 2009; Ebarvia et al., 2020).

By consciously choosing diverse and inclusive texts that have barriers that can be (re)moved by teachers, "we can push open doors" (Enriquez et al., 2021, p. 105), challenging readers and ourselves to have difficult conversations. To (re)move barriers, teachers must notice an aspect of a text, topic, or activity that may hinder students' abilities to step through the sliding glass door and make deliberate moves to help their students navigate the divide. There is no singular way to do this; instead, (re)movement is always conducted considering the local context. As re-often denotes something that is done again (as in repeated), we use parentheses to imply that teachers' pedagogical moves may provide access to an unfamiliar world, either real or imagined, for the first time. Multivoiced narratives are ripe with opportunities to push open doors. They piece together individual characters' stories, often through first-person narration. Multivoiced narratives juxtapose a series of similar opposing perspectives to provide entryways into multiple perspectives on shared storylines.

Recently published YA multivoiced narratives were intentionally written for youths' critical consumption and often offer insights into how white supremacy operates systematically and repositions people of color as subjects of their liberation (Morrison, 1992) through counterstories (Solórzano & Yosso, 2002). While traditional narratives may also present counterstories, multivoiced narratives decenter the importance of a singular character's identities, perceptions, and realities. Readers see characters as they see themselves and how others perceive them.

By presenting characters in this complex manner, they may become more real to the students reading them. This may also allow readers to feel that "Within the pages of this book, [readers] can be who [they] wholly are. And perhaps this might be empowering enough to at least add a bit of significance to their lives" (Reynolds, as cited in Gonçalves, 2020).

We take up CREE to explore how pedagogical moves were used in conjunction with three multivoiced YA novels—*Clap When You Land* (Acevedo, 2020), *The 57 Bus: A True Story of Two Teenagers and the Crime That Changed Their Lives* (Slater, 2017), and *All American Boys* (Reynolds & Kiely, 2015)—to discuss issues of race and racism with youth. These titles were selected because they offered deep explorations into multiple perspectives on race and racism, removed a barrier within the texts themselves, and were rich with possibilities for fostering love for humanity. Within each vignette, we outline the use of one text and include sample assignments and student responses. Following the third vignette, we discuss obstacles that remained, despite the use of specific pedagogical moves and offer suggestions for how educators can continue to develop pedagogical actions that open doors for youth.

Pedagogical Move #1: Centering Voices From the Diaspora Through Deliberate Text Selection

Clap When You Land features two teens, Camino Rios living in the Dominican Republic, and Yahaira Rios living in New York City. After a plane crash claims their father's life, they discover they are sisters. The story begins with each learning of her father's death and her sister living a lifetime away. Narration alternates between Camino and Yahaira. Readers are introduced to richly presented landscapes of both settings and are invited along the journey of self-discovery as both girls wrestle with their grief and their understanding of family. The book challenges readers' understanding of identity, as the girls differ in skin color, sexuality, and class.

Clap When You Land removes barriers by illustrating how each sister walks through a sliding glass door through a unique convergence of the two stories. The sisters develop empathy and love for each other, metaphorically moving through the door within the plot. The reader accompanies them and must consider the same story from two perspectives, complicating the reader's understanding of whose story is right/better and ultimately empathizing with both.

One strategy teachers can use is to center characters' lived experiences. Tenth-grade students in Sarah Fleming's classroom engaged in literature circles (Daniels, 2002), particularly considering texts related to one of the course's driving questions: (a) "Who tells your story?" (b) "In telling histories, whose voices are included and excluded?" and (c) "How do we use inquiry and activism to tell our truths?" Sarah believed literature circles would help students explore these

TABLE 3.1 Inquiry and Advocacy Literature Circles Booklist

Title and Author
Clap When You Land by Elizabeth Acevedo
We Are Not from Here by Jenny Torres Sanchez
The Grief Keeper by Alexandra Villasante
X by Ilyasah Shabazz with Kekla Magoon
The Black Kids by Christina Hammonds Reed
Brown Girl Dreaming by Jacqueline Woodson
Hearts Unbroken by Cynthia Leitich Smith
Sanctuary by Abby Sher and Paola Mendoza
The Lines We Cross by Randa Abdel-Fattah
Punching the Air by Ibi Zoboi and Yusef Salaam
Wicked Fox by Kat Cho
This Is My America by Kim Johnson
Under a Painted Sky by Stacey Lee
Legendborn by Tracy Deonn
I Hope You Get This Message by Farah Naz Rishi
The Education of Margot Sanchez by Lilliam Rivera
Slay by Brittney Morris
Cemetery Boys by Aiden Thomas

questions because of the number of stories and voices her students could inter-act with throughout the unit. While no individual student read every book in Table 3.1, through Sarah's planned activities, every student interacted with ele-ments of every book at some point in the unit.

Five students selected *Clap When You Land*. Circle members created reading schedules and completed the self-assigned readings by their weekly meetings in which they discussed their reactions to the plot. Students completed close reading strategy activities, sometimes with classmates from their circles and other times with peers reading other novels. The focus of these activities changed each time; for example, for one meeting, students kept their annotations focused on how the author used dialogue to progress the story. Students differentiated between and evaluated moods in scenes across their novels in another task. Tasks were some-what generic so they could be applied to multiple novels simultaneously, allowing the teacher to focus on a particular skill set as it occurred across various narratives (see Figure 3.1 for an example).

Students wrote final reflections in which they connected their reading to their work throughout the school year. Students who read *Clap When You Land* spe-cifically discussed the experience of reading a multivoiced narrative. Catherine (pseudonyms for all students) explained that the multivoiced structure "[brought] the story together and [made] it feel as one." Meg felt it made the story better because both characters "add their own take on how they are dealing with the

Inquiry and Activism Literature Circle Activity

1. For today's lit circle meeting, you are going to talk about how your book (so far) is prompting you to think about **a particular topic or issue relevant to the lives of young people: relationships, family, mental health, social status, issues of difference, education,** etc. Prepare your response to the following two questions, to share out with your classmates:

What does this book make you want to learn more about? (Inquiry)	How might this book be inviting you to do something or act in response to that issue? (Activism)

2. Talk to three people in class who are reading a different book, and then complete the chart.

Name	Book	Liking it? Why?	What does your classmate want to learn more about or do in response? (Use your Qs above)

Literature Circle Reflective Prompt

Q4 lit-circle reading: end-of-book reflection

Now that you've finished the book, consider how this narrative fits in with the other work we've done this year. Ask yourself, how does it answer one of (if not all) of the driving questions?

- Who tells your story?
- In telling histories, whose voices are included and whose are excluded?
- What do speculative stories teach us about the past, present and future?
- How do we use inquiry and activism to tell our truths?

Response more personally to the text. Why did you like it? Who should read it, and why? What would you like to read next, if there were time?

FIGURE 3.1 Sample Assignments From Literature Circle Unit

situation and their views on their father. Their voices were very much included." Stefan took this a step further; he said,

I felt as a reader that I wasn't hearing two separate stories, but really one, compartmentalized by intervening cultural, social, and personal factors shaping their lives. It really shows how a story can not only be greatly influenced by the conspiring events, but the perspectives from which it is told from.

Some responses were more superficially focused on their exposure to new topics and cultural experiences rather than being focused on the narrative structure itself. For example, Catherine said, "I loved this book because it gave me a look into other cultures, as well as the different grief process, which I only have so much knowledge about." Allison expressed that "Typically minority voices are excluded in novels; this novel gives the perspectives of Yahaira and Camino, whose voices would typically be excluded." In other words, students' reflections spoke to the inclusion of others' stories as being unique to their reading experiences. Still, they did not necessarily move beyond a voyeuristic sense of peering through the glass to a more sincere and sophisticated understanding of empathy with the characters and their experiences. It is clear from these responses that students felt they were stepping through the door into new worlds and experiences. Yet, we notice that the barrier of potential voyeurism remains.

While their statements speak to the desired sensitivity toward the characters' different experiences, there too remained an objectification of those characters and their stories as the students maintained a safe distance from the text's racial themes by focusing their comments on textual structures. Centering traditionally othered stories through deliberate text selection is necessary but insufficient without additional pedagogical moves that ask students to unpack not just what those stories are, but why they exist as they do and how students' perceptions of those stories are filtered through their lenses of whiteness and privilege.

Pedagogical Move #2: Challenging Ethnocentrism Through Activist Literacies

The 57 Bus: A True Story of Two Teenagers and the Crime That Changed Their Lives is a complex nonfiction narrative of an assault in Oakland, California, on November 4, 2013, and its aftermath on the victim, the perpetrator, their families, and community. Richard, a 16-year-old Black teen, sets fire to the dress of Sasha, a gender-nonconforming white teen while riding the bus. The story follows these youth as Sasha lives through the surgeries needed to recover from the assault—and the difficulties of being an agender teen in various heteronormative environments— and as Richard attempts to survive in juvenile detention under the threat of being charged with a hate crime and of being tried as an adult. Slater tells the story of both teens' lives before, during, and after the assault, providing readers with the opportunity to discuss gender identity and expression and the various systemically racist structures of the criminal justice system. The book (re)moves barriers by challenging readers' understanding of what nonfiction storytelling can look like and providing factual information about the complicated forces that prevent some teens from realizing their greatness.

One strategy to foster students' adoption of an activist stance is to create a collaborative, multimodal assignment written for a real audience requiring students to address issues of race and racism specifically. Keith's English 11 class students read this text as part of their summer reading assignment. After their independent reading and multiple weeks of discussion in the final project, students created informational brochures about social issues and ideas presented in the text of which they thought their peers should be aware. Students engaged in a mini-lesson about using school-provided databases and other online research sources to gather reliable, relevant sources of information. Students completed a source credibility checklist and met with Keith to review their sources and checklist. Students were told that these brochures would be on display on bulletin boards throughout the school and available in the library and guidance office. See Figure 3.2 for the trifold brochure requirements and an example student brochure.

Thirteen students collaboratively produced seven informational brochures featuring gender identity, racial inequality in the justice system, restorative justice, gun control, education reform, poverty, and juveniles tried as adults in the criminal justice system. Students wrote for real audiences around taboo topics like anti-black racism, whiteness, white supremacy, patriarchy, and violence that unfolds in out-of-school spaces, as displayed in Slater's non-fiction text.

One brochure provided an embedded hyperlink to a *Wikipedia* page for "Race in the United States criminal justice system" (2022). It offered an infographic from the U.S. Bureau of Justice Statistics to state:

> In the story, *The 57 bus*, racial inequality in the justice system is portrayed in statistics showing how black [sic] youths are more likely to go to adult or juvenile correctional facilities than their white [sic] counterparts. "Just one third of white [sic] youths were sentenced to adult or juvenile state correctional centers while two thirds were given probation or sentenced to time in jail" (Slater, 2017, p. 164). For kids of color the ratios were reversed. This shows how the author acknowledges the existence of racial inequality in the justice system (Student A Informational Brochure, see Table 3.3 for materials accessed/created by students).

This call to action was profound and simple: "You can be an ally to help these issues become a thing of the past by protesting racial injustice, advocating for legislation that could make racial injustice illegal or at least make things more equal in the justice system in terms of prosecuting and sentencing."

Two additional brochures focused on this issue, stating that "According to the article *Unjust Burden* (Hinton et al., 2018), racial disparities in the criminal justice system are not an accident, but instead, are rooted in the history of oppression and discrimination that have targeted black [sic] people." They provide an infographic from the University of Washington Task Force on Race and the Criminal Justice System about incarceration rates in the United States and Washington State from 2005 (Anthony, 2011). The call to action provided an embedded hyperlink to an online document that provided information about being strong white allies who work for social justice (Kivel, 2006).

The 57 Bus: A True Story of Two Teenagers and the Crime That Changed Their Lives
Final Project

Directions: Work with a partner to create an informational brochure about the social issues and/ideas presented in the text that you think your peers should be aware of.

Brainstorming:
What are some social issues or ideas presented in this text which you think your peers should be aware of?

Requirements:
Use the Trifold Brochure Template on Google Classroom.

Panel One should include an original cover for the book. Think of it like a movie poster. Be sure to include the full title, the author's name, awards won, and a tagline. Go here to see some examples of movie posters and taglines.

Panel Two should include a character description of the important characters in the book. This should be a narrative explanation of who each character is before, during, and after the incident. See the back cover of the book for a creative example. This section will be evaluated on how well you map the important characters' journeys in the book—from page 1 to page 295, and maybe beyond.

Panel Three should include a heading with the social issue you want to bring attention to, a paragraph explaining how this topic was addressed in the text (including direct quotes and discussion of the importance of the topic in the text), an infographic with a representation of the idea, an explanation of the importance of this topic in society.

Panel Four should include a heading with the social issue you want to bring attention to, a paragraph explaining how this topic was addressed in the text (including direct quotes and discussion of the importance of the topic in the text), an infographic with a representation of the idea, an explanation of the importance of this topic in society.

Panel Five should include a heading with the social issue you want to bring attention to, a paragraph explaining how this topic was addressed in the text (including direct quotes and discussion of the importance of the topic in the text), an infographic with a representation of the idea, an explanation of the importance of this topic in society.

Panel Six should include a call to action. Provide a statement about what it means to be an ally and specific resources where the reader can go to learn more about how to become an ally for the specific social issues discussed in the inside of your brochure.

FIGURE 3.2   Brochure Guidelines and Student Example

These artifacts illustrate the pedagogical and social value of writing for authentic audiences in their communities, structuring students' exploration of taboo topics in multivoiced narratives. One wonders: could a similarly poignant depiction of real-world issues affecting youth be garnered if, for example, *To Kill a Mockingbird* was the class text—as it often is in secondary English Language Arts classrooms (Stotsky et al., 2010)? Many of the same topics explored by students in this unit of study and the final project could be similarly discussed with Lee's text, but would the outcome be as relevant and purposeful?

Pedagogical Move #3: Expanding the Concept of Blackness by Incorporating Curated Multimodal Texts

All American Boys relates an all-too-common incident of police brutality within Black communities. Rashad, a Black teen, is assaulted by a police officer while shopping at a local corner store. Quinn, a white classmate of Rashad's, witnesses the assault but remains a bystander. Rashad is presumed a criminal; however, he is not. The officer assumes Rashad is guilty because he is Black and brutalizes Rashad. Rashad's assault heightens the story's tension and mimics many real-life concerns of Black families.

The narrative alternates between the lives of these two teens as Rashad recuperates from the physical and emotional trauma while navigating multiple family issues, including a father who was previously a police officer. At the same time, Quinn considers his privilege and next steps only after realizing that he and Rashad are connected socially. Once Quinn realizes that he has bought into racialized bias, he takes action and participates in a die-in protest to raise awareness of police brutality. This text reminds the tragic reality of police brutality, the challenge of understanding white privilege, the bonds of community, and the power of youth as agents of change.

All American Boys removes barriers through co-authorship. Each author was responsible for crafting the character's narrative whose identities most closely mirrored their own, providing authenticity to each character and allowing them to be perceived as nuanced and fully human, thereby facilitating students' journeys as they step between perspectives. Yet, a barrier remains which requires teacher (re)movement. The functional setting and storyline can allow some readers to put distance between what's happening in the book and their communities.

Teachers can open the door to focus on the Black histories, stories, and experiences within a text rather than only focusing on the tragic stories to understand the breadth and depth of Black experiences. To do this, Keith's English 9 students engaged in the Past as Present activity outlined in Figure 3.3. Students learned about Aaron Douglass, a Harlem Renaissance artist alluded to within *All American Boys*, to add depth to Rashad's story and to assist students in understanding the rich history of Black art in contemporary and present times. One student's

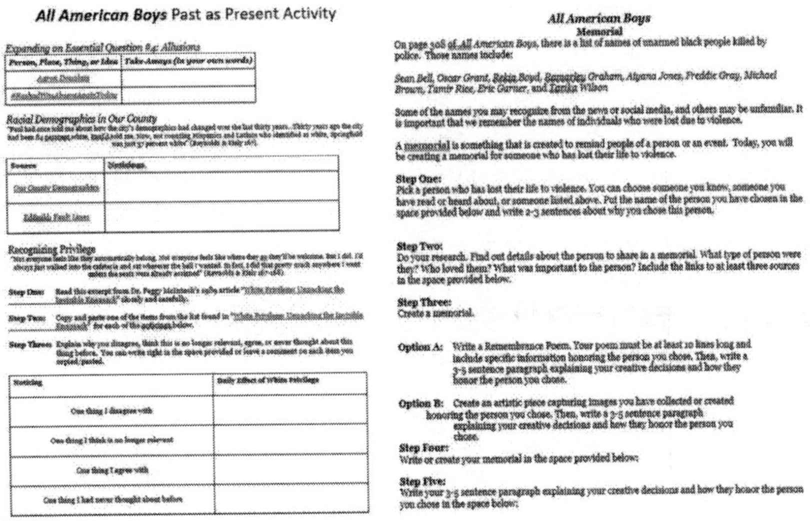

FIGURE 3.3 Assignment Examples From *All American Boys* Unit

summary of *The Art Story* webpage ("Aaron Douglass Artist Overview and Analysis," 2022) dedicated to Douglas stated:

> [Douglas' art] seemed to be an attempt to empower people of color. It alluded to the struggle of black [*sic*] people and the people who helped to try and stop it. The paintings were non-descript, as if to say that anyone can be their own hero, you have the power within you to become great, to stand up for yourself.
>
> *(Student C Summary Response)*

A subsequent lesson picks up this theme to include a discussion of current activists and social movements (Johnson, 2021) seen in the text. For instance, after reading the names of unarmed Black people killed by police in *All American Boys* (Reynolds & Kiely, 2015, p. 308), students researched a person on that list. They wrote a Remembrance Poem honoring this person, as outlined in Figure 3.3. One student's poem, titled "Ramerley Graham," states:

> It is sometimes hard to put in words.
> The loss of a family member is hard.
> People who were loved,
> People who were brothers,
> Sisters,
> Moms and Dads and unfortunately more.
> Gun violence is real,

And cannot go unheard.
Today we remember Ramarley Graham
A human being,
That was loved.
          (Student D Memorial Response)

These student artifacts poignantly depict the importance of expanding youths' notions of Blackness to include the rich history and humanity of Black folks and all individuals from historically marginalized communities. As before, would students have come to the same conclusions about contemporary, real-world issues affecting youth if *To Kill a Mockingbird*, for example, had been the focal text? Is the history of Blackness and the power of antiracist social movements similarly realized when (white) authors co-opt narratives?

Discussion

We often hear that teachers need to give students time and space to unpack taboo topics. However, simply giving time and space is not enough. Much like the phrase "thoughts and prayers" frequently heard in response to violent crimes rooted in oppression, "giving time and space" is passive, requiring little planning and even less action. When we talk about books as windows, mirrors, and sliding glass doors, we acknowledge the need for these tools *in addition* to time and space, yet we, as teachers, outsource our integral and active role to a text—hence the verbs in this chapter's title. Teachers need to *slide* the door. It is what teachers *do* with time and space that matters: deliberately structure and curate both. Similarly, CREE's four tenets are rooted in action, calling for teachers to *challenge, examine, work*, and *stand*.

When we examine how Sarah and Keith constructed time and space in their classrooms, we first notice that we must reconsider what counts as best practice. Consider how Sarah's essential questions shaped the year-long course and the selection of *Clap When You Land:* she considered her class to be a time and space to unpack taboo topics, including race. Her literature circles provided sliding glass doors for students to step through and unpack racial themes. Students noted the presence of racial elements in the text but did not unpack them or step through the door into other worlds. While her use of generic activities across all book selections gave students access to many doors, it limited her ability to deliberately shape each literature circle's discussions of text-specific racial themes. If students were guided to question more precisely the effects of reading this story on the students' developing understanding of race and racism, what could they have said? Would they have expressed more nuanced perspectives or explored their ability to navigate the story and enter previously unknown spaces? Despite Sarah's use of "best practice," a barrier remained between her students and the transformative conversations she intended to foster.

To (re)move the barrier, a teacher's assignments must specifically structure opportunities for students to be reflexive and to challenge various systems and regimes of oppression that are relevant in their world and as read in young adult multivoiced narratives, even if these issues aren't immediately seen or felt in their daily lived experiences—or, one could argue, *because* they aren't. Consider Keith's students' brochures: the social issues they chose to represent suggest a critical understanding of the multiple narrators' experiences within the text and the effect that those experiences have on the students' knowledge of the world. This assignment aimed to push students beyond a voyeuristic understanding of the lives of individuals from communities different from their own. However, some students' projects continued to "other" Black youth, depicting them as victims. While this unit addressed multiple CREE tenets, it fell short in its ability to stand on and celebrate Black literacies and lived experiences to include Black joy, love, and action (Love, 2019).

To (re)move this barrier, a teacher's pedagogy must immerse students in the richness of historical and contemporary artistic narratives written by people of color, including those written within activist social movements. Because these antiracist social movements are so immediately accessible by youth through social media, students must be allowed to understand how those narratives "stand on Black literacies that Black people have created over time and continue to form" (Johnson, 2021, p. 57).

Consider Keith's *All American Boys* unit and students' interactions with counternarratives to the "histories" often presented in school curricula. Students demonstrated a willingness to consider these "new" histories, but not without hesitancy and missteps. Much like Keith's English 11 class activity, some students' projects continued to focus on the trauma of the individuals. While this pedagogical move addressed multiple CREE tenets, it similarly fell short in assisting students in understanding how Black joy and love are tools for liberation. The results of both activities point to the need to continue to do antiracist work with youth, refine how time and space are curated, and consider how antiracist pedagogies often get stalled in tropes of guilt and trauma and rarely (and unfortunately) get to love.

Not all barriers are (re)movable simultaneously by even the most skillful teachers. If the barriers presented by a text are insurmountable, students remain voyeurs into the experiences of others. Each of our vignettes' focal texts offers characters with rich intersectional identities (Crenshaw, 1991). Characters are not just Black and not just white. Yet, here we've only taken up moves to push students to consider their racial identities.

We acknowledge that the pedagogical moves described in this chapter are just a start. Each time we engage white youth in taboo conversations, we find another barrier to (re)move. This work is never finished. Table 3.2 presents our recommendations for teachers seeking to engage in this work, and Table 3.3 provides access to some of the instructional materials used/created by Sarah and Keith's students. Given that all K–12 authorial team members are

TABLE 3.2 Suggestions for Sliding the Glass Door With Youth

Suggestion	Discussion
1. Find your North Star.	Dr. Bettina Love (2019) reminds us that theory is a "location for healing" and, like the North Star which marked the way to freedom for enslaved folks, educators need to embrace theory as a means of freedom-dreaming with youth. You can begin by reading sources referenced in this chapter. What works might serve as your "North Star"?
2. Center the voices, histories, counternarratives, and lived experiences of people of color in the curriculum.	Listen and learn. Then, get to work disrupting texts (see Ebarvia et al., 2020). You can begin by exploring the literature and other sources used with students in this chapter. What might resonate with your students?
3. Be deliberate and intentional.	Rather than "give them time," take time before you teach a unit to consider the potential barriers topics, texts, and activities may present for your students. Then, structure and curate time and space for students to make sense of race and racism for themselves and with each other through activities that require students to step between multiple perspectives.
4. Challenge yourself and your students to fight against forms of oppression.	In the words of James Baldwin (1962), "Not everything that is faced can be changed; but nothing can be changed until it is faced"(p. BR11). It is past time that we face that which needs to be changed. Don't wait in fear of facing barriers you hadn't anticipated or don't know how to (re)move. Adopt a stance of continual reflection and improvement. When in doubt, return to your "North Star" (Love, 2019)!

white, we acknowledge that our identities and ignorance also present barriers. Race, gender, and sexuality might be taboo in white suburban communities and high schools.

Teaching taboo topics through multivoiced YA texts is a risky pedagogical choice. Done incorrectly, viewing perspectives through colonial and depreciating lenses, the reading experience can lead to more extensive walls and stronger animosity. Such reading experiences (re)center whiteness rather than the experiences of BIPOC and reifies voyeuristic positions. Yet, as we learn more about doing it correctly, we reaffirm the belief that adolescence is the time and space to have these conversations. Students find themselves at a critical crossroads. Teachers may serve as proverbial forks in the road and signposts toward more socially just futures. However, teachers also need waypoints. Theories, like CREE, can act as our "north star" (Johnson, 2021; Love, 2019). We hope that the pedagogical moves described previously, and those we envision next, help teachers (re)move as many barriers as possible between our realities and the world we envision all students creating and prospering within together, rather than at the expense of

TABLE 3.3 Resources Used/Created With/By Students

Resource	Hyperlink
Literature Circles Mood Task	https://bit.ly/37gDEqB
Literature Circles Dialogue Task	https://bit.ly/3O7KrU2
Literature Circles Inquiry and Activism Task	https://bit.ly/37JuTFi
Literature Circles Final Reflection Prompts	https://bit.ly/3E8KudH
An Unjust Burden	https://bit.ly/UnjustBurdenVera
Guidelines for being strong white allies	https://bit.ly/WhiteAlliesGuidelines
Race in the United States criminal justice system	https://bit.ly/RaceinCriminalJustice
Website Evaluation Checklist	https://bit.ly/34CIxZX
The 57 Bus Information Brochure Assignment	https://bit.ly/57bBusBrochure
Student A Informational Brochure	https://bit.ly/StudentABrochure
Student B Informational Brochure	https://bit.ly/StudentBBrochure
Aaron Douglass Biography	https://bit.ly/ADouglassBio
All American Boys: The Past as Present Assignment	https://bit.ly/AABPastAsPresent
Student C Summary Response	https://bit.ly/StudentCResponse
All American Boys Memorials Assignment	https://bit.ly/AABMemorials
Student D Memorial Response	https://bit.ly/StudentDMemorial
Additional Resource: The Argument Essay	https://bit.ly/81Debate

one another. We hope that you ask students to take risks, but to take "risks [as] an act of love" (Freire, 1970/2000, p. 50) and realize that "the moment we choose to love, we begin to move towards freedom, to act in ways that liberate ourselves and others" (hooks, 2006, p. 250).

Note

1 This article intentionally uses white (lowercase w) as a form of linguistic justice in order to further dismantle white supremacy.

References

Aaron Douglass Artist Overview and Analysis. (2022). *The art story.* www.theartstory.org/artist/douglas-aaron/

Anthony, C. (2011, March 12). LSJ professor addresses race issues to Washington supreme court. *University of Washington.* https://lsj.washington.edu/news/2011/03/12/lsj-professor-addresses-race-issues-washington-supreme-court

Baker-Bell, A., Butler, T., & Johnson, L. (2017). The pain and the wounds: A call for critical race English education in the wake of racial violence. *English Education, 49*(2), 116–129.

Baldwin, J. (1962). As much truth as one can bear. *New York Times Book Review,* p. 14.

Bhattacharya, K. (2009). Othering research, researching the other: De/colonizing approaches to qualitative inquiry. In L. W. Perna (Ed.), *Higher education: Handbook of theory and research* (pp. 105–150). Springer.

Borsheim-Black, C. (2015). "It's pretty much white": Challenges and opportunities of an antiracist approach to literature instruction in a multilayered white context. *Research in the Teaching of English, 49*(4), 407–429.

Borsheim-Black, C., & Sarigianides, T. (2019). *Letting go of literary whiteness: Antiracist literature instruction for white students.* Teachers College Press.

Botelho, M. J., & Rudman, M. K. (2009). *Critical multicultural analysis of children's literature: Mirrors, windows, and doors.* Routledge.

Crenshaw, K. (1991). Mapping the margins: Intersectionality, identity politics, and violence against women of color. *Stanford Law Review, 43*(6), 1241–1299.

Daniels, H. (2002). *Literature circles: Voice and choice in book clubs and reading groups.* Pembrooke Publishers Limited.

Ebarvia, T., Germán, L., Parker, K. N., & Torres, J. (2020). #DISRUPTTEXTS. *English Journal, 110*(1), 100–102.

Enriquez, G. (2021). Foggy mirrors, tiny windows, and heavy doors: Beyond diverse books toward meaningful literacy instruction. *The Reading Teacher, 75*(1), 103–106.

Florida Senate. Reg. Sess. 2022. S.B. 148. Individual Freedom. flsenate.gov/Session/Bill/2022/148/BillText/Filed/PDF

Freire, P. (2000). *Pedagogy of the oppressed.* Continuum. (Original work published 1970)

Gonçalves, D. (2020, February 7). 'I get to whisper to them, I love you': Jason Reynolds on writing for youth, growing up in DC and his mission. *WUSA9.* www.wusa9.com/article/news/local/dc-native-author-jason-reynolds-mission-writing-for-youth/65-ef42a5db-8423-4149-8f18-ae8e1f52d845

Hinton, E. K., Henderson, L., & Reed, C. (2018, May). An unjust burden: The disparate treatment of Black Americans in the criminal justice system. *Vera.* www.vera.org/publications/for-the-record-unjust-burden

hooks, b. (2006). *Outlaw culture: Resisting representations.* Routledge.

Johnson, L. L. (2021). *Critical race English education: New visions, new possibilities.* Routledge.

Kendi, I. (2019). *How to be an antiracist.* Bodley Head.

Kivel, P. (2006). Guidelines for being strong white allies. *Racial Equity Tools.* http://paulkivel.com/wp-content/uploads/2015/07/guidelinesforbeingstrongwhiteallies.pdf

Love, B. (2019). *We want to do more than survive: Abolitionist teaching and the pursuit of educational freedom.* Beacon Press.

Moll, L. C., Amanti, C., Neff, D., & Gonzalez, N. (1992). Funds of knowledge for teaching: Using a qualitative approach to connect homes and classrooms. *Theory into Practice, 31*(2), 132–141.

Morrison, T. (1992). *Playing in the dark: Whiteness and the literary imagination.* Harvard University Press.

Parker, K. (2022). *Literacy is liberation: Working toward justice through culturally relevant teaching.* ASCD.

Sims Bishop, R. (1990). Mirrors, windows, and sliding glass doors. *Perspectives, 6*(3), ix–xi.

Solórzano, D. G., & Yosso, T. J. (2002). Critical race methodology: Counter-storytelling as an analytical framework for education research. *Qualitative Inquiry, 8*(1), 23–44.

Stotsky, S., Traffas, J., & Woodworth, J. (2010, May). Literary study in grades 9, 10, and 11: A national survey. In *Forum: A publication of the ALSCW* (Vol. 4, pp. 1–75). Association of Literary Scholars, Critics, and Writers.

Thomas, E. E. (2015). "We always talk about race": Navigating race talk dilemmas in the teaching of literature. *Research in the Teaching of English,* 154–175.

Vasquez, V. M., Janks, H., & Comber, B. (2019). Critical literacy as a way of being and doing. *Language Arts, 96*(5), 300–311.

Literature Cited

Acevedo, E. (2020). *Clap when you land*. Harper Teen.

Lee, H. (1960). *To kill a mockingbird*. J.P. Lippencott & Co.

Reynolds, J., & Kiely, B. (2015). *All American boys*. Simon & Schuster.

Slater, D. (2017). *The 57 bus: A true story of two teenagers and the crime that changed their lives*. Farrar, Straus and Giroux.

SECTION 2

4

EXPLORING GENDER IDENTITY AND EQUITY THROUGH *LILY AND DUNKIN*

Jennifer S. Dail, Julie M. Koch, Shelbie Witte, and Lauren Vandever

That students struggle with identity during adolescence presents nothing new; however, identity presents great opportunities for exploration in classroom contexts when taken up as critical civic empathy, defined by Mirra (2018) as the consideration of how issues of power and inequity play out in the literacy classroom, envisioning literacy practices as a means of civic engagement. Traditional models of literature instruction focus on building empathy in individual readers through engagement with texts. Mirra (2018) argues for a "concept of critical empathy to push the dialogue toward recognizing ourselves (and other individuals) within a political context as members of socially constructed groups with different levels of power and privilege while reimagining caring in terms of engagement with public life" (p. 20). Identity is politicized in society; yet, schools overlook discussing that in the context of exploring broader issues of identity with students.

The concept of gender identity as just one layer of the human experience creates a complex web of terms and viewpoints that students struggle to understand and master. Literature provides a core means for teachers to address identity issues in the English Language Arts classroom. Drawing on the foundational research of Dr. Rudine Sims Bishop (1990), who discusses texts providing readers with mirrors, windows, and sliding glass doors, literature can help students feel more connected regarding challenges they face and can even give them more courage in facing them. As Dail and Leonard note (2011), adolescent "identity extends well beyond safer mainstream topics, such as family and friends, and that topics like sexual orientation and gender identity are often skirted during open discussions" (p. 50). Schools do not always support these frank discussions of gender identity, without which there cannot be gender equity. The Gay, Lesbian, and Straight Education Network (GLSEN) notes, "When asked to describe how staff responded to reports of victimization, LGBTQ students most commonly said that

DOI:10.4324/9781003302216-6

staff did nothing or told the student to ignore it; 2 in 10 students were told to change their behavior (e.g., to not act 'so gay' or dress in a certain way)" (Kosciw et al., 2020, p. 31). This does not demonstrate a shift from the National School Climate Survey from a decade ago where GLSEN noted that high incidences of harassment toward students identifying as LGBTQ in schools are "exacerbated by school staff rarely, if ever, intervening on behalf of LGBT students" (Kosciw et al., 2010, p. xvi). Research also indicates that students who identify as transgender report more negative school climate perceptions than those who identify as cisgender (Ioverno & Russell, 2021). Students report a more positive school climate and more supportive adults in the later high school years and a more negative school climate/fewer supportive adults in the middle school years (Ioverno & Russell, 2021). In short, schools, particularly middle schools, need to do better in creating cultures of empathy around gender identity and equity.

Lily and Dunkin by Donna Gephart

Lily and Dunkin (2016) is a highly engaging read for middle grades students focusing on the friendship of Lily Jo McGrother and Dunkin Dorfman. Lily, born Timothy McGrother, is a girl living in a boy's body. Dunkin, named Norbert Dorfman, is dealing with bipolar disorder. Norbert has moved from New Jersey to the Florida town where Lily lives. They meet over the summer when Norbert, returning from a Dunkin Donuts run, spies Lily perched in her favorite hiding place, the great banyan tree in front of the local library. When Norbert spies Lily sitting in the tree, he sees a girl with piercing blue eyes in a dress and sandals.

When they meet, both characters face the challenge of naming how they prefer to be addressed by the other. Norbert expresses dislike for his birth name, and Lily nicknames him Dunkin while Lily remains silent about her preferred name. The novel is structured with alternating stories, as Lily and Dunkin narrate their own. These alternating stories often offer differing perspectives on the same incident. Through Lily and Dunkin's stories, we see their tight thread of friendship grow and strengthen as we learn about their secrets and the consequences of those secrets.

While the novel deals with serious issues such as gender identity and bipolar disorder, it does so in a manner that focuses on friendship and adolescent struggles accompanying that at its core. The characters experience typical middle school issues such as bullying and family tensions. The novel also expresses the tensions adolescents experience between authentically balancing who they truly are on the inside with the persona they project to the world.

Building Literacy Around Issues of Gender Identity

In the novel, Lily struggles with acceptance related to her gender identity. Mental health professionals consider concerns around transgender identity concerning a diagnosis of *gender dysphoria* (American Psychiatric Association [APA], 2013). According to APA, gender dysphoria is people's negative feelings when their bodies and gender identity do not match. We define gender identity based on the definition provided by the APA and Guidelines for Psychological Practice with Transgender and Gender Nonconforming People:

> A person's deeply-felt, inherent sense of being a boy, a man, or male; a girl, a woman, or female; or an alternative gender (e.g., genderqueer, gender non-conforming, gender-neutral) that may or may not correspond to a person's sex assigned at birth or to a person's primary or secondary sex characteristics.

When babies are born in the United States, a physician will assign a sex based on physical characteristics; sometimes, "assigned" sex and gender identity are different. When this causes discomfort and distress, mental health professionals may label it gender dysphoria.

Not all gender-diverse peoples experience a sense of dysphoria. Those who do may also struggle with anxiety and depression resulting from rejection by peers or family members or feeling like they do not fit into society (Rood et al., 2016). As we see with Lily, support from her mother and sister increases her confidence, and she can be herself, thus reducing gender dysphoria and negative feelings. On the other hand, the rejection Lily experiences from her father makes her feel worse, thus increasing her dysphoria and negative feelings. In one instance, Lily cuts her hair to please her father and her bullies, and she then spends the rest of the novel experiencing dysphoria from the loss. Approximately 1.8% of adolescents identify as transgender (Trevor Project, 2019); therefore, it may be that teachers who see 100 students or more a day likely have had at least two who identify as transgender or experience gender dysphoria.

Transgender youth have much higher rates of depression and suicidality than other adolescents (Trevor Project, 2019). In one study, almost half of all transgender youth reported thinking about suicide in the last year compared to 16% of cisgender youth. These mental health struggles may be related to how society treats transgender people. In the same study, almost one-third of transgender youth felt unsafe at school, while one-fourth had been threatened or injured with a weapon at school (Trevor Project, 2019). These numbers are much higher than those reported by cisgender youth: 6% felt unsafe, and 5% had been threatened or injured with a weapon at school.

Building a Foundation With Language

Students will bring different experiences and background knowledge to reading *Lily and Dunkin*, which will inform how they read the novel. We advocate engaging students in some thinking before the text to gauge where they fall in their knowledge. Some preliminary scaffolding with theories as lenses, specifically queer theory or queer theory frameworks, could assist students in focusing their analyses. For a deeper discussion of queer theory and the ways that queer theory can be used as a framework for discussions with and among students, Blackburn et al. (2015) share an overview of queer ideologies and elements to consider. Many students will need support in understanding precisely what gender identity means and how gender identity is separate from sexual orientation, which they *may* be more familiar with.

To begin helping students understand gender and identity in a broad context, teachers can lead students through an activity to establish their own identity and how a book would "mirror" them. Using the acronym RESPECTFUL (D'Andrea & Daniels, 2001), students explore ten aspects of their own identity. Religious/spiritual identity, Economic/class background, Sexual identity, Psychological maturity, Ethnic/racial identity, Chronological age, Trauma and threats to well-being, Family background and history, Unique physical characteristics, Location of resident, and language. Students can first identify all or some of these aspects of their identity in a list format (see Figure 4.1). Then, students can turn to reflective writing with one of the following prompts:

1. How does your identity shape your day-to-day life?
2. What aspect of your identity do you feel is more important and why?
3. If you were to read a book about a character with the same RESPECTFUL traits as you, what would that story be about?

Once students have explored their own identity, have students share their responses with classmates. This will allow students to see how their worldview is not the only worldview, even among students living in similar circumstances.

Following the RESPECTFUL activity, a good starting point for supporting students in understanding gender and how it differs from sexual orientation is through the Gender Unicorn (Trans Student Educational Resources, 2022) and GLSEN's terminology visual (www.glsen.org/activity/gender-terminology) (GLSEN, 2019a). For example, a person could be assigned female at birth and express themselves as feminine ("gender expression"), while their actual gender identity could be masculine. Some people are very open about their gender identity, while others may feel the need to keep their identity hidden or "in the closet" due to fears about how others will react and safety concerns. Another term often used is "cisgender," which refers to a match between a person's gender identity and sex assigned at birth. These resources can help build some understanding around the concept of gender identity, and gender expression specifically. The Gender Unicorn helps clarify the differences between sexual orientation and gender identity. In contrast, the GLSEN visual focuses on gender by breaking down the relationships between gender attribution (our gender as perceived by others), assigned sex at birth, and gender expression (how we want to display our gender). Working through these terms carefully

R
E
S
P
E
C
T
F
U
L

Name: _Elsabeth_____

Every one of us has a unique identity that is shaped by many different parts of our personality. In this worksheet, we are going to explore 10 aspects of your identity that make you uniquely you.

Directions: Fill out each box below with as much information about yourself as you can or are willing to share.

Religious/spiritual identity	Christian (dad) /Catholic (mom and abuela)
Economic/class background	? Not Poor
Sexual identity	N/A
Psychological maturity	15
Ethnic/racial identity	Mexican
Chronological age	12
Trauma and threats to well-being	N/A
Family background and history	Grandparents moved here from Mexico.
Unique physical characteristics	Glasses, Brown skin, Black hair
Location of resident and language	Oklahoma Spanish & English

On the back of this page, answer one of the following prompts:
1. How does your identity shape your day-to-day life?
2. What aspect of your identity do you feel is more important and why?
3. If you were to read a book about a character with the same RESPECTFUL traits as you, what would that story be about?

1. Being Mexican is the big part of my identity. At home, I speak Spanish with my Abuela and Mom. At school, we have no classes for Spanish speakers. Many of my friends make fun of my year long "tan" and ask why I miss school every year to visit Mexico. They complain about not getting their chips and salsa while we are closed, but I only see my Mexican cousins 10 days a year.

FIGURE 4.1 RESPECTFUL Example

and thoroughly will set students up for a better view through Lily and Dunkin's window. As a point of clarity, this discussion should not position students (or teachers) as feeling the need to identify these aspects of their own identity for the class.

Discussing gender identity and equity issues requires building common and acceptable language with students, particularly where pronouns are concerned. GLSEN (2019b) offers a Pronoun Guide resource to support teachers and students in applying pronouns correctly to align with how people identify. This applies to students both within reading the text and beyond the classroom as they work to engage more empathetically in society. Modeling gender pronouns via the novel can help students consider their use of identifying language for themselves and others. For example, some students may not understand why an individual's preferred pronoun is "they," which can often create tension with traditional pronoun/antecedent rules governing grammar. The guide's goal and accompanying classroom conversations are to help schools advocate "for the inclusive use of pronouns for all" (GLSEN, 2019c). Similarly to gender, we do not ever want to mandate that students share their pronouns; although we can invite it for those who are comfortable. We can also model it for our students by sharing our pronouns.

To bring these ideas around gender identity together, teachers may want to implement GLSEN's lesson activity on Misgendering and Respect for Pronouns. Engaging students with this can help solidify their thinking around language and use where people and identity are concerned. It ties in with other resources offered by them on gender identity and utilizes a video, the terminology, and a structured discussion to engage students in further exploring the concept of gender identity in preparation for reading *Lily and Dunkin*.

Creating a Safe Learning Environment for Students

Facilitating pre-reading discussions offers a prime opportunity for setting expectations regarding classroom discourse and conduct to promote a safe environment for all students. A good place to begin this is by articulating overarching goals for students to frame the work. Some goals might include using inclusive language, listening to each other, and understanding how to ask effective questions for empathy.

Just as we strive to create a safe learning community in our reading and writing classrooms, we advocate drawing upon these same principles in extending that environment and those practices into literature discussions with complex issues. Teachers might start by developing and articulating some non-negotiables for classroom discourse and behavior. We recommend involving students in creating this list. Some examples of non-negotiables include no name-calling, bullying, or pejorative or inaccurate use of language. As the teacher, model kindness in responding to your students so that they can see what that looks like in action and develop it in their responses to each other. We also recommend being vulnerable and taking the same risks you ask your students to take in the classroom. For example, if something is funny, it is okay to laugh with students about it. It is okay to say that you do not understand or correct your language use. This takes failures and turns them into learning opportunities where teachers position themselves as growing alongside their students in the learning community. Once terminology and rules of engagement for a safe classroom space are in place, you are then ready to guide students through the text.

Guiding Readers Through the Text

Facilitating Discussion of the Text

There are many opportunities in whole-novel study to invite students into a deeper exploration of the text and its issues through discussion. These questions cause moments of pause and to purposefully reconnect students with the gender identity and equity issues presented in the book. We advocate providing students with opportunities to write in response to questions before entering into the whole class discussion. We recommend helping students make explicit connections between the issues presented in the text and the pre-reading work around identity and language. Questions of this nature, in particular, may require more space for some students to process to have a productive discussion. Here are a few potential options to use:

1. Lily was born as Tim. She lives life in a boy's body but identifies as a girl. She is eager to have her physical body reflect how she internally views herself. This makes her want to start hormone therapy to facilitate a physical transition into a girl's body. Why does Lily believe it is best to begin hormone therapy now? Why do you think her father is resistant to that even though her mother and sister are supportive?

2. Lily loves the great banyan tree so much she named it Bob. She fights to save the tree, which many view as an act of bravery. As she takes steps to become Lily, the tree becomes even more important to her. Why do you think that is? Do you think Lily exhibits bravery when she stands up to the city in an attempt to save Bob, the tree? What is Lily's ultimate act of bravery?

3. A tension in Lily and Dunkin's friendship is when Dunkin wants to sit with the basketball players at lunch, yet the basketball players bully Lily in the hallways and call her derogatory names like "fag." How does Dunkin feel about this? What evidence in the text can you find to support your answer?

4. Even though they are both bullied, Lily and Dunkin are both reluctant to report the bullying at school. Why do you think that is? What do you think the school might have been able to do to help Lily and Dunkin with bullying?

5. Consider the courage it takes for Lily and Dunkin to share their secrets. What risks do they take by sharing their secrets? What obstacles might they each face due to their sharing of secrets?

6. In what ways is Lily and Dunkin's friendship about tolerance and understanding?

Often teachers present questions on a text as something students should answer as they read and use them to prepare for a test. This is not the context in which we advocate using these questions. In fact, we encourage you to pause at various points in the reading to simply discuss the events in *Lily and Dunkin* with students. The names alone and when to use them can be confusing in this novel. For example, we encourage you to use the name "Lily" and she/her/hers pronouns when talking about this character. Also, discussing the events allows students opportunities to clarify the names, gender identity issues, and family issues. Before these summary discussions, we encourage allowing students a few minutes to free write in reflection on and respond to the second reading. Here, students might summarize what they think is occurring and record any questions or points of confusion they may have.

To help minimize confusion for students as they write/annotate, utilizing a Facts/Questions/Responses (FQR) three-column chart will allow students to separate their thoughts from the basic facts of the story. In FQR, students place Facts from the story in the left-hand column, questions about the story in the middle column, and responses to the text or the questions in the right-hand column. This allows students a more in-depth look into their thoughts and allows the teacher to quickly see where gaps in understanding are happening. After reading *Lily and Dunkin*, the in-depth discussion questions can be used alongside these freewriting responses as appropriate for a deeper dive.

Helping Readers Respond to the Text

One-pager responses offer a structured, visual way to invite students to respond to *Lily and Dunkin* and the issues explored in it. In asking students to create a one-pager response, you can provide them with a template, which can be found via a quick online search using the phrase "one-pager templates," but you can also invite them to create their own structure (Figure 4.2). We recommend providing them examples you identify through an online image search of "one-pager responses." This search will show a wide range of responses for inspiration. There are two possibilities for supporting students in creating one-pager responses: (1) talking about components included in one-pagers that students can choose to draw from, or (2) involving students in generating a required list for the class to reference in creating their responses. Possible components for examination in a one-pager response include, but are not limited to, making connections to the text by using quotations, big ideas such as the gender identity issues highlighted, images, analysis of the text (e.g., figurative language, structure, etc.), key names,

FIGURE 4.2 One-Pager Example

or key places. Involving students in identifying the components of their responses will give them more ownership.

This assignment is simple but powerful. Because students mix images and information, what they present on the page becomes more memorable. Because the brain processes information visually and verbally, asking students to combine the two response modes leads to more robust results. In short, we remember more when we mix language and imagery. Students may feel intimidated by creating something visual or artistic, and this is where offering them a template can provide some support. One useful template is to divide the paper into sections around a circle or square in the middle. In that middle space, have students put a direct quotation from the text and build their response around that. This sort of response to literature allows you to evaluate students' understanding of the text and concepts beyond the discussion while not relying on a test, which we do not advocate for in this context.

Guiding Readers Out of the Text

A Call to Action

A novel such as this offers opportunities to normalize stigmas around gender identity and advocate for inclusive language and behaviors around gender identity. We offer some strategies for helping guide students in doing this.

Acts of Healing

Art presents another means through which expression of feelings and thoughts can occur; therefore, we think this offers an opportunity to invite students to connect what they have learned and express empathy for others through art. As an act of healing to wrap up the reading and discussion of *Lily and Dunkin*, gather art supplies and invite students to create a composition that expresses how they are feeling as a result of the study of this text. It will likely help if you develop some prompts to guide them in this because staring at a blank page or canvas can be highly intimidating for many students. The prompts should be created based on issues and questions raised during the reading and discussion of the novel. You might record questions students asked, interesting things they said, especially around their or characters' feelings, or broad questions that extend beyond the text and promote empathy and equality. You could also ask them to show how their identity can be evolved into an advocate and how they can use their identity for good.

To prepare students for this, you might also share and discuss images with them. A basic online search of "art depicting gender dysphoria" will yield many images to draw from for discussion and inspiration with students. Encourage students to take risks with this and have some fun in their composing process. One way to do this is to assure students that you are not evaluating their artistic ability but their thinking. To emphasize and support this, have students share an artist's statement explaining their piece and their reflection on creating it. This turns the focus back to their thinking and the content and away from their artistic ability. Other ideas for acts of healing include advocacy activities (such as a table in the cafeteria supporting LGBTQ students and providing information on these topics) or writing "letters" to Dunkin or Lily or one of the other characters in the book (e.g., Dunkin's mom or Lily's dad) (Pizzo & Zucker, 2020).

Challenges and Censorship Toolkit

Educators who include books focusing on LBGTQ characters and topics are often met with backlash. In recent years, the challenges and censorship of LBGTQ books have been on an upward trend. The American Library Association (2021) released a statement stating, "In recent months, a national campaign demanding the censorship of books and resources that mirror the lives of those who are gay, queer, or transgender, or that tell the stories of persons who are Black, Indigenous, or persons of color have surfaced . . . More than 330 unique cases were reported to ALA's Office for Intellectual Freedom (OIF) in the three months between September 1 and November 30, 2021. Thus far, challenge totals in 2021 have doubled the number of reports from 2020 (156 challenges) and most likely will outpace 2019 figures (377 challenges)."

When utilizing LGBTQ books in the classroom, the potential pushback can come from many different angles and look different ways. When looking at school and public libraries combined, the ALA (2021) notes 50% of the challenges are initiated by parents, 20% are initiated by public library patrons, 11% are initiated by board or administration, 9% are initiated by political or religious groups, 5% are initiated by librarians or teachers, and elected officials initiate 4%, with only 1% initiated by students. These statistics are also incomplete because the ALA estimates that 82%–97% of challenges are never reported to the ALA Office of Intellectual Freedom.

Teachers need to understand the potential pushback they will receive from many possible angles when including a book like *Lily and Dunkin* in their curriculum and strategies to protect themselves and their students.

Potential Issues

The majority of book censorship issues might come in informal complaints from parents or colleagues about a book currently being utilized in a classroom. Informal complaints are typically handled by the teacher and the principal in a meeting with the challengers to resolve the issue. However, if an informal complaint does not solve the problem, districts must have an official book review form on file. Challengers can submit a formal complaint on a book that will go through the district's process. These formal complaints will be a combination of what the challenger finds valuable about the book and the complaints. Typical complaints about LGBTQ books are "religious viewpoint," "political viewpoint," "glorifying gay marriage," "brainwashing children," "perverted," "indecent," "confusing for students," "liberal ideas," "not meeting community standards," and so on (American Library Association, 2021). It is then up to the school to form an approved book review committee, including the affected teacher. However, this is the civil route taken when a challenger wants a book removed.

If a challenger wishes to make a stand or does not feel that the book challenge is handled satisfactorily, teachers have also had to deal with social media blasts with personal attacks about the educator, parents requesting the student be removed from the educator's classroom, censorship by administration on LGBTQ books in classroom and school libraries, as well as administrative pressure to resign or take unpaid leave to "handle" the situation. It is often easier to remove the problem, whether that is the teacher or the book, rather than advocate for the inclusion of representation of people from many different walks of life.

Teacher Preparedness

Well-meaning educators can be blindsided by these potential challenges and make snap decisions to censor books that do not align with community beliefs or students' rights. Educators need to know their rights and do prep work ahead of time to create a better experience for everyone involved. Listed here are action steps every educator should take to feel prepared to tackle any challenge.

1. Learn your community. Every community is different, and educators must respond to the needs and ideals of their community in curriculum planning.
2. Read the book in its entirety before assigning and note particularly controversial sections.
3. Know yourself and your limits. Know what you are comfortable tackling before anything else happens and how you will respond to potential student questions.
4. Meet with a school librarian to review book selection policies for the district and reviews for the book you want to include.
5. Develop a rationale for the book that includes the connection to state standards, awards the book has won, scholarly sources on the impact of LGBTQ literature in the classroom.
6. Read and know your school district's anti-discrimination policy.
7. Understand the book challenge process at your school and your role. School librarians should be well versed in this.
8. Meet with your principal/department chair/curriculum director beforehand to discuss the book, your rationale, potential solutions to foreseeable complaints, and their potential response.
9. Know your rights as an educator by connecting with the local Education Association.
10. If necessary, reach out to the Office of Intellectual Freedom at the ALA for advice, information on previous challenges to your book, or resources to fight a challenge. The OIF can be contacted at oif@ala.org.

Conclusion

We recognize that engaging in discussions of gender identity with middle grades students can induce anxiety for many teachers; however, we believe it is vital. Schools typically have limited capacity to address gender identity and equity issues. While teachers are not counselors, they can partner with school counselors, school social workers, and other community professionals to create bridges for students exploring these issues. Young adult literature offers the foundation for that bridge. Talking about matters through characters removes the stigma of publicly identifying those issues and creates a safe space where students can explore their own identity and support others' identity from a place of empathy.

References

American Library Association. (2021). *Surge in book challenges press kit.* www.ala.org/news/mediapresscenter/presskits/surge-book-challenges-press-kit

American Psychiatric Association. (2013). *Diagnostic and statistical manual of mental disorders* (5th ed.). American Psychiatric Association.

Blackburn, M. V., Clark, C. T., & Nemeth, E. A. (2015). Examining queer elements and ideologies in LGBT-themed literature: What queer literature can offer young adult readers. *Journal of Literacy Research, 47*(1), 11–48.

Dail, J. S., & Leonard, J. (2011). Creating realms of possibilities: Offering mirrors and windows. *The ALAN Review, 38*(2), 50–57. https://doi.org/10.21061/alan.v38i2.a.6

D'Andrea, M., & Daniels, J. (2001). RESPECTFUL counseling: An integrative model for counselors. In D. Pope-Davis & H. Coleman (Eds.), *The interface of class, culture, and gender in counseling* (pp. 417–66). SAGE.

Gay, Lesbian, and Straight Education Network (GLSEN). (2019a). *Gender terminology.* www.glsen.org/acitvity/gender-terminology

Gay, Lesbian, and Straight Education Network (GLSEN). (2019b) *Misgendering and respect for pronouns.* www.glsen.org/sites/default/files/2020-04/Misgendering-and-Respect for-Pronouns.pdf

Gay, Lesbian, and Straight Education Network (GLSEN). (2019c). *Pronoun guide.* www. glsen.org/activity/pronouns-guilde-glsen

Gephart, D. (2016). *Lily and Dunkin.* Delacorte Press.

Ioverno, S., & Russell, S. T. (2021). School climate perceptions at the intersection of sex, grade, sexual, and gender identity. *Journal of Research on Adolescence, 32*(1), 325–336.

Kosciw, J. G., Clark, C. M., Truong, N. L., & Zongrone, A. D. (2020). *The 2019 national school climate survey: The experiences of lesbian, gay, bisexual, and transgender youth in our nation's schools.* GLSEN. https://files.eric.ed.gov/fulltext/ED608534.pdf

Kosciw, J. G., Greytak, E. A., Diaz, E. M., & Bartkiewicz, M. J. (2010). *The 2009 national school climate survey: The experiences of lesbian, gay, bisexual, and transgender youth in our nation's schools.* GLSEN.

Mirra, N. (2018). *Educating for empathy: Literacy learning and civic engagement.* Teachers College Press.

Pizzo, J., & Zucker, L. (2020). Conveying sympathy through carefully crafted words: Rehearsal meets reality. In S. Witte (Ed.), *Writing can change everything: Middle-level kids writing themselves into the world* (p. 7). National Council of Teachers of English.

Rood, B. A., Reisner, S. L., Surace, F. I., Puckett, J. A., Maroney, M. R., & Pantalone, D. W. (2016). Expecting rejection: Understanding the minority stress experiences of transgender and gender-nonconforming individuals. *Transgender Health, 1*(1).

Sims Bishop, R. (1990). Mirrors, windows, and sliding glass doors. *Perspectives, 6*(3), ix–xi.

The Trevor Project. (2019). *National survey on LGBTQ mental health.* www.thetrevorproject. org/wp-content/uploads/2019/06/The-Trevor-Project-National-Survey-Results-2019.pdf

Trans Student Educational Resources. (2022). *The gender unicorn.* www.transhealthsa.com/ wp-content/uploads/2017/05/The-Gender-Unicorn.pdf

5

REMIXING FOR RELEVANCE

Talking Gentrification in Pride

Brooke Bianchi-Pennington and Arianna Banack

"It's a truth universally acknowledged that when rich people move into the hood, where it's a little bit broken and a little bit forgotten, the first thing they want to do is clean it up" (Zoboi, 2018, p. 1). The first sentence of Ibi Zoboi's novel, *Pride*, a remix of Jane Austen's *Pride and Prejudice*, doesn't pull punches as it opens with a strong comment on gentrification. While *Pride and Prejudice* provides a critique of gender norms and social class through Elizabeth's initial resistance to marry Mr. Darcy, it reinforces the racial exclusivity of the Western literary canon that centers white characters and voices. *Pride* by Ibi Zoboi stands in stark contrast to majority white texts in the canon (Bissonnette & Glazier, 2016) as it centers the Benitez family and Zuri the protagonist who describes "all the things that make me up: Haitian, Dominican, and all black" (Zoboi, 2018, p. 32). Zoboi's text offers multiple perspectives from Black families and centers joy in ways that students do not often get to see in traditional ELA curricula. *Pride* is set in a present-day, rapidly gentrifying neighborhood in Bushwick, NY. When Darius and Ainsley, teenagers from a wealthy family, move in across the street, Zuri resents the change they represent in her neighborhood and life. However, Zuri and Darius find commonalities, and their first impressions of each other shift. *Pride* offers opportunities for educators to engage with their students around a story centering complex and diverse portrayals of adolescents, better reflecting the increasingly culturally and linguistically diverse students in the United States overall (deBrey et al., 2019; Hussar & Bailey, 2013). We argue that using critical literacy (Luke, 2012) and centering a young adult (YA) text when paired with a canonical text can allow for rich and complex discussion around social justice topics like gentrification.

As there are countless bills being passed to restrict the teaching of Critical Race Theory (CRT), the history of racism, and discussing white privilege (Natanson, 2021; Stout & LeMee, 2021), conversations around gentrification are certainly

DOI:10.4324/9781003302216-7

taboo in our political climate. While Critical Race Theory (CRT) originated in legal studies (Bell, 1995), it is a tool that researchers use to understand the role race plays in education (Ladson-Billings, 1995). Understanding relationships among race, racism, and power helps to explain how systemic racism serves to privilege white people (Bell, 1995). In the field of education, CRT can help educators think critically about how curricula can act as a "master script" of white supremacy in our classrooms and schools (Ladson-Billings, 1995). Despite new censorship, teaching *Pride* may be a way in for teachers facing restrictions. Zoboi centers two Black families in her text which could benefit teachers who wish to include it as the narrative isn't focused on race explicitly. Students in Brooke's class even discussed why they thought Zoboi centered two Black families, noting "maybe the author didn't want the message to be too racial because the message is supposed to be the separation between the poor family and rich family and the class differences not race differences." The emphasis on class in Zoboi's text could be a way for teachers to creatively subvert restrictions around race-based texts.

This chapter and partnership came together because *Pride and Prejudice* is a summer reading text for sophomores at Brooke's school. This text as well as others written in a similar style have generally been considered essential reading as they feature heavily in state and advanced placement (AP) exams. Brooke and Arianna connected through a mutual professor and wanted to try pairing *Pride and Prejudice* with Ibi Zoboi's remix, *Pride*. While Brooke has abandoned the institutionalized idea that the understanding of any particular text or style is the goal of language arts education, it did seem that, by pairing texts, meeting this school-district goal could neatly align with more personal objectives, like teaching the ways context affects style and exploring real-world issues of social justice—two concepts connected by the need to value others' perspectives. Through funding from the ALAN Foundation Grant, Brooke was able to get a class set of *Pride*, and Arianna went into Brooke's class weekly to observe. In this chapter, we offer suggestions and reflections on how to center *Pride* (Zoboi, 2018) alongside *Pride and Prejudice* (Austen, 1813) to invite students to participate in critical discussions around social context, perspective-taking, and gentrification.

As gentrification is a major theme in *Pride*, teachers may want to provide a history of white property ownership, redlining, and racially restrictive covenants in order for students to have a deep and nuanced understanding of gentrification, which can be taboo depending on the teacher's school context. These "taboo" topics are important for students to understand how the choices of the wealthy affect the people whose communities are gentrified. Teachers can share resources like the following video from YouTube (https://bit.ly/3DrjUML) and article from Georgetown Law (https://bit.ly/3Do4OHI) to scaffold discussion around gentrification. Discussing the CRT tenet of whiteness as property would be relevant to *Pride*, and teachers who have the freedom may wish to give an overview of what whiteness as property means and how it contributes to gentrification. Historically, "only white possession and occupation of land was validated and therefore privileged as a basis for property rights. These distinct forms of exploitation each contributed in various ways to the construction of whiteness as property" (Harris, 1993, p. 1716). As Harris (1993) explained, there are privileges associated with being born white, materializing in owning property, in turn creating long-lasting inequities for Black, Indigenous, People of Color (BIPOC). And while the one main wealthy family in *Pride* is Black, there are instances where Zuri references wealthy white families gentrifying her neighborhood in Bushwick—instances that are worthy of being discussed throughout the course of the novel study even if it is taboo to do so.

Critical Literacy in the Classroom to Teach the Taboo

Critical literacy extends comprehension to ask students to consider the connections between language, power, and the literature read in classrooms (Luke, 2012). Knowledge of important plot points from *Pride* and *Pride and Prejudice* can serve as a foundation for teachers and students to engage in discussion that offers different perspectives on the same topic. To ensure students had an understanding of connections between the two novels, Brooke required her students to annotate as they read each chapter and provide text-to-text connections. However, the purpose of critical literacy instruction is not for students to recite plotlines and character traits (Luke, 2012), but rather is a way of thinking about how texts are never neutral as they are socially constructed and can help students make sense of sociopolitical systems (Vasquez et al., 2019). Once students understand the plot of a novel, they can begin discussing questions central to critical literacy as posed by Luke (2012): "What is 'truth'? How is it presented and represented, by whom, and in whose interests? Who should have access to which images and words, texts, and discourses? For what purposes?" (p. 4). *Pride* provides students with opportunities to discuss class, race, and privilege across texts and related to their worlds.

Through a critical lens, students may begin to focus on topics including inequities between socioeconomic classes when discussing *Pride* paired with *Pride and Prejudice* and applying that thinking to the world around them. Discussions centering on social issues require students to think in depth about the two connected novels and further their thinking by examining how/if the social issues are relevant to their own life or cultural context. For example, when comparing *Pride and Prejudice* to *Pride* the following conversation relies on an understanding of plot. Brooke asked the students why they thought Zuri liked Warren (a character from a similar socioeconomic class to Zuri's), and her students brought up critical discussions of class:

Student 1:   I think Zuri thinks she knows Warren even before she meets him because she has stereotypes about people just like Darius because she thinks he's stuck up so she thinks she'll have more in common with Warren.

Student 2:   They are also closer in terms of class than Zuri and Darius so it's not as big of a leap for her.

Student 2 demonstrated an understanding of the perceived differences in socio-economic class by saying: "They are also closer in terms of class than Zuri and Darius so it's not as big of a leap for her." Implied in this statement is the assumption that liking someone from a different socioeconomic class, contextualized from the plot of *Pride* and *Pride and Prejudice*, is outside of the norm. As critical literacy encourages readers to understand power and sociopolitical structures, pairing *Pride and Prejudice* and *Pride* allowed us to explore the sociopolitical act of gentrification. The previous conversation then prompted the teacher to ask students what they know about gentrification and then assign students the task of researching and sharing resources about gentrification (see more specific details in the During Reading section). Students then extended their discussion about socioeconomic class to learning about how gentrification applies from a historical perspective and to the world today. Using critical literacy can further student learning in meaningful and authentic ways that go beyond literal interpretations of a text.

Before Reading: Establishing Perspective

Students were assigned *Pride and Prejudice* to read over the summer. Upon returning to school in August, the class engaged in a four-to-five-week unit pairing *Pride and Prejudice* and *Pride*. Unsurprisingly, students had difficulty understanding *Pride and Prejudice* with its unfamiliar social setting and style. Indeed, upon encountering this difficult text, several students did not read the novel at all. Because the major goal in assigning *Pride and Prejudice* as summer reading is to engage students in the difficult style and unfamiliar context, several activities throughout the unit gave students the opportunity to engage in these areas with more scaffolding to make up for lack of engagement over the summer.

To begin assisting students with understanding and engaging with the perspective of *Pride and Prejudice*, whether they had read it or not, and to prepare them for perspective taking in *Pride*, the students engaged in a group research project geared toward increasing their background knowledge of the social context of *Pride and Prejudice* while simultaneously asking them to engage with how their own social context affects contemporary style. For this project, Brooke provided students with topics and baseline information on different aspects of the social context of Jane Austen including dancing, dating, marriage, gender roles, and manners. Students then completed further research and presented on their topic using found or created memes that satirized their topic. The goal was for students to gain deeper insight into both how Austen satirized her world as well as how style can be an outgrowth of context and perspective.

In Figure 5.1 you will also find an anticipation guide that can be used to get students to think about themes in the novel before beginning *Pride*. Students can complete this independently and then discuss the statements in either a small or whole group setting. Students can then reflect on if their opinions changed or which statement they felt the strongest about.

PERSONAL STANCE			
Statement	**Agree**	**Disagree**	**Unsure**
Gentrification ruins neighborhoods.			
"Home" is a specific place and structure.			
A person's culture is an important part of everyday life.			
It is okay to judge someone based on their appearance.			
Having pride in your neighborhood is important.			
People from different social classes shouldn't be together.			
I would speak out against injustices in my society.			

FIGURE 5.1 Anticipation Guide for *Pride*

To further prepare students to think about how gentrification is an important theme in *Pride*, students can read an interview Turner (2018) did with Zoboi about the inspiration behind her novel. In it, Turner (2018) asks Zoboi what aspects of Brooklyn were extremely important to capture, and Zoboi responded:

> The changes, rapid gentrification, how the landscape is changing right before our eyes. The demographics are changing, but also it could be an intra-cultural change [in which] a community can be mostly black and brown working class or lower income, and other black and brown people can move in. They can have more disposable income to use in the community in ways that people who have been living in the community for years have not been able to.
>
> *(para 3)*

Teachers can provide a definition of gentrification after reading the interview to scaffold students' understanding. This will help students be prepared to discuss gentrification, which Zoboi addresses in the opening sentence of *Pride*. Students can continue to develop their understanding of gentrification as they read *Pride* and see how Zoboi weaves it into the plot.

During Reading: Deepening Discussions

While reading *Pride*, class structure centered around text annotation and discussion. Students annotated each chapter of *Pride* with a note on plot or theme, two notes on style, and two notes on connections: One connection to their personal experience and one connection to *Pride and Prejudice*. The annotations made sure students were attentive to the different social contexts between *Pride* and *Pride and Prejudice*, the differences in style, as well as ways in which they could compare their own world to *Pride*. Class discussion often stemmed from these annotations as students earned discussion points for asking and responding to questions with text evidence through a visual point-tracking system. For example, one conversation stemming from annotations, particularly connections, allowed the class to delve into a cultural perspective that was not their own:

Student 1:   In Chapter 1 she's analyzing her neighbors, but for me it doesn't play a huge role in my life and is that because of her culture or is it a remix of *Pride & Prejudice*?

Brooke: We do have to keep in mind culture. Because it's more contemporary we can relate to it a lot better, but it's still a different culture. What does anyone else think?

Student 2:   In government class we're talking about social capital and not a lot of Americans have a lot of social capital because they don't talk to a lot of people, but it seems like she has that (social capital) because she talks to her neighbors.

Student 3:   It ties back to [Student 4's] question about change because the new neighbors are messing with the whole block.

Brooke: Getting back to is it normal? I think what she's getting across is that this is a type of community—this small neighborhood within the larger city, kind of like a small town here, and this is a small neighborhood where everyone gets to know everyone.

In this exchange, students drew on their connection annotations and discussed the ways in which their experiences differed from Zuri's, resulting in a more nuanced understanding of Zuri's perspective as well as the larger social forces at work. Brooke helped foster critical literacy by asking students to consider how culture is important in *Pride*.

Students also used the same point-tracking system when engaging in small group discussion with prepared questions, scribing their group's responses. This system asked students to earn a total number of points across the course of the unit with two points awarded for thoughtful responses, four points for asking thoughtful questions, and six points for responses with text evidence. We noticed during these conversations, topics of social justice were brought up by the students. In one instance, Brooke posed the question: *Why did Zoboi remix the book?* While one student responded "to make it more relatable, to make it more modern because a lot of people say *Pride and Prejudice* is boring and hard to read," another student replied, "they're shifting the focus to more on inequality and wealth instead of inequality and gender." Through Brooke's use of critical literacy practices and having students consistently think about the sociopolitical nature of the text, students were able to identify that inequity and class are driving factors in *Pride*, contributing to the gentrification of Zuri's neighborhood. Figure 5.2 provides a list of some discussion questions geared toward fostering personal connections, perspective taking, and critical literacy.

Chapters 1-10
What is the style of speaking of our narrator? (How is it different from *Pride and Prejudice*? How is it different from your own voice?) How do each of the characters compare to the characters in *Pride and Prejudice*? How is Zuri's attitude different than Elizabeth Bennet's?
11-20
Why does Darius seem nicer in D.C.? How does the change in setting/context affect him? We've got important plot points – the visiting Howard, the sexy pictures. How do these compare with *Pride and Prejudice*?
21-29
What is their trip to the roof on page 255 symbolic of? How does this compare to when Elizabeth Bennet saw Pemberly? What is Zuri's perspective on gentrification based on her letter? What is the main thing that upsets her?

FIGURE 5.2   Relevant Discussion Questions

While reading, students also engaged in activities to promote an understanding of the contexts of both texts. With a focus on gentrification in *Pride*, students created an open-source document of multimedia resources on gentrification on a national and local level. Students were asked to post two resources, one text and one multimedia resource, about affordable housing and/or gentrification and provide a description of both the format and the content of their resource. Later, students were asked to look for similarities and differences among their sources. Not only did this activity deepen students' real-world understanding of gentrification, but it also reinforced concepts about context and style by asking students to look for and compare visual or audio texts to traditional texts. Out of any activity, this one most brought the issue of gentrification to the forefront of students' minds as they found many local news articles about gentrification in our city. The nuances of social class discussed in *Pride* are particularly taboo topics for many of Brooke's students who belong to the middle class because in discussions they spoke of class as an issue of the past, occurring in countries other than the United States. Even when students are aware of differences in wealth among themselves, there is a strong sense that these disparities are unconnected, that one person's wealth has no bearing on another's experiences of poverty. The gentrification discussed in *Pride* not only allowed students to understand the class implications in *Pride and Prejudice* with a more accessible and engaging text, but it also illuminated the ways in which class is a communal, not solely individual, issue in modern society. Taking on Zuri's perspective in the text allowed them to take on a different perspective on themselves. While Brooke's students' city is minuscule in comparison to *Pride's* New York, it is a city experiencing rapid growth, displacement, and, in some areas, gentrification. The school's own community is one of the fastest-growing areas of the region where suburban sprawl is quickly eating away farmland. By practicing perspective taking in *Pride and Prejudice* and taking on perspectives in *Pride*, students in this suburban community were able to view themselves in a different light.

One way students could also focus on gentrification is through tracking how the theme of gentrification shows up throughout the novel. Students could create

a chart and every time they see a character reference gentrification, either implic-
itly or explicitly, they could write the quote down and provide an analysis of the
quote. As stated earlier, the first sentence of the novel addresses gentrification,
and teachers can model analysis using that sentence. Students and teachers can
fill in the chart together and provide an analysis before asking students to complete a chart on their own throughout the duration of the novel. This history is
particularly applicable to *Pride* as Zoboi addresses the ability to own property in
Zuri's neighborhood. Zoboi explicitly describes the effects of gentrification on
neighborhoods and the people who live in those neighborhoods (see Figure 5.3).

In another activity, to compare how each text's style was affected by its social
context, students first participated in a teacher-created matching game in which
they matched quotes from *Pride and Prejudice* to a corresponding element of
Regency era social context. They then created their own version of the game,

Quote	Analysis
"It's a truth universally acknowledged that when rich people move into the hood, where it's a little bit broken and a little bit forgotten, the first thing they want to do is clean it up" (p. 1).	The first sentence of the novel alerts readers to the fact that gentrification can be seen as a negative though the rich people wanting to "clean up" the neighborhood and as Zuri keeps talking she says they'll throw people out too. Gentrification pushes people out of their neighborhoods.
"bet a whole twenty dollars that it's a young white family moving in, because that's what's been happening all over Bushwick" (p. 3)	Zuri connects white families with home ownership echoing Harris (1993) about gentrification and white possession of land being seen in Zuri's neighborhood. In this instance, Zuri was wrong and it was a rich Black family, she notes that in other instances white families are moving in.
"rent is going up all over the place and people are not getting paid more" (p. 257)"	Zuri comments how gentrification often raises living costs, but wages don't increase which disproportately affects people who originally lived in the neighborhood as they get pushed out with rising costs of living.
Sometimes love is not enough to keep a community together. There needs to be something more tangible, like fair housing, opportunities, and access to resources. Lifeboats and lifelines are not supposed to just be a way for us to get out. They should be ways to let us stay in and survive. And thrive. (p. 273, emphasis in original)	Zuri recognizes that fair housing, opportunities, and resources are needed for the people of color in her neighborhood. However, they *aren't* provided those opportunities, and instead are pushed out of the neighborhood by rich, white people as they "polish and erase" the neighborhood Zuri grew up in reinforcing whiteness as property ownership (Harris, 1993).

FIGURE 5.3   Quote Analysis Chart

generating elements of social context for *Pride* and quotes that exemplified that social context. This activity not only reinforced how context affected style in each individual text but also allowed students to see that both texts were created with meaningful messages about context through differing styles. This activity drove home the idea that *Pride* was not a text being used to gain a better understanding of *Pride and Prejudice*. Rather, it was a text worthy of study on its own. Like *Pride and Prejudice*, the issues *Pride* discusses and the style of writing that is an offshoot of those issues are important classroom topics.

The activities described previously not only served to teach the taboo but also to meet classroom standards. Several Common Core standards were central to the during reading activities. RL.9–10.4 states "determine the meaning of words and phrases as they are used in the text . . . analyze the cumulative impact of specific word choices on meaning and tone (e.g., how the language evokes a sense of time and place)" (NGO/CCSS, 2010). Annotations, discussion, and the matching activity all featured this standard in their focus on style, specifically on how style was dependent on context or, as this standard puts it, "a sense of time and place." Addressing RL.9–10.9, "analyze how an author draws on and transforms source material in a specific work"(NGO/CCSS, 2010) is obviously a strength of this unit because it demonstrates how Ibi Zoboi translated Jane Austen's text into a modern context while writing a unique text worthy of study on its own.

Finally, from the beginning of this chapter, we have noted the flaws in demanding only certain types of texts be taught in schools. The text complexity guidelines associated with the common core (e.g. RL.9–10.10) have often been used to limit the diversity of texts and the teaching of taboo topics. While these guidelines are not appropriate educational measures, as teachers, working within the frameworks given while still advocating for better practices is necessary. To that end, this unit allows for the incorporation of a "complex text," *Pride and Prejudice*, while not sacrificing engagement, relevance, or inclusivity by pairing with *Pride*. Indeed, this unit allows for a deeper understanding of both texts, addressing goals created by external forces as well as goals rooted in more forward-thinking teaching practices.

After Reading: A Personal Remix

Finally, students extended their knowledge of both *Pride* and *Pride and Prejudice* by translating the stories into a third social context, their own school. After watching a movie adaptation of *Pride and Prejudice*, groups of students recreated five scenes key to the central plot of both novels through making a video that had the following elements:

- Stylistic elements (in dialogue or visuals) that show the social context
- Thematic elements that parallel a theme of both novels or show character development
- Thematic elements that reflect class or social differences in the school context

After filming the videos, students then completed a written analysis in which they described how each scene in their video illustrated the required components from this list. This after reading activity directly addressed RL.9–10.7 "analyze the representation of a subject or a key scene in two different artistic mediums, including what is emphasized or absent in each treatment." Ultimately, this final activity had students relate to both *Pride* and *Pride and Prejudice* by recreating the tensions of the stories in a context most relevant to them. Through the process, they had to use a format and style that reflected their culture, just as Ibi Zoboi and Jane Austen did. Not only did this require analyzing the author's choices but it also required making similar choices themselves and reflecting on the process.

Conclusion

Reflecting upon the unit allowed us to see how centering *Pride* in the classroom allowed for Brooke's students to have meaningful conversations around gentrification, class, and context. For educators whose districts will allow *Pride* as a focal text, we would encourage them to take up the theme of gentrification as a focus of the unit to have students incite critique of the sociopolitical structures that create gentrification. We noticed students were particularly excited when learning about gentrification and relating it to their own neighborhood. Investigating gentrification and redlining in their local context proved to foster discussions where students were animated and invested. Discussing with students how gentrification is a "taboo" topic, especially in states with restrictive legislation, can lead to meaningful conversations about power and privilege. We see endless opportunities for educators to use *Pride* as a starting point for critical thinking, writing, and reading.

Pairing texts like *Pride* and *Pride and Prejudice* can accomplish what Muhammad (2020) refers to as "layering texts," when "texts can support the mandated curriculum" (p. 147). For educators whose curriculum mandates canonical texts be taught, they can bring in texts like *Pride* and continue to layer on Austen's texts and other supplemental materials with BIPOC-authored texts. Layering texts and bringing in multiple perspectives can help students "incite social critique" (Muhammad, 2020, p. 147) as they look across texts to locate instances of power and privilege. For educators who engage in pairing texts, Toliver and Hadley (2021) remind us to avoid "situating diverse texts as support toward the sacred goal of canonical texts" (p. 12). We advocate for teachers to reverse the positioning of YA texts as scaffolds and instead center *Pride* and use excerpts from *Pride and Prejudice* to discuss class and gentrification, allowing students to make connections across texts, cultures, and media to their own lived experiences. In this way, teaching the taboo not only fosters critical thinking about texts and the world, but also engagement and empowerment in the classroom.

Fiction Cited

Austen, J. (1813). *Pride and prejudice.* Penguin Classics.
Zoboi, I. (2018). *Pride.* Balzer & Bray.

References

Bell, D. A. (1995). Who's afraid of critical race theory. *University of Illinois Law Review,* *1995*(4), 893–910.

Bissonnette, J. D., & Glazier, J. (2016). A counterstory of one's own: Using counterstory-telling to engage students with the British canon. *Journal of Adolescent & Adult Literacy,* *59*(6), 685–694. https://doi.org/10.1002/jaal.486

de Brey, C., Musu, L., McFarland, J., Wilkinson-Flicker, S., Diliberti, M., Zhang, A., Branstetter, C., & Wang, X. (2019). *Status and trends in the education of racial and ethnic groups 2018* (NCES 2019–038). National Center for Education Statistics. https://nces.ed.gov/pubs2019/2019038.pdf

Harris, C. I. (1993). Whiteness as property. *Harvard Law Review,* *106*(8), 1707–1791.

Hussar, W. J., & Bailey, T. M. (2013). *Projections of education statistics to 2022* (41st ed., NCES 2014–051). National Center for Education Statistics, Institute of Education Sciences, U.S. Department of Education.

Ladson-Billings, G. (1995). Toward a theory of culturally relevant pedagogy. *American Educational Research Journal,* *32*(3), 465–491.

Luke, A. (2012). Critical literacy: Foundational notes. *Theory into Practice,* *51*(1), 4–11.

Muhammad, G. (2020). *Cultivating genius: An equity framework for culturally and historically responsive literacy.* Scholastic.

Natanson, H. (2021, December 6). A White teacher taught White students about White privilege. It cost him his job. *The Washington Post.* https://www.washingtonpost.com/education/2021/12/06/tennessee-teacher-fired-critical-race-theory/

National Governors Association Center for Best Practices & Council of Chief State School Officers [NGA Center & CCSS]. (2010a). *Common Core State Standards for English language arts and literacy in history/social studies, science, and technical subjects.* Authors.

Stout, C., & LeMee, G. L. (2021, June 9). Efforts to restrict teaching about racism and bias have multiplied across the U.S. *Chalkbeat.* www.chalkbeat.org/22525983/map-critical-Race-theory-legislation-teaching-racism

Toliver, S. R., & Hadley, H. (2021). Ca(n)non fodder no more: Disrupting common arguments that support a canonical empire. *Journal of Language and Literacy Education,* *17*(2), 1–28.

Turner, P. (2018, September 17). Ibi Zoboi on gentrification and how motherhood informs her work. *Culture Trip.* https://theculturetrip.com/north-america/usa/new-york/articles/ibi-zoboi-on-brooklyn-gentrification-and-how-motherhood-informs-her-work/

Vasquez, V. M., Janks, H., & Comber, B. (2019). Critical literacy as a way of being and doing. *Language Arts,* *96*(5), 300–311.

6

LAYERING DISCOURSE

Encouraging Diverse Perspectives in a High School Literature Class

Renee Stites Kruep and Lauren Popov

It is the fifth day of class, and a quick scan of the room reveals that every kid is reading, every book is young adult (YA) literature, and a non-White author is writing every title. After 15 minutes, we beg them to put their books away so we can begin the day's lesson, a viewing of Chimamanda Ngozi Adichie's 2009 TED Talk, *The Danger of a Single Story*.

In her talk, Adichie recounts several examples in which she, as a child, believed book characters and people were to be "white and blue-eyed" (Adichie, 2009, 00:27) because she only had access to British and American children's books. Likewise, when she—a Nigerian—arrived in America for university, she found that many people carried short-sighted and false assumptions about her and Nigeria. Adichie (2009) warns this is the "danger of a single story," where society will "show a people as one thing, as only one thing, over and over again, and that is what they become" (9:14). In this cycle, we develop biases and perpetuate stereotypes. She challenges her audience to use stories to "empower and to humanize" (17:24). She wants people to "reject the single story" (18:05) by reading widely, as this helps to define people's differences and similarities in a more robust and dignifying way.

When the TED Talk ends, we, their teachers, ask our students to discuss some immediate takeaways and highlight a few key lines from the transcript with a partner. Next, we direct them to their journals to reflect on how Adichie's message relates to them. The next day, after giving them a few minutes to revisit those journals, we talk. They begin in small groups to flesh out their thinking and then transition into a whole class discussion about our semester's work together.

Students often tell us that, until now, they are unaware that most books they read are written by white authors and include mostly white characters. Many of them express interest in reading more diverse books. Others share how hard it

DOI:10.4324/9781003302216-8

is to break their old beliefs, but thinking about this message helps them listen to others and learn from their points of view. Jackson (all student names are pseudonyms) shares a memory of when he was told, "you don't sound like a Black person," and then asks the class, "how do you sound like a color?"

As teachers, we must offer space for students to read and confront their biases and stereotypes; this is a role we take seriously. We guide our students to uncover the single stories they have accepted without question. After a semester of work, Emily wrote in her journal that "a lot of the time, you just have these thoughts and ideas drilled into your head, but just because you hear something, doesn't make it wholly accurate." After reading and discussing diverse texts all semester, our students walk away believing that reading diverse literature provides new perspectives on reading books and the world (Freire & Macedo, 1987; hooks, 1994/2020; Janks, 2010).

We are impressed by our students' honesty and vulnerability to engage in our work together. By the end of the first week, our students are already establishing a community of readers that are reflective and willing to challenge themselves and each other through the discussion of taboo topics.

The Class: Global Voices in Literature

We, the authors, teach in a relatively politically conservative, suburban, midwestern high school district with a primarily white, middle-to-upper-middle-class student population. The pressure of diverse English curricula is primarily placed on two specific courses—a mandatory sophomore course, World Literature, and a junior/senior elective called Global Voices in Literature, which is the focus of this chapter. While there are no guarantees that upper-level students will choose the latter course among the elective options (not including AP or honor track), this particular course has grown in popularity because it offers unique reading and learning opportunities for our student population. For many, it may be one of the only classes where they are consistently provided the choice in what they read and opportunities to engage in critical literacy, which "focuses on the interplay between discursive practices and unequal power relations—and issues of social justice and equity—in support of diverse learners" (Vasquez et al., 2019, p. 302). It may be one of the only high school courses that invites them to study themselves and their current perspectives.

As the two teachers (both white and female) teaching this course, our positionality is complicated; we acknowledge our privilege when teaching texts that are not representative of our own lived experiences (Baker-Bell et al., 2017). We are "honest with students about [our] professional commitment to bringing diverse voices into the classroom," and we openly share that we "might not fully understand the cultures and communities contained in the stories" that we teach (Ginsberg & Glenn, 2019, p. 193). We are passionate about this work and believe courses like this offer students opportunities to advance their literacy skills and "develop empathy and understanding" for all lives and experiences (Ebarvia, 2021, para. 6). Our goal is to help them consider other perspectives.

Over the years, the course has evolved and is now almost exclusively designed around independent and small group reading. We are not teaching texts; we are teaching students how to be critical thinkers, reflective learners, and articulate speakers about the taboo topics we present in our classroom. To do this effectively, we rely on three layers of discourse: personal writing about reading, small group conversations over shared reading experiences, and teacher monitored— but student-guided—whole-class discussions (both in-person and online) that promote courageous conversations across texts. We scaffold the discourse to give students plenty of experience interpreting, analyzing, and considering the texts (Gee, 2011).

The openness of the reading curriculum may be uncomfortable for some. It does require us as the teachers to read a lot. Still, the diversity and volume of texts allow our students to (a) read widely, thus challenging their assumptions and limiting their risk of trusting a single story (Adichie, 2009; Janks, 2010), (b) think about how different characters, cultures, and situations relate and talk to each other (Freire, 1970/2010; Freire & Macedo, 1987; Janks, 2010; Vasquez et al., 2019), (c) talk through these challenging new perspectives and reflect on their assumptions (Freire, 1970/2010; Freire & Macedo, 1987; Janks, 2010; Vasquez et al., 2019), and (d) learn from and with each other as respected and trusted peers (Gee, 2011; hooks, 1994/2020).

Selecting the Texts

We ask our students to read in three ways over the semester: independently, in small book clubs, and whole-class texts. Like the layers of discourse, the forms of reading are essential as they allow our students a variety of reading experiences while also exposing them to volumes of diverse texts. Figure 6.1 illustrates our reading patterns in the course.

When selecting books that will invite respectful discussions and reflective thinking on taboo topics, we consider Sims Bishop's (1990) "Windows, Mirrors, and Sliding Glass Doors," where windows allow readers to see the experiences of others, mirrors enable readers to see themselves, and sliding glass doors invite readers into the text for the window and mirror opportunities. We want windows so our students can read and challenge the single story—or mainstream narratives— that they have seen or heard about marginalized groups in society. We use young adult literature that includes relatable, meaningful stories about teens facing similar circumstances as our students for mirrors. We hope for sliding glass doors through the layers of discourse that surround our students' interactions with these texts.

While we encourage our students to read texts through a critical lens, books written by non-white authors are our only rule for book selection. To do the

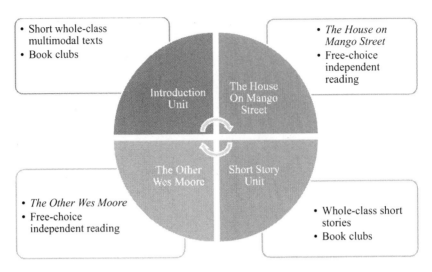

- Short whole-class multimodal texts
- Book clubs

Introduction Unit

The House On Mango Street

- *The House on Mango Street*
- Free-choice independent reading

The Other Wes Moore

Short Story Unit

- *The Other Wes Moore*
- Free-choice independent reading

- Whole-class short stories
- Book clubs

FIGURE 6.1 Reading Schedule With Layered Discourse

work of critical literacy, we select texts where taboo topics like race, class, and social injustice are present but not central to the story (Vasquez et al., 2019). We know these topics are essential, but we also aim to avoid any potential censorship from our district. We strive for students to notice similarities and acknowledge differences with the diverse characters and situations they read. See Table 6.1 for our current book club listings for our two whole-class texts and the taboo topics addressed in each text.

When book clubs were first implemented into the Global Voices curriculum, we wanted students to have input on the texts chosen. We asked our certified teacher-librarian to organize a book tasting where students could sample numerous texts and rank their top choices. We then read through the student feedback and brought several texts to our classrooms. Over the next few months, we set aside time in class to read the top choices aloud to our students. Interested students read some of the other titles independently. Finally, after our students had the opportunity to fully engage with multiple texts, we gathered feedback on their top choices. The students' top choices became our first set of book club books and were implemented the following year.

We update our book club selections as often as possible to keep the options fresh and exciting for students. Each day we set aside a minimum of 10 minutes of quiet reading time, and during this time, we (teachers) also read YA books. Sharing in the reading experience keeps us aware of new YA texts and allows us to have authentic conversations with students about reading.

To gather feedback from students and help us make the best text selections for book clubs, we provide students with a living document of recommended independent reading. The document lets our students explore cultures and contexts that our book club offerings do not invite them to find a title to form their

TABLE 6.1 Book Club and Whole Class Texts and the Taboo Topics They Present

Book	Summary	Taboo Topics
Acevedo, E. (2021). *With the fire on high.* HarperCollins.	High school senior Emoni is a single mother and relies on the help of her Abuela as she navigates what comes after high school. She works hard to stay true to her passion for culinary school.	teen pregnancy, racism, abortion, non-traditional families, financial distress
Ali, S. K. (2020). *Love from A to Z.* Simon & Schuster.	After confronting her teacher about his racism, Zayneb is sent to stay with her aunt in Qatar, where she falls in love with Adam, who has just been diagnosed with multiple sclerosis. The novel is told from both of their perspectives.	Islamophobia, chronic illness, teen romance, racism, drone warfare
Boulley, A. (2021). *Firekeeper's daughter.* Henry Holt and Co.	Daunis is asked to go undercover to investigate the string of deaths tied to meth addiction on the Ojibwe reservation. As a biracial, unenrolled tribal member, she faces challenges of acceptance while also navigating teen life and what comes after high school.	drug addiction, illegal distribution of meth, murder, suicide, sexual assault, racism, teen romance
Cisneros, S. (1984). *The house on Mango Street.* Vintage Books.	A novel written in vignettes; it's a story of Esperanza's life growing up in a Latino Chicago neighborhood.	racism, sexual assault, sexism, language barriers, financial distress, discrimination
Giles, L. (2015). *Fake ID.* HarperCollins.	Nick and his family live in the witness protection program, but after a series of mysterious events, he sets out to uncover the conspiracy about his new town.	gun violence, bullying, death, racism, mixed-race relationships, religious stereotypes
Moore, W. (2010). *The other Wes Moore: One name, two fates.* Spiegel & Grau.	This is the true story of two Wes Moores from Baltimore who found themselves on very different paths while trying to overcome the systemic racism in America.	alcohol use, drug use, addiction, illegal distribution of drugs, financial distress, high school dropout, systemic racism, housing segregation
Noah, T. (2019). *Born a crime.* Random House.	Told with humor and honesty, Noah recounts his younger years as a mixed-race child growing up in South America.	Apartheid, racism, domestic abuse, poverty
Phillippe, B. (2020). *The field guide to the North American teenager.* HarperCollins.	A Black French-Canadian finds himself living in Austin, Texas, where he navigates the highs and lows of high school as the new kid.	mental illness, suicide, homophobia, mixed-race relationships, racism, police brutality (minor), divorce

(Continued)

TABLE 6.1 (Continued)

Book	Summary	Taboo Topics
Reynolds, J. A. (2020). *Opposite of always.* HarperCollins.	This is a love story told through time travel. Jack is given several chances to sacrifice almost everything to save the girl he loves from sickle cell anemia.	chronic illness, mixed-race relationships, police brutality, racism, teen alcohol use
Sáenz, B. A. (2014). *Aristotle and Dante discover the secrets of the universe.* Simon & Schuster.	Two boys with very little in common forge a surprising friendship that helps them find their true selves and discover love.	same-sex relationships, homophobic violence, language
Stone, N. (2019). *Jackpot.* Random House.	Rico is working harder than any teen should to help her single mother keep them housed and fed. When she discovers a winning lottery ticket, she and an unexpected friend (one of the wealthiest kids in school) set out to find the ticket's owner.	socio-economic status, mixed-race relationships, alcoholism, bullying, mental illness, chronic illness
Zoboi, I. (2018). *American street.* HarperCollins.	A Haitian immigrant is separated from her mother and living with her family in Detroit, where she realizes that her freedom in America is not guaranteed. She wants to reunite with her mother, but instead, she learns the secrets and the struggles of her family.	alcohol use, drug use, immigration, police brutality, gun violence, bullying, domestic abuse

unofficial book club groupings, allows them to make suggestions for additional titles, and provides us insight into what is most interesting and essential to our students. By the end of the semester, students read a minimum of two whole-class books, two book club books, and two independent reading books. Many students exceed this count.

Table 6.1 illustrates that race is a topic found across nearly all selected texts. For the sake of this chapter, we will focus on how students develop their thinking and engage in discourse around this taboo topic. However, we often encourage them to consider the intersectionality of race, socio-economic status, gender, education, and other taboo topics that appear in the texts. Students often find themselves relating to the everyday turmoil of teenage life. There are days when the discussion is strained because of substantial differences in characters' race and actions. Yet, students demonstrate a desire to respectfully participate in open dialogue about systemic inequalities they witness and experience locally and globally each day and always have the option to continue the conversation online.

Establishing Norms in Global Voices Class

By selecting books that present teens in situations related to taboo topics like racial inequality, socio-economic differences, mixed-race relationships, and teen pregnancy, our students quickly engage in reading. Many are very open about how surprised they are to suddenly enjoy reading. We credit this to the choice and time we offer them (Miller, 2009). On the first day of class, before we even review syllabi and expectations, we ask our students to browse the book club books and select their top choices. We have them meeting in their book clubs by day two of class.

In the first book club meeting, we give students time to just talk. We invite them to introduce themselves, chat about why they are interested in the book, and set a schedule for their reading. These early and easy conversations help establish a welcoming community where students feel safe to engage in future discussions about complex topics (hooks, 1994/2020). Before we have our first whole-class discussion, we establish the expectation that everyone's voice and opinion are valid. We want to encourage them to expand their thinking and consider other perspectives. We promise we will ask them to do meaningful work. We ask that they show respect to themselves, their classmates, and their teachers as we openly and honestly talk about topics that matter to us and the characters in our books.

We build reading time into every class period, so we know they always have something to discuss. They start reading their book club books on day two of the semester, and by day three, they are ready to talk. As previously mentioned, we use a layered discourse method to allow students to engage in individual and social learning experiences around literature. We aim to "help students think, not tell them *what* to think" (Probst, 2004, p. 51).

Layered Discourse

Using three layers of discourse gives students space for slow, patient, honest reflection and learning. Some days students encounter just one layer, but other days we scaffold their progress as they work through all three layers. We understand and value the students' desire and need first to have a safe space to think about the texts they are reading because they are much more likely to participate in the second and third layers of discourse (Gee, 2011; hooks, 1994/2020). The following sections highlight the three components of layered discourse our students participate in as we are "striving not just for knowledge in books, but knowledge about how to live in the world" (hooks, 1994/2020, p. 15).

Reading Journals

After reading a text, we give students reflective space in the form of reading journals. We developed this idea from autoethnographic self-studies, where researchers use their journals and personal narratives "as window to the world, through which they *interpret* how their selves are connected to their sociocultural contexts and give meaning to their experiences and perspectives" (Chang et al., 2013, pp. 18–19). Students are encouraged to be honest because this is a judgment-free journal that only their teachers see.

We often offer very general and open prompts for the journals, something like "what was your takeaway" or "what did you notice" so that students truly have the room to utilize the transactional theory of texts. They can ask themselves, "What in this book, *and in me*, caused this response?" (Rosenblatt, 2005, p. 70), going back and rereading and analyzing how and why they may feel that way. We invite them to ask tough questions of themselves to use the writing to uncover their biases and discover their perspectives on taboo topics (e.g., race and privilege) related to the books they are reading.

This is the first course where they see themselves in the class texts for many of our students. Tana wrote:

> I like how they talk about [being] African American and the difficulties with hair stuff. It was awesome because I can relate to the part where she is talking about doing hair and how if it is humid, it gets frizzy.

For this teen reader, her connection to the text was a mirror—she felt valued and seen. Tana was eager to share more about herself and her lived experience in the journal and later with her classmates in discussions.

Other students confront their biases and think critically about why they hold the biases. Luke wrote:

> I would have never thought that Wes Moore would have had a very interesting and hard life. I would have thought he was just another criminal that robbed a store. Now knowing the ins and outs of his life, I am sympathetic for him and I feel genuine empathy for him.

Often, students enter class believing there are right and wrong or good and bad choices. Still, after spending time reading, writing, and talking about challenging concepts, they realize the multitude of factors that influence one's decisions and that it is not as simple as they once thought. We see these personal reflections later in small group and whole-class discussions. Some of our best discussions stretch across texts as students point out where the characters face obstacles and make challenging, sometimes questionable decisions because they face systemic racism and injustices. These are issues that many of our students have never considered before.

We gather feedback on how students are faring in their journaling processes throughout the semester. Sophie reflected that her journal "helped [her] take a deeper dive into the book" and made her "stop and think about what [she] read and some of the deeper meanings behind it." It does not take long for students to find value in the reflective work of reading journals, and by not giving them a prompt for these journals, we get more open and honest reflections. Rarely can students not find a way to relate to and understand the text, but when this happens, we guide our whole class or group discussions in that direction if it seems warranted.

Small Groups

Next, students study their independent journals for possible discussion topics to bring to the small groups where they realize that others share their wonderings and misunderstandings. Often, students work through the confusion found in their journals through the simple task of talking with others (Hash, 2019, p. 49). We do not assign roles or require a transcript of their conversation; instead, we allow the exchanges to be student-guided. We monitor the room, note what we notice across the groups, and carefully read the conversation extensions. These extensions take place in online spaces where students continue the unfinished work of our in-person book club meetings.

While reading Trevor Noah's (2019) *Born a Crime*, one book club discussed a chapter where Noah's family moves into a predominantly white neighborhood. During class, the students showed empathy and anticipated that his family would face racism. In the online discussion, days after their in-class conversation, Max asked, "what if it was you and your family making that move?" Two Black students immediately responded that they would experience fear. Two white students showed support for that emotion, acknowledging they had not experienced it but could empathize with the fear. A week later, they were still thinking about this. The group ended up reflecting on how racism still exists today. They talked about how many of our upper-class neighborhoods in town are still predominantly white, and they wondered what it was like for Black families to move into and live in those spaces. Lana wrote online, "Even here . . . it can be worse than bullying . . . people are still living apart and maybe in fear when they are the only ones [Black families] living in those neighborhoods." This is evidence of our students' evolving perspectives when they synthesize themes across multiple texts and connect them to real-world scenarios through their layered discourse.

Even when we read whole-class texts, we ask students to take this step of small group work before a whole-class discussion. For whole-class texts—which include two books, several short articles, short stories and poems, and a few

TABLE 6.2 Recurring Themes and Concepts to Shape the Semester's Work

Culture	Representation	Action
• Cultural expectations vs. cultural realities • Culture can mean different things to different people • Family dynamics are discussed in relationship to culture • Different definitions of culture can strain relationships • Seeking identity within and beyond "your culture"	• People form groups based on similarities • People often have limited exposure to outside groups • Misjudgment and misrepresentation is often due to lack of knowledge or experience	• We must face and fix challenges together • Call for approaching differences among people with full perspective • We have on-going societal problems that have yet to be solved • How? Because stereotypes are so easily created when we're trying to avoid the creation or perpetuation of them

TED Talks like *The Danger of a Single Story*—we always follow the discourse layers of journaling, small group, whole class. After reading shorter whole class texts during the first unit, students independently reflect on what they have read or viewed and answer the question, "how do our course texts talk to each other?" Then we put students into small groups and ask them to compare those reflections as a way to practice our layered discourse approach for the semester. Students share parts of their reflections in their groups and draw connections between the texts before sharing out with the whole group. We talk as an entire class about how the texts communicate a counternarrative or challenge stereotypes. We categorize their thinking to compile something like Table 6.2, which illustrates a synthesis of these ideas. These themes and concepts serve as foundational concepts and themes that we refer to as we read texts throughout the semester. It is not unusual for someone to bring up *The Danger of a Single Story* in our final days of class or for someone to reference their first book club book during our final whole-class discussions about *The House on Mango Street* (Cisneros, 1984) in the middle of the semester. We challenge them early on to seek these connections. We model it and demonstrate how it helps us as readers and people to navigate taboo topics.

Whole Class

The final layer of discourse is whole class discussion. We begin our whole class discussions by reminding them that we are reading a diverse set of authors and literature to "widen our own views" (Green, 2021, p. 12) and challenge the mainstream narrative while also being cautious to question what else is not said or what other texts have presented differently. Here is where we use our position as teachers to help students make connections across texts, world events, personal experiences, and their book club conversations. In many instances, the whole class discussion is where students find validation of their new understandings and perspectives and where we can cultivate more opportunities for continued questions and growth that we later witness in their journals. During our study of *The House on Mango Street* (Cisneros, 1984), Andrew reflected that:

> After we discussed how men mistreat Esperanza, I see why she has a strong distrust in men. . . . I never really thought about how the men did horrible things to her, and I would be hesitant to trust a group of people, too.

As a participant in the cycle of reflection, discussion, and evolution, Andrew expands his perspective of the text. He builds a connection to his own life by considering how he might react.

We read two books we inherited with the course as a whole class, *The House on Mango Street* (Cisneros, 1984) and *The Other Wes Moore: One Name, Two Fates* (Moore, 2010). Having whole class novels between the book club sessions enables our reading community to continue answering the question, "how do our texts talk to each other" and the overarching themes found in Table 6.2. Students have discussed that change happens from a single person, and they witness this through the racism and systemic challenges that the characters face. They relate Esperanza's story and the stories of the Wes Moores to other characters they have read and their own lives. This course is a place for them to start that critical work.

Because of the course design, students make connections from text to text throughout the entire semester allowing their thinking and self-reflective practices to continually grow and develop as they synthesize information. As Vasquez and colleagues (2019) explain, "students learn best when what they are learning has importance in their lives; as such, using the topics, issues, and questions that they raise should be central" (p. 306). The layered discourse prompts students to make relevant and valuable connections between the class texts, their book club books, and their independent reading. Because of these connections, their contributions to the class discussion are insightful and robust.

Conclusion

Our students evolve in their thinking and understanding of the world through individual reflection, small group conversations, and whole-class discussion (Freire & Macedo, 1987; Janks, 2010; hooks, 1994/2020). At the end of the course, students consider how their identities and stories impact the larger collective of lived experiences. Olivia's response is representative of what many students write. She says she now understands "how many authors in the world use their diversity, experiences, and culture as fuel. Not just for the books they write, but how they navigate the world." When students realize that books have the power

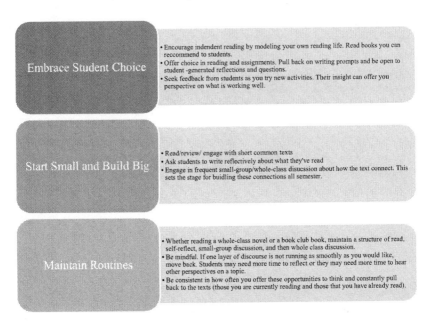

Embrace Student Choice
- Encourage indendent reading by modeling your own reading life. Read books you can recommend to students.
- Offer choice in reading and assignments. Pull back on writing prompts and be open to student -generated reflections and questions.
- Seek feedback from students as you try new activities. Their insight can offer you perspective on what is working well.

Start Small and Build Big
- Read/review/ engage with short common texts
- Ask students to write reflectively about what they've read
- Engage in frequent small-group/whole-class disucssion about how the text connect. This sets the stage for buidling these connections all semester.

Maintain Routines
- Whether reading a whole-class novel or a book club book, maintain a structure of read, self-reflect, small-group discussion, and then whole class discussion.
- Be mindful. If one layer of discourse is not running as smoothly as you would like, move back. Students may need more time to reflect or they may need more time to hear other perspectives on a topic.
- Be consistent in how often you offer these opportunities to think and constantly pull back to the texts (those you are currently reading and those that you have already read).

FIGURE 6.2 Establishing Layered Discourse in the Classroom

to help us navigate the world, we have not only helped our students foster a love of reading but also cultivated tools to navigate their world through reading and writing. Students also understand the importance of dismantling single stories and checking their biases.

When we share our reading lives and offer our students choices, students genuinely find value in the coursework and often rediscover how amazing reading can be. While choice and authentic conversations around reading create buy-in from our students, the three layers of discourse are necessary to give students time, space, and grace to navigate their current understandings of the world and open them up to varying perspectives. See Figure 6.2 for a list of steps to get started in your classroom. We genuinely hope these perspectives make them more empathetic and better citizens in our world as they read, reflect, discuss, and confront the single narratives they know. We will give the final word to our student Jess, "My perspective has changed by not just seeing what is in front of me but going more into it and looking for the true meaning in everything."

References

Adichie, C. N. (2009, July). The danger of a single story [Video]. *TED*. www.ted.com/talks/chimamanda_ngozi_adichie_the_danger_of_a_single_story?language=en

Baker-Bell, A., Butler, T., & Johnson, L. (2017). Editorial: The pain and the wounds: A call for critical race English education in the wake of racial violence. *English Education, 49*(2), 116–129.

Chang, H., Ngunjiri, F., & Hernandez, K. (2013). *Collaborative autoethnography*. Routledge.

Ebarvia, T. (2021, January). January 2021 statement. *#DisruptTexts*. Retrieved September 20, 2021, from https://disrupttexts.org/2021/01/02/january-2021-statement/

Freire, P. (2000). *Pedagogy of the oppressed* (30th-anniversary ed.). Continuum. (Original work published 1970)

Freire, P., & Macedo, D. (1987). *Literacy: Reading the word and the world*. Routledge.

Gee, J. (2011). *Social linguistics and literacies: Ideology and discourses*. Taylor and Francis.

Ginsberg, R., & Glenn, W. J. (Eds.). (2019). *Engaging with multicultural YA literature in the secondary classroom: Critical approaches for critical educators*. Routledge.

Green, K. L. (2021). Counterstorytelling this historical moment. *English Journal, 111*(1), 12–14.

Hash, P. (2019). Theoretical book clubs: Social experiences with required reading. *English Journal, 109*(2), 47–53.

hooks, b. (2020). *Teaching to transgress education as the practice of freedom*. Routledge. (Original work published 1994)

Janks, H. (2010). *Literacy and power*. Routledge.

Miller, D. (2009). *The book whisperer*. Jossey-Bass.

Probst, R. (2004). *Response and analysis* (2nd ed.). Heinemann.

Rosenblatt, L. (2005). *Making meaning with texts*. Heinemann.

Sims Bishop, R. (1990). Mirrors, windows, and sliding glass doors. *Perspectives, 6*(3), ix–xi.

Vasquez, V., Janks, H., & Comber, B. (2019). Research and policy: Critical literacy as a way of being and doing. *Language Arts, 96*(5), 300–311.

Literature Cited

Cisneros, S. (1984). *The house on Mango Street*. Vintage Books.

Moore, W. (2010). *The other Wes Moore: One name, two fates*. Spiegel & Grau.

Noah, T. (2019). *Born a crime*. Random House.

7

CURATING SOCIALLY JUST CLASSROOM LIBRARIES FOR MIDDLE GRADE READERS

Kristie W. Smith and Erica Adela Warren

The classroom of the 21st century is filled with considerable challenges and opportunities and characterized by immense complexities and demands (Darling-Hammond et al., 2017; Hansen, 2008) while being situated against a backdrop of social change, political unrest, and re-considerations of the purposes of schooling (Hess & Noguera, 2021). Further, classrooms are highly diverse, with "students of color making up a majority of public school enrollment" (Love, 2020, p. 29) despite the persistence of diversity deficits among classroom teachers (Love, 2020). There is also an intensifying call for culturally informed curricula, pedagogies, and practices (Ladson-Billings, 1995, 2014; Picower, 2021). Given this, it is essential to reimagine ways of teaching and serving all students equitably, with empathy and social care.

Additionally, it has become increasingly important to support in-service teachers' instructional work and professional development through a lens of equity in instructional practice (Aguilar, 2020). This is true across all disciplines and content areas, but these ideas take on a particular significance in the middle grades (Bishop & Harrison, 2021) as adolescents engage in critical identity exploration during this time, including their racial identity formation (Cross & Cross, 2011; Umaña-Taylor, 2014). Further, in humanities disciplines, such as English language arts and social studies, the prevalence of teaching through literature and historical narratives presents multiple opportunities to disrupt "the danger of single stories" (Adichie, 2009) and counter "racialized curricular violence" (Picower, 2021, p. 63). Additionally, there are opportunities to diversify literary and historical representations (Cho, 2019; Muhammad, 2020b) prevalent in the traditional classroom and curricular canons.

Responsive to this backdrop, 21st-century teachers and teacher educators often seek to identify the knowledge, skills, and commitments that are the most essential (Darling-Hammond & Bransford, 2005) in the classroom while working

DOI:10.4324/9781003302216-9

to maintain an awareness of the connections between society, culture, and schooling (Ladson-Billings, 1995). Teaching in the 21st-century middle grades context, in particular, presents a setting filled with "complexity and shape-shifting characteristics" (Smith & Falbe, 2021). Among these complexities are the challenges of teaching during the COVID-19 pandemic and the existence of socio-political turmoil that touches the educational context. Both the realities of the COVID-19 pandemic, which has exacerbated issues of teacher shortages and pushed forward a Great Resignation (Diliberti et al., 2021), and heightened socio-political debates have thrust schools into a plethora of unprecedented and complex trends and issues. Significant issues include heated debates around K–12 curricular content, such as arguments that focus on fears about Critical Race Theory (CRT) taught in the K–12 classroom.

CRT is a complex framework that is only "one of many research-based theoretical frameworks" (NCTE Educators' Right and Responsibilities to Engage in Antiracist Teaching Position Statement, 2022). Teaching CRT is not generally considered part of K–12 or middle-level curricula (Harrison et al., 2021). However, when applied to the educational context, the ideas of CRT provide a lens to "theorize race and use it as an analytic tool for understanding school inequity" (Ladson-Billings & Tate, 1995). Connected to debates about CRT and "ban(s) of teaching concepts such as systemic racism, conscious or unconscious bias, and privilege" (Harrison et al., 2021), there has been a wave of heated arguments about book selections in K–12 schools, escalating to book bans and challenges (Alter & Harris, 2022). While these realities and complexities exist as real-time issues within the current educational climate, contemporary school settings also present an opportunity-filled landscape for classroom teachers interested in centering diverse perspectives while using a lens of social justice to curate curricular resources.

What and Why—The Socially Just Classroom Library

While there are many ways to qualify and define "social justice," for the purposes of this chapter, social justice definitions align with the perspectives of Nieto and Bode (2018), who articulated the following connections between key tenets of social justice within the educational context:

- "challenging, confronting, and disrupting (social) misconceptions and stereotypes that lead to structural inequality and discrimination" (p. 8)
- "providing all students with the resources necessary to learn to their full potential" (p. 8)
- "drawing on the talents and strengths that students bring to their education" (p. 8)
- "creating a learning environment that promotes critical thinking and supports agency for social change" (p. 8)

Additionally, Nieto and Bode (2018) discussed the ideals that social justice seeks to disrupt. These ideals include disrupting social disparities "[based upon] race, ethnicity, social class, language use, gender and gender identity, sexual orientation, religion, ability, and other social and human differences" (p. 18). These principles describe the integration of social justice within the educational context and illuminate the broad possibilities for centering diverse perspectives and representative histories (Muhammad, 2020b) as part of middle grades classroom resources and curricula.

Diverse Representations, Social Justice, and the Middle Grades Classroom Library

In the middle grades classroom, students must encounter various ideas and perspectives in their learning. "Students need to consider points of view beyond their own, so they come to recognize that their perspective is one of many ways to view the world, not the norm against which to measure other viewpoints" (Short et al., 2016, p. 17). Additionally, Bishop and Harrison (2021) noted that effective and high-quality curricula should expose students to multiple perspectives and ways of understanding the world at the middle level. About this, they stated the following:

> Not only do young adolescents develop an increased awareness of diversity and, subsequently, stereotypes, but they also have a heightened understanding of how power and privilege result in differences among groups of people. Notably, young adolescents reflect on and question how their own cultural and social identity groups relate to, differ from, and are in position to other groups.
>
> *(p. 31)*

Further, given the unique positioning of the 21st-century teacher of middle grades students, imparting the tools of critical and diverse reading and response to reading, particularly within the humanities classroom, has become an important role. Ward et al. (2017) argued that there is a curricular responsibility for 21st-century teachers to engage students in civil discourse around historical and contemporary social injustices. Furthermore, they posit that a pathway for exploration and conversation for these civil discourses is supported by reading young adult literature (YAL). "In the classroom, honest conversations allow adolescents to share feelings, tell stories, construct meaning, and grow intellectually" (Ward et al., 2017, p. 139). These conversations can be connected to and spurred by engagement with literature that challenges and disrupts the traditional literary classroom canon (Cho, 2019).

It is vital to present and allow students to encounter diverse perspectives through children's literature. In her seminal piece, *Mirrors, Windows, and Sliding Glass Doors*, Dr. Rudine Sims Bishop (1990) explained the power of literature to open and expand readers' world views. She noted, "literature transforms human experiences and reflects it back to us . . . in that reflection, we can see our own lives and experiences as part of the larger human experience. Reading . . . becomes a means of self-affirmation . . . readers often seek their mirrors in books" (para. 1). Through the ideas of Sims Bishop (1990), educators understand the necessity of diverse representations in children's literature. Drawn from these ideas, in its *Children's Rights to Read* (n.d.), the International Literacy Association noted that "children have the right to read texts that mirror their experiences and languages, provide windows into the lives of others, and open doors into our diverse world." Likewise, in her TEDTalk, "The Danger of a Single Story," Adichie (2009) described not only how "impressionable and vulnerable we are in the face of a story, particularly as children," but also the idea that power is exacted through selective storytelling. About this, she noted the following:

> It is impossible to talk about the single story without talking about power. . . . How (stories) are told, who tells them, when they're told, how many stories are told, are really dependent on power. . . . Power is the ability not just to tell the story of another person, but to make it the definitive story of that person. . . . But to insist on only these negative stories is to flatten (one's) experience, and to overlook the many other stories that formed (us). The single-story creates stereotypes. And the problem with stereotypes is not that they are untrue, but that they are incomplete. They make one story become the only story.

Adichie's words help underscore the need to curate classroom libraries with attention to author diversity and representation and develop awareness about the balance and tone of stories told and represented within the classroom library collection.

In addition to considerations about diverse representations for the 21st-century classroom library, a reflection of social justice integrations through contemporary YAL is significant. In *Teaching Social Justice Through Young Adult Literature*, Glasgow (2001) noted, "social justice education has the potential to prepare citizens who are sophisticated in their understanding of diversity and group interaction, able to critically evaluate social institutions, and committed to working democratically with diverse others" (p. 54). Further, discussing the unique potential for social justice integrations through literature in the ELA classroom, Boyd (2017) noted the following:

> When teachers and students look at context, they can ask questions about who was privileged in that era and how this fits with their own. They can choose to look at historic events through texts that were pivotal in fights for justice, as there are both nonfiction and fiction documents readily available for such study. Students can examine not only the meanings of words, but how those meanings are attached to power and how they affirm or negate social positions. When educators draw connections to students' lives, they

can focus on validating their students' stories and they can craft bridges to current local, national, and global events that are connected to social issues.

(pp. 7–8)

These ideas point to the power and possibility of curating the middle grades classroom library with explicit attention to social justice.

How—The Socially Just Classroom Library

After providing a foundational understanding of the "what" and "why" of creating the middle-level classroom library with attention to diverse perspectives and social justice, it is essential to consider the "how" of this task. As teaching contexts and learning communities vary, approaches will likewise vary according to the unique needs of each community, social setting, or school context. The following sections present overarching possibilities, resources, customizable strategies, and examples for envisioning this work.

Considering Teacher Reading Identities

Given the work of curating titles with attention to various social identities, teachers' engagement in their critical reflections and self-identity explorations is significant. A possible starting place in the work of curating classroom libraries with attention to diverse perspectives is to do some introspective thinking about self-identity. About this, Boyd (2017) put forth the following:

> (Educators) coming to know who they are as socialized beings is a crucial first step in reading the world and being critical teachers. The experiences that have shaped them, both related to education and to their familial backgrounds, influence the way that teachers interpret events and filter information.
>
> *(p. 7)*

In his "textual lineages" approach, literacy scholar Alfred Tatum (2009) offered a model for self-exploration around one's reading, identity, and texts. Muhammad (2020a) described textual lineages as a way to "represent . . . students' reading lives . . . capture(ing) students' relationships to books and other texts." In the classroom, as Muhammad (2020a) pointed out, the use of textual lineages helps to "value family and cultural influences; (to) understand that everyone has a unique mosaic of textual influence; (and to) honor different types of texts and ways of reading." These principles, applied through the teacher lens, can help provide a pathway for critical reflection and launch the independent and collaborative work of curating the classroom library. The teacher's exploration of their textual lineage can precede student work in this area and create a foundation for a conversation about thoughtful and diverse classroom library selections.

A Survey of Texts and Authors

Another step in the work of curating middle-level classroom libraries with attention to diverse perspectives is to work within school-based professional learning communities (PLCs) to survey YAL texts, discovering authors who have written toward themes of social justice. Figure 7.1 summarizes a survey of authors and texts assignment that a group of preservice middle-level ELA teachers (PSTs) explored while centering social justice in a class project—*The Socially Just Classroom Library Project*.

Author Talks & Text Selection

To launch the Social Justice Classroom Library Project, preservice teachers briefly surveyed the work of several YAL authors, viewing and discussing short, publicly available video clips of author talks. In particular, PSTs considered the following texts and author talks:

- *All American Boys* by Jason Reynolds and Brendan Kiely
- *Free Lunch* by Rex Ogle
- *Amal Unbound* by Aisha Saeed
- *Melissa's Story* by Alex Gino

After the author talks and discussion, these and other social justice-themed YAL texts were presented to PSTs for checkout. The texts in the choice collection ranged across various social justice themes, issues, and literary genres (prose, narrative poetry, and graphic novels). Additionally, PSTs used publicly available sites to survey text summaries, YAL authors, and text reviews to help make selections about appropriate middle-level titles. PSTs used the following sample list of sites:

- We Need Diverse Books (https://diversebooks.org/)
- Social Justice Books (https://socialjusticebooks.org/)
- Project Lit Community (https://twitter.com/projectlitcomm?lang=en)
- Nerdy Book Club (https://nerdybookclub.wordpress.com/)
- Book Riot (https://bookriot.com/)

PSTs made text selections based on their reading identities, interests, and teaching contexts. The selected texts became independent reading, about which PSTs would later create reader response artifacts.

FIGURE 7.1 Author Talks & Text Selection

TABLE 7.1 Top Book Titles in PSTs Classroom Libraries

Book Title	Book Author
This Book Is Anti-Racist: 20 Lessons on How to Wake Up, Take Action, and Do the Work	Tiffany Jewell
Ain't Burned All the Bright	Jason Reynolds and Jason Griffin
All Boys Aren't Blue	George M. Johnson
Monday's Not Coming	Tiffany D. Jackson
When Stars Are Scattered	Victoria Jamieson and Omar Mohamed
A Journey Toward Hope	Victor Hinojosa, Coert Voorhes, Susan Guevara
Unbroken: 13 Stories Starring Disabled Teens	Marieke Nijkamp
A Snake Falls to Earth	Darcie Little Badger
Resilient Black Girl: 52 Weeks of Anti-Racist Activities for Black Joy and Resilience	M.J. Fievre
Ace of Spades	Faridah Àbíké-Íyímídé

Table 7.1 presents a list of top titles that PSTs selected as part of their middle-level-facing social justice-focused classroom library curations.

A similar process for the in-service classroom teacher to include a survey of authors and genre, deliberated text selection, and text reading could be taken, with attention to teaching contexts and community, instructional standards of focus, and student needs. It is important to note that not only does a survey of texts and authors spark teachers' familiarity with current social justice-themed YAL, but also the role of "teacher as reader" in this subgenre is important. Similar to their reading of texts that center on other themes, "teachers create readers in the class by teaching students how to read, by being a role model, and by creating a classroom culture where reading for pleasure is encouraged and supported" (Teachers Creating Readers, 2011). These ideas are significant in the realm of reading for social justice; middle-level classroom teachers must be active model readers of these texts. Further, PLC conversations about how the texts explored might be windows or mirrors (connected to teacher reading identities) could add an essential dimension to the work of discovering a variety of diverse authored and social justice-themed texts for the classroom.

Standards-Based Text Curation

In addition to selecting texts through author surveys and making connections to teacher reading identities, another approach to curating the socially just classroom library might include considering student-friendly social justice standards paired with existing humanities (e.g., ELA or Social Studies) content standards. A combination of social justice and content standards could anchor classroom library curations. For example, the organization, Learning for Justice, a coalition with a "strong foundation of providing educational resources (toward) creating justice" (Learning for Justice, 2017), published a "Framework for Anti-bias Education" that maps explicit social justice standards (Learning for Justice IDJA Framework, 2021). Within the standards, Learning for Justice identified four broad domains—identity, diversity, justice, and action (IDJA)—which recognize that "in today's diverse classroom, students need knowledge and skills related to both prejudice reduction and collective action" (Learning for Justice, 2021). Table 7.2 lists the IDJA domains with excerpts from related anchor standards and provides sample connections to YAL texts with social justice themes.

TABLE 7.2 IDJA Domains, Excerpts from Anchor Standards, and YAL Text Examples

Domains	Excerpts From the Anchor Standards	YAL Text Examples
Identity Standards 1–5	"Students will develop positive social identities based on their membership in multiple groups in society." "Students will recognize that people's multiple identities interact and create unique and complex individuals."	*Black Brother, Black Brother* Jewell Parker Rhodes
Diversity Standards 6–10	"Students will express comfort with people who are both similar to and different from them and engage respectfully with all people." "Students will respond to diversity by building empathy, respect, understanding and connection."	*Melissa's Story* Alex Gino
Justice Standards 11–15	"Students will recognize stereotypes and relate to people as individuals rather than representatives of groups." "Students will recognize that power and privilege influence relationships on interpersonal, intergroup and institutional levels and consider how they have been affected by those dynamics."	*Stamped* Jason Reynolds, Ibram X. Kendi
Action Standards 16–20	Students "speak up with courage and respect when they or someone else has been hurt or wronged by bias." Students "make principled decisions about when and how to take a stand against bias and injustice in their everyday lives . . . despite negative peer or group pressure."	*Finding Junie Kim* Ellen Oh *Run* John Lewis

Learning for Justice also breaks the standards into grade-level bands with related outcomes and scenarios that clarify the embedded competencies and provide student-friendly connections. While the texts in Table 7.2 represent only a small sampling of possibilities connected to the IDJA framework, at the school level, the collective wisdom of a PLC would be essential to connecting social justice standards with necessary content standards to refine a robust classroom library curation.

Considering What Is—A Classroom Library Audit

Another step, or possibly an independent phase that can support the work of curating socially just classroom libraries for middle-level readers, is considering "what is" or auditing the existing classroom library. For example, a "bookshelf equity audit (serves the purpose of) fostering school conversations about the books we read and teach" (Fishman-Weaver, 2019). To conduct a bookshelf or classroom library audit that centers on diversity and equity, Nguyen (2021) provided the following sample guiding questions:

"How many of your books do the following:"

- "Feature people of color as the central character, rather than a sidekick"
- "Feature LGBTQ and gender-expansive characters"
- "Feature characters with differing physical and intellectual abilities"
- "Feature characters who are not lanky, scrappy, skinny, or small"
- "Feature characters from nontypical family backgrounds"
- "Treat incarcerated characters with dignity"
- "Do too many of the books depict worlds that are utopian and trouble-free?"
- "Do the books rely too heavily on caricatures or promote harmful stereotypes in subtle ways?"
- "Are typical gender roles dominant across the library?"
- "Are women frequently represented as powerful leaders or as instigators of action and change, for example?"
- "Are language and cultural heritages honored?"

Another example of the kinds of considerations that could apply to an audit of bookshelf materials derives from the National Council of Teachers of English (NCTE) (2020) *Position Statement on Indigenous Peoples and People of Color (IPOC) in English and Language Arts Materials*. This position statement includes the following considerations about curricular resources:

- "texts represent Indigenous peoples and People of Color in a fashion which respects their dignity as human beings and accurately mirrors their contributions to American culture, history, and letters, meaning that depictions of these communities should be balanced and realistic"

- "illustrations and photographs of Indigenous peoples and People of Color accurately portray historical and socioeconomic diversity and do not play purposefully or inadvertently to stereotype"
- "dialect is realistic, consistent, and appropriate to the setting and characters"

These kinds of questions and considerations are examples of ways to begin an examination of current classroom library materials using a critical lens. This step would precede waves of revised curation with attention to how to best include themes of social justice and positive representations of marginalized communities and characters within the collection.

Acknowledging Challenges and Moving the Work Forward

The work of curating classroom libraries with attention to themes of social justice presents a range of approaches and opportunities. The possibility of facilitating storytelling and reading through windows, mirrors, and sliding glass doors (Sims Bishop, 1990) is hugely important for the learning needs of 21st-century young adolescents (Bishop & Harrison, 2021). However, this work is not without explicit challenges. Middle-level teachers who seek to disrupt extant curricular traditions, such as the classroom canon, will face the challenge of needing to carefully and thoughtfully curate texts that reflect the diverse identities of young adolescent readers and global human experiences. Additionally, practical, social, and political pushback may challenge teacher efforts toward carrying out this work. According to NTCE, at least "27 states with legislation either passed, pending, or under discussion would severely limit K–12 and university educators' ability to engage with critical race theory and antiracist teaching" (NCTE Educators' Right and Responsibilities to Engage in Antiracist Teaching Position Statement, 2022). This reality also brings opposition to teachers' efforts to center themes of social justice within selections for the middle-level classroom library.

However, despite challenges to the work, there exists strong support in the field for continued efforts to push forward educational equity and attention to diverse perspectives and representations within the curriculum. For example, NCTE (2022) "express(ly) declar(ed) . . . solidarity with people of diverse human, cultural, and racial backgrounds (toward the goal of) eradicating all forms of racism, bias, and prejudice in spaces of teaching and learning" (NCTE Educators' Right and Responsibilities to Engage in Antiracist Teaching Position Statement, 2022). Further, in doing this work, even as it pertains to curating the socially just classroom library, teachers may find themselves in a "search for that (practical) space between the radical and the possible" (Miller, 2019, p. 7). In this space, it is vital to seek out allies "who believe (in the work) even if they are not leading it" (Miller, 2019, p. 5) and to sustain teacher courage, persistence, and collegiality. Most importantly, it will be imperative to maintain a belief in the critical and transformative power of text curation for the middle-level classroom library.

References

About Learning for Justice. (2017, June 28). *Learning for Justice*. www.learningforjustice.org/about

Adichie, C. N. (2009). The danger of a single story. *TED Talks*. www.ted.com/talks/chimamanda_adichie_the_danger_of_a_single_story?language=en

Aguilar, E. (2020). *Coaching for equity: Conversations that change practice*. Jossey-Bass.

Alter, A., & Harris, E. (2022). Attempts to ban books are accelerating and becoming more divisive. *New York Times*. https://www.nytimes.com/2022/09/16/books/book-bans.html

Bishop, P., & Harrison, L. M. (2021). *The successful middle school: This we believe*. Association for Middle Level Education.

Boyd, A. S. (2017). *Social Justice literacies in the English classroom: Teaching practice in action*. Teachers College Press.

Children's Rights to Read. (n.d.). *International Literacy Association*. www.literacyworldwide.org/docs/default-source/resource-documents/ila-childrens-rights-to-read.pdf

Cho, N. (2019). Why I teach diverse literature. In L. Delpit (Ed.), *Teaching when the world is on fire* (pp. 208–213). The New Press.

Cross, W. E., & Cross, T. B. (2011). Theory, research, and models. In S. M. Quintana & C. McKown (Eds.), *Handbook of race, racism, and the developing child* (1st ed., pp. 154–181). John Wiley & Sons. https://doi.org/10.1002/9781118269930.ch8

Darling-Hammond, L., & Bransford, J. (Eds.). (2005). *Preparing teachers for a changing world: What teachers should learn and be able to do*. Jossey-Bass.

Darling-Hammond, L., Bransford, J., & LePage, P. (2017). Introduction. In *Preparing teachers for a changing world: What teachers should learn and be able to do* (pp. 1–39). Jossey-Bass.

Diliberti, M. K., Schwartz, H. L., & David, G. (2021). *Stress topped the reasons why public school teachers quit, even before COVID-19*. Rand Corporation. www.rand.org/pubs/research_reports/RRA1121-2.html

Fishman-Weaver, K. (2019). How to audit your classroom library for diversity. *Edutopia*. www.edutopia.org/article/how-audit-your-classroom-library-diversity

Glasgow, J. N. (2001). Teaching Social Justice through young adult literature. *The English Journal*, *90*(6), 54. https://doi.org/10.2307/822056

Hansen, D. T. (2008). *Why educate teachers?* (ed. Cochran-Smith et al.) Routledge.

Harrison, L. M., Hurd, E., & Brinegar, K. M. (2021, August 31). But is it really about Critical Race Theory?: The attack on teaching about systemic racism and why we must care. *AMLE*. www.amle.org/but-is-it-really-about-critical-race-theory-the-attack-on-teaching-about-systemic-racism-and-why-we-must-care/

Hess, F. M., & Noguera, P. (2021). *A search for common ground: Conversations about the toughest questions in K-12 Education*. Teachers College Press.

Ladson-Billings, G. (1995). But that's just good teaching! The case for culturally relevant pedagogy. *Theory into Practice*, *34*(3), 159–165. https://doi.org/10.1080/00405849509543675

Ladson-Billings, G. (2014). Culturally relevant pedagogy 2.0: A.K.A. the remix. *Harvard Educational Review*, *84*(1), 74–84. https://doi.org/10.17763/haer.84.1.p2rj131485484751

Ladson-Billings, G., & Tate, W. (1995). Toward a critical race theory of education. *Teachers College Record*, *97*(1), 47–68.

Learning for Justice. (2021). Social justice standards. *Learning for Justice*. Retrieved September 15, 2021, from www.learningforjustice.org/frameworks/social-justice-standards

Love, B. (2020). *We want to do more than survive: Abolitionist teaching and the pursuit of educational freedom*. Beacon.

Miller, H. (2019). Being a radical pragmatist: Reflections on Introducing LGBTQ YA lit to an ELA Department. *English Leadership Quarterly, 41*(3), 5–8. https://library.ncte.org/journals/ELQ/issues/v41-3/29995

Muhammad, G. (2020a). Cultivate the genius in your students at home with a textual lineage tree. *Scholastic*. http://teacher.scholastic.com/education/reachteach/pdfs/textual_lineage_tip_sheet.pdf

Muhammad, G. (2020b). *Cultivating genius: An equity framework for culturally and historically responsive literacy*. Scholastic Inc.

National Council of Teachers of English (NCTE). (2020). *Position statement on Indigenous Peoples and People of Color (IPOC) in English and language arts materials*. https://ncte.org/statement/ipoc/

National Council of Teachers of English (NCTE). (2022). *Educators' right and responsibilities to engage in antiracist teaching*. https://ncte.org/statement/antiracist-teaching/

Nguyen, H. (2021). 5 Ways to audit your classroom library for inclusion. *Edutopia*. www.edutopia.org/article/5-ways-audit-your-classroom-library-inclusion

Nieto, S., & Bode, P. (2018). *Affirming diversity: The sociopolitical context of multicultural education*. Pearson.

Picower, B. (2021). *Reading, writing, and racism: Disrupting whiteness in teacher education and in the classroom*. Beacon.

Short, K. G., Day, D., & Schroeder, J. (2016). *Teaching globally: Reading the world through literature*. Maine. https://eric.ed.gov/?id=ED583546

Sims Bishop, R. (1990). Mirrors, windows, and sliding glass doors. *Perspectives: Choosing and Using Books for the Classroom, 6*(3).

Smith, K. W., & Falbe, K. N. (2021). Middle grades teacher education for equity and social justice: A research summary. *AMLE*. www.amle.org/research/middle-grades-teacher-education-for-equity-and-social-justice/

Tatum, A. W. (2009). *Reading for their life: (Re)building the textual lineages of African American adolescent males*. Heinemann.

Teachers Creating Readers. (2011). *Govt.nz*. https://natlib.govt.nz/schools/reading-engagement/strategies-to-engage-students-as-readers/teachers-creating-readers

Umaña-Taylor, A. J., Quintana, S. M., Lee, R. M., Cross, W. E., Rivas-Drake, D., Schwartz, S. J., Syed, M., Yip, T., Seaton, E., French, S., Knight, G. P., Markstrom, C., & Sellers, R. M. (2014). Ethnic and racial identity during adolescence and into young adulthood: An integrated conceptualization. *Child Development, 85*(1), 21–39. https://doi.org/10.1111/cdev.12196

Ward, B., Day-Wiff, D., & Young, T. (2017). Civil rights and social justice: Then and now—How much progress have we made? In *Teaching young adult literature today: Insights, considerations, and perspectives for the classroom teacher*. Rowman & Littlefield.

Literature Cited

Àbíké-Íyímídé, F. (2021). *Ace of spades*. Fiewel and Friends.

Darcie Little Badger. (2021). *A snake falls to earth*. Levine Querido.

Fièvre, M. J. (2021). *Resilient black girl: 52 weeks of anti-racist activities for black joy and resilience*. Mango Publishing.

Gino, A. (2018). *Melissa's story*. Scholastic Inc.

Hinojosa, V., Voorhees, C., Guevara, S., & Baylor University. (2020). *A journey toward hope*. Six Foot Press.

Jackson, T. D. (2019). *Monday's not coming*. Katherine Tegen Books, An Imprint of Harper Collins Publishers.

Jamieson, V., & Mohamed, O. (2020). *When stars are scattered*. Penguin Group USA.

Jewell, T. (2020). *This book is anti-racist: 20 lessons on how to wake up, take action, and do the work*. Quarto Publishing Group.

Johnson, G. M. (2020). *All boys aren't blue: A memoir-manifesto*. Farrar, Straus and Giroux.

Lewis, J., Aydin, A., & Nate Powell. (2018). *Run*. Abrams ComicArts.

Marieke Nijkamp. (2018). *Unbroken: 13 stories starring disabled teens*. Farrar, Straus and Giroux.

Ogle, R. (2019). *Free lunch*. W. W. Norton & Company, Inc.

Oh, E. (2021). *Finding Junie Kim*. Harper Collins.

Reynolds, J., & Griffin, J. (2022). *Ain't burned all the bright*. Atheneum.

Reynolds, J., & Kendi, I. X. (2020). *Stamped-racism, antiracism, and you: A remix of the national book award-winning stamped from . . . the beginning*. Little, Brown.

Reynolds, J., & Kiely, B. (2017). *All American boys*. Turtleback Books.

Rhodes, J. P. (2020). *Black brother, black brother*. Little, Brown and Company.

Saeed, A. (2020). *Amal unbound*. Puffin Books.

SECTION 3

8

'I DON'T UNDERSTAND, I DON'T SPEAK SPANISH'

Exploring Linguistic and Cultural Differences Through Picture Books

Julia López-Robertson and Maria del Rocio Herron

James:	Señora Julia, I don't understand, I don't speak Spanish. There is Spanish in that book, I don't understand it.
Sra. Herron:	James, that's okay, I know some of our friends speak Spanish and they will love to help you.
Rafael:	I will help you; I know lots of Spanish.
Sra. Julia:	Yes, see James, you have friends who will help you.
Samantha:	Wait, wait, look I speak Spanish, see—uno, dos, tres, cuatro. I can help you too. I know Spanish and I can speak Spanish, and I can help you speak Spanish.
James:	Wait, I do know too, uno, dos, tres . . .
Rafael:	We all know Spanish.

The above vignette is from a discussion a group of 4-year-old children in María del Rocio [Rocio] Herron's Pre-Kindergarten class had during a read aloud. I (Julia) had just introduced the book, *Isabel and her colores go to school* (Alessandri, 2021), and one of the children, James (a mono-lingual English speaker), became a little distressed when he did not immediately recognize all the words I read. As seen in the excerpt, his classmates, Rafael, (a bilingual Spanish/English speaker), and Samantha (a mono-lingual English speaker), immediately offered to help him and Samantha (all children's names are pseudonyms) even demonstrated her knowledge of Spanish by counting from one to four in Spanish. It seems that Samantha's counting reminded James that he did in fact know Spanish which Rafael affirmed by stating that "we all know Spanish." In this classroom, children's engagement with diverse children's literature is foundational; children engage in daily explorations with books representing a variety of languages, cultures, and ways of being in the world.

DOI:10.4324/9781003302216-11

Rocio has been a teacher of young children for over 20 years in her native country, Costa Rica, and the United States. Before becoming a teacher educator, Julia spent 17 years as a bilingual primary teacher in Boston, MA, and Tucson, AZ. We met 13 years ago when Julia's youngest son was a student in Rocio's class. In addition to our shared identities as Spanish-speaking Latina educators, we share a passion for multicultural children's literature, specifically Latinx children's literature, and engaging young children with that literature.

Conceptual Framework

We ground our work upon a sociocultural perspective (Freire & Macedo, 1987/2005) and view literacy as a set of social and cultural practices (Lewis et al., 2007) that comprise specific ways of using language and interacting with people (Street, 1995) within specific sociopolitical contexts (Nieto, 2009). We believe that (a) children and their families have a right to their own language (González et al., 2005; Scott et al., 2009); (b) children's learning begins and is continuously influenced by the home (Bartolomé, 2011; López-Robertson et al., 2010); and (c) we must build on the knowledge and experiences that they bring with them to school (González, 2001).

In classrooms where teachers let children know that they value the range of languages, literacies, and knowledge represented in childrens' communities and where teachers create contexts for privileging and using those resources, children have opportunities to draw on what they already know to enrich and support their learning interactions. We engage children with literature in ways that view their lived experiences as a foundation upon which to build (López-Robertson, 2021) and use multicultural literature as an instrument to provide children experiences with literature that allow them to see themselves and explore different ways of being—what Sims Bishop (1990) referred to as mirrors, windows, and sliding glass doors. Our work examines the potential role of multicultural picture books in helping young children develop a strong sense of self and a positive view of those who represent linguistic and cultural backgrounds with which they may be unfamiliar.

The Potential of Multicultural Picture Books

Recognizing that "complex topics and difficult histories are always and already present in classrooms" (Clark et al., 2021, p. 274) and that "literary interpretations are influenced by readers' ethnic backgrounds as well as the cultural milieu embedded in the stories they read" (Brooks & Browne, 2012, p. 76), we are intentional in our book selection. We choose books written by authors who represent various cultural, linguistic, and racial backgrounds and whose stories reflect the children's languages, cultures, and ways of making meaning of the world and books that will extend their worldview keeping in mind Arizpe's (2021) notion that picture books are "ideological and cultural objects that can speak meaningfully to certain groups of readers, but at the same time potentially misrepresent or silence some of them" (p. 261).

Context

Palmetto Elementary is in a mid-size southeastern city surrounded by older established neighborhoods, a couple of brand-new apartment complexes, ethnically diverse shopping centers, and several family-owned restaurants. Palmetto Elementary is a Title One school serving about 630 children in grades PreK–5; 74% of the school population is African American, 13% are Latinx, 5% are two or more races, 4% are white, and 4% are Asian or Pacific Islander. Rocio's classroom is characteristic of the diversity found within Palmetto Elementary; she has 20 students representing diverse ethnicities, languages, religions, socioeconomic status, and immigration experiences. Of the 20 children, 14 are African American, 1 is African, and 5 are Spanish-speaking Latinx children from Mexico, Guatemala, or Honduras.

While there are a few Latinx support staff members at Palmetto, Rocio is the only Latina classroom teacher. Rocio works conscientiously to nurture strong relationships with her students and their families beginning well before the school year. Although home visits are not required, Rocio visits all families and maintains close ties with them throughout the year. Latinx families at Palmetto seek Rocio out for assistance with various issues and not always school-related; families have confianza in Rocio. As explained by González et al. (2005), confianza is a mutual trust based on respect and cultivated over time. The confianza the families place in Rocio is evidenced by the openness with which they share their lived experiences and/or hardships. Although it is not immediate (and never expected), this confianza is given to me; as someone who has been with Rocio for years, is seen often in the classroom, and openly shares my lived experiences—the families know that I work alongside Rocio to advocate for them and their children.

Through constant and consistent communication with families, home visits, open and honest two-way conversations with families, and love, Rocio lays the foundation for our work. Confianza from the families opens space for us to engage the children in read alouds and discussions about what some may consider "taboo topics" with young children—issues of immigration, racism, and linguicism. Some may deem these inappropriate for school, especially for children 4–5 years old, while others believe that these are topics to be discussed only at home. We believe that preparing students for participation in a global society includes discussing these topics; it is our responsibility to create safe spaces to explore their thoughts and provide them with strategies and tools that teach them how to think.

Latinx Children's Literature

Children engage in whole class read alouds, play, and the writing center throughout the week with Rocio, and on Friday, Julia joins the class for read aloud, singing, and movement. During the read aloud, Julia encourages conversation by asking the children questions such as: does this story remind you of anything, has anything like this ever happened to you, or what questions do you have? Rocio clarifies connections the children are making, engages them through questions, and often participates in the read aloud. The children actively listen and participate by sharing stories, connections, and asking questions. Many of the books are bilingual, Spanish/English, providing space for our Spanish-speaking students to share their linguistic abilities with their classmates.

While we infuse the curriculum with multicultural children's picture books, the present study, and this chapter, focused on Latinx children's literature. Like multicultural children's literature, Latinx children's literature is for all children; for Latinx children, the literature strengthens their sense of self and identity; positively contributes to academic achievement; and may amplify pride in their linguistic abilities. Latinx children's literature exposes non-Latinx children to different languages, cultures, and ways of making meaning leading to increased cultural understanding (López-Robertson, 2021).

We deeply value the opportunities multicultural children's picture books present us to engage in conversations about things that matter and are of interest to the children; the books serve as catalysts that spark conversations about issues like the right to one's language, what it means to be bilingual, why people move, the right to be safe, and what it means to have pride in one's linguistic and racial heritage. While some might question young children's ability to understand and talk about these issues, we believe that "existing classroom practices underestimate and constrain what Latino/Latina and other children are able to display intellectually" (González et al., 2005, p. 27); our instruction connects and draws from the lived experiences of our students, their families, and our community.

The Right to One's Language

In *Dreamers* (2018), Yuyi Morales takes us on her immigration journey to the United States with her baby. While reading the book, we came upon the page that reads, "Unable to understand and afraid to speak, we made a lot of mistakes." The children delighted in the illustration of Yuyi and her baby playing in the fountain and were puzzled by the police officer standing before them, "he looks mad," one child said. Another wondered, "Why are they afraid to speak?" and added, "it doesn't matter what language, you can talk in any way you like." The conversation continued when Marta said, "Sometimes I don't understand what Janelle is saying so I ask Rafael, and he helps me." We asked the children why Yuyi might be afraid to speak, and Marco shared,

> Sometimes people get mad at my mom when she talks in Spanish, but I tell her no matter, she can talk any way she likes. They are not the boss of her. She [Yuyi] doesn't need to be scared just like my mom doesn't need to be scared.

Marco supported his mother's right to speak her language and provided reassurance that neither his mother nor Yuyi needed to be scared to speak their language, and he was correct. Scott et al. (2009) remind us that "language is a uniquely human quality of people who live in a world with authentically equal rights to language, especially rights to their own language" (p. xix). As several of the children said, "you can talk any way you like."

What It Means to Be Bilingual

Children learn to communicate by using their communities' language and linguistic codes in their social interactions (Schieffelin & Ochs, 1986) and are influenced by the language ideologies held by those around them, their families, teachers, and peers. In this classroom, Rocio's beliefs about language and the importance of being bilingual are clearly communicated to the children through all that she does; she believes that language is a resource (Ruiz, 1984), that children must help each other, and that being bilingual is something to be proud of. The children have internalized this, as they are always prepared to use their bilingualism to support each other and are proud to call themselves bilingual.

The book *Pepita Talks Twice/Pepita Habla Dos Veces* (Lachtman, 1995) is about a little girl, Pepita, who has grown tired of talking twice. In her community, she is bilingual and offers translation from Spanish to English and/or English to Spanish. Pepita decides that she will only speak English, a decision she has not thoroughly thought through. The story climaxes when the family dog runs out of the yard and almost gets hit by a car; Pepita yells, "Wolf! Wolf!" and he does not respond. It is not until she yells ¡LOBO! that the dog stops and barely misses being hit by a car. That near-miss taught Pepita the importance of being bilingual.

Rocio gave an example of what it means to be bilingual in their classroom; she reminded the children that Marisela is learning English and that Marco helps her. Marco happily added, "Yes, I am like Pepita. I can talk in Spanish and English." Cecilia connected to helping her grandmother, "I help my abuelita when we go to the store. The people don't speak Spanish, and I tell her what they say. I am like Pepita too." While we recognize that bilingualism is a gift (López-Robertson, 2014), we are also keenly aware that due to the anti-Spanish sentiment in the United States, linguicism, prejudice based on the language one speaks, is widespread. As a result some families painfully choose not to give their children the gift of language. In this classroom, being bilingual means using your language to help others and being proud of having access to two languages.

Why People Move

My Shoes and I: Crossing Three Borders/Mis Zápatos y Yo: Cruzando Tres Fronteras by René Colato Laínez (2019) tells René's story of moving from El Salvador to the United States as a child. This story is one that children might connect with, perhaps because they may have experienced something similar or know someone who has. Additionally, while they may not have personal experiences with this type of moving, children can connect with the excitement of having a new pair of shoes and even feelings of fear. While listening to the book, there were many connections to the page depicting the angry dogs chasing René and his shoes. The text read, "racing cars and fleeing hungry dogs." The children were excited to share their thoughts and connections to the dogs: Michael shared, "I have seen dogs when they growl and bark like that. I don't like it. They scare me a lot!" Sheryl added, "When dogs are hungry, they are mean. You are not supposed to touch their bowls when they are eating."

Tomás shifted the conversation and wondered, "why doesn't his mamá live with them? Where is she?" Michael responded, "she had to get money, so she moved, and now the dad and boy are coming to see her so they can be together." "Yeah," Samantha added, "you can't buy food with no money, so she went to get money and then told them to come and be with her." The children comment on their awareness of the necessity of money and how one might need to move to "get money" in some cases. As noted earlier, picture books are "ideological and cultural objects" (Arizpe, 2021, p. 261) representing life conditions and experiences; in the case of *My Shoes and I: Crossing Three Borders/Mis Zápatos y Yo: Cruzando Tres Fronteras*, the children's connections were to fear, specifically of dogs as illustrated in the book, and to the idea of lack of money necessitating a move to obtain money and provide for the family. One of our goals in sharing this type of literature with the children is the desire for them to learn to identify with different communities and develop empathy and accept others' differences.

The Right to Be Safe

Bright Star (Morales, 2021) tells the story of a young fawn's separation from her mother and subsequent survival in the Sonoran Desert. The children were immediately drawn to the book's illustrations and the embroidered words throughout the book. As I held up the book, one child commented, "I know what that says, '*mira*'!" Rafael replied, "That means look in Spanish. She [Yuyi] wants us to look at pictures."

We continued to read, and Felicity looking at the picture of the fawn in the desert, said, "Why is the baby deer alone? She is not going to be safe." A discussion ensued where the children commented on safety issues and being taken care of. Many children were concerned that the fawn was too little to take care of herself, "who is going to take care of the baby?" "How is she going to eat and get food?" "How will she be safe?" Diana responded, "I can't take care of myself. My mom and dad have to make my food and take me to school." Felicity came back to her question, "How will she be safe, where is her mommy?" Tomás commented, "It's like in that book with the shoes, the mom left them to get money. And the dad stayed to take care of the boy and to keep him safe." Sheryl added,

"But there is no daddy in this book. Who will take care of her? She is little and needs to be safe."

As children try to make sense of their world, which they do every day, it is only natural that they would be concerned with safety issues; after all, safety is a basic human need. Adults worry about safety; parents worry about their child's safety when they play, when they are in the car—all the time! Teachers are also concerned with children's safety, and we explain why we have rules and procedures "to keep everyone safe." Everyone has a right to be safe, guaranteed by the Universal Declaration of Human Rights (UG, 1948).

Pride in One's Linguistic and Racial Heritage

Inspired by her own life story, Supreme Court Justice Sonia Sotomayor's *Just Ask!: Be Different, Be Brave, Be You* (2019) celebrates children with different abilities and reframes these abilities as special powers. As children interact in the book, they ask each other questions about their abilities, modeling what children (and adults) should do in the real world; when we come across someone different and would like to know why, just ask! While none of the children in Rocio's class have different abilities, she works very hard to establish a classroom community where children "just ask" each other about their curiosities, including linguistic, cultural, and racial heritage.

During the read aloud of *Just Ask: Be Different, Be Brave, Be You*, a discussion about bilingualism as a superpower ensued,

Rafael shared, "I have super special powers."
Michael agreed and added, "Yeah, I do too. I can run really fast."
Rafael responded, "But my power is super, and some other people have it too. Señora Herron has it, and Diana, and Sofia, and Señora Julia too!"

Michael:	"They are girls?"
Diana:	"No, we are bilingual. We speak two languages, Spanish and English."
Rafael:	"Yeah, we all speak both, so we are all super!"

As discussed here, being bilingual in this classroom is a source of pride and something all the children strive to achieve. Rocio is an example of the "role that a caring teacher can play . . . when they praise and encourage students' efforts to reach their full potential, and when they permit Latino students to experiment with the two languages at their disposal" (Reyes, 2011, p. xv). Crucial to our work with the children is a shared desire to "reclaim the language practices of Latinx students" (Sánchez & García, 2022, p. 2) since for far too long, students have suffered (and in some cases continue to suffer) linguicism in schools. The Latino children in the classroom are encouraged to speak Spanish and share their superpower with others from the first day of school. Being bilingual is something desirable and to be proud of in this classroom.

Racial Heritage

In the opening vignette, we discussed *Isabel and Her Colores Go to School* (Alessandri, 2021). In the book, a little girl named Isabel is very nervous about going to school because she does not speak much English. Isabel begins the school day feeling nervous and uncomfortable, but she soon learns that she can communicate with others through drawing. The read aloud discussion also brought up issues of racial heritage, namely skin color. In the book, Isabel's skin is brown, and according to Sofia, "it looks like chocolate."

Mira happily added, "Yes, she is black like me!"
Brandon: "Yeah, and like me. I am dark brown!"
Mira: "But I am from Africa and her skin looks like mine, see."
Brandon: "I am dark brown, see. It looks like my color too."

As this discussion proceeded, the children, seated on the carpet, began holding up their arms and talking about their skin color too. "Mine is like cinnamon." "Mine is like hot chocolate mix." Rocio had recently introduced the skin color crayons and engaged the class in a discussion about their skin color; they recognized that their skin color was like some children's and different from others. The children brought that discussion into the one we were having about *Isabel and her colores;* they talked about difference as something positive. Mira shared, "My mommy says that I am Black and beautiful" and Sofia responded, "Your black is beautiful, and you do look like Isabel."

Rather than have the children believe that "we are all the same," together, they explore their differences and learn that there is beauty in their differences and that those differences enrich our classroom. We recognize that children are not blind to issues of race and difference (e.g., Tenorio, 2009); they are surrounded by it; moreover, they "learn covert and overt messages from many sources including television, home, literature, and peers" (Boutte et al., 2011, p. 338); it is a part of our world. Reading and then talking about these issues, unfamiliar places, and experiences can raise our students' level of understanding, engagement, and empathy (e.g., Arizpe et al., 2014).

Discussion

It is imperative to note that conversations such as those described previously do not happen overnight; through concerted and consistent effort, Rocio works to establish close relationships with the families so that they feel confident to ask questions, seek help, and participate in school. Cultivating relationships can become complicated when including someone who is an outsider; Rocio's role was even more critical as she extended her classroom to Julia. The families hear about Julia from the children, engage with her during events held at school and in the community, and are accustomed to seeing her at school. The families feel heard, respected, and safe and have given us their confianza, which forms the foundation of our work. Julia created relationships with the families through the children.

Patience is one of our most significant assets; we have been at Palmetto Elementary since it opened its doors four years ago, and along with the excitement of a new school comes some fear of the unknown. While some families had preconceived notions of what PreK should look like (free play all day), families new to the United States did not know what to expect. One of the most significant challenges we [continue to] face is having our Spanish-speaking Latinx families understand the importance of sharing their language with their children. Linguicism, as explained above, is rampant in the United States, and Latinx families fear for their children. We often have discussions with families centering on the power of being bilingual and the importance of "passing along the home language" (López-Robertson, 2021, p. 71). We share our experiences as Spanish-speaking Latinas raising bilingual children to have pride in their Latinx and linguistic heritage.

It is critical that we thoughtfully engage our young students with carefully selected multicultural picture books; these books offer children the opportunity to "immerse themselves in story worlds, gain insights into how people feel, live, and think around the world, while they also come to recognize their common humanity as well as to value cultural differences" (Short, 2009, p. 1). All children need to feel a sense of pride in who they are, in the languages they speak, and they need to be able to talk about their skin color, recognize that they are different, and feel valued. These picture books provide the avenue to discuss issues that are important and relevant to our students while opening the space for "meaningful connections with others" (Zentella, 2005, p. 27). Viewing our students as holders and creators of knowledge (Bernal, 2002) allows us to build a curriculum based on the knowledge, experiences, and languages they bring to school.

Closing Thoughts

While "silence on racial issues sends a strong message to children that it is taboo to discuss these issues in school and left with no avenues for discussing issues, children often develop misconceptions and stereotypes about various racial groups" (Boutte et al., 2011, p. 339), engaging young children in discussions about skin color, difference, language, and race signals to them that these are important topics, that we respect their thoughts about these issues, and that we want to listen to what they are telling us.

References

Arizpe, E. (2021). The state of the art in picturebook research from 2010 to 2020. *Language Arts, 98*(5), 260–272.

Arizpe, E., Colomer, T., & Martínez-Roldán, C. (2014). *Visual journeys through wordless narratives: An international inquiry with immigrant children and the arrival.* A&C Black.

Assembly, U. G. (1948). Universal declaration of human rights. *UN General Assembly*, *302*(2), 14–25.

Bartolomé, L. I. (2011). Literacy as *Comida*: Learning to read with Mexican novellas. In M. L. Reyes (Ed.), *Words were all we had: Becoming biliterate against the odds* (pp. 49–59). Teachers College Press.

Bernal, D. D. (2002). Critical race theory, Latino critical theory, and critical raced-gendered epistemologies: Recognizing students of color as holders and creators of knowledge. *Qualitative Inquiry*, *8*(1), 105–126.

Boutte, G. S., López-Robertson, J., & Powers-Costello, E. (2011). Moving beyond colorblindness in early childhood classrooms. *Early Childhood Education Journal*, *39*(5), 335–342.

Brooks, W., & Browne, S. (2012). Towards a culturally situated reader response theory. *Children's Literature in Education*, *43*(1), 74–85.

Clark, C. T., Chrisman, A., & Lewis, S. G. (2021). Using picturebooks to teach with and against social and emotional learning. *Language Arts*, *98*(5), 246–259.

Freire, P., & Macedo, D. (2005). *Literacy: Reading the word and the world*. Routledge. (Original work published 1987)

González, N. (2001). *I am my language: Discourses of women and children in the borderlands*. University of Arizona Press.

González, N., Moll, L., & Amanti, C. (2005). *Funds of knowledge: Theorizing practices in households and classrooms*. Erlbaum.

Lewis, C., Enciso, P. E., & Moje, E. B. (Eds.). (2007). *Reframing sociocultural research on literacy: Identity, agency, and power*. Routledge.

López-Robertson, J. (2014). My gift to you is my language: Spanish is the language of my heart. In B. Kabuto & P. Martens (Eds.), *Linking families, learning, and schooling: Parent—researcher perspectives* (pp. 80–91). Routledge.

López-Robertson, J. (2021). *Celebrating our cuentos: Choosing and using Latinx literature in elementary classrooms*. Scholastic.

López-Robertson, J., Long, S., & Turner-Nash, K. (2010). First steps in constructing counter narratives of young children and their families. *Language Arts*, *88*(2), 93–103.

Nieto, S. (2009). *The light in their eyes: Creating multicultural learning communities*. Teachers College Press.

Reyes, M. L. (2011). *Words were all we had: Becoming biliterate against the odds*. Teachers College Press.

Ruiz, R. (1984). Orientations in language planning. *NABE Journal*, *8*(2), 15–34.

Sánchez, M. T., & García, O. (Eds.). (2022). *Transformative translanguaging espacios: Latinx students and their teachers Rompiendo fronteras sin miedo*. Multilingual Matters.

Schieffelin, B. B., & Ochs, E. (1986). Language socialization. *Annual Review of Anthropology*, *15*(1), 163–191.

Scott, J. C., Straker, D. Y., & Katz, L. (Eds.). (2009). *Affirming students' right to their own language: Bridging language policies and pedagogical practices*. National Council of Teachers of English and Routeledge.

Short, K. (2009). Critically reading the word and the world: Building intercultural understanding through literature. *Bookbird: A Journal of International Children's Literature*, *47*(2), 1–10.

Sims Bishop, R. (1990). Mirrors, windows, and sliding glass doors. *Perspectives*, *6*(3), ix–xi.

Street, B. V. (1995). *Social literacies: Critical approaches to literacy in development, ethnography and education*. Longman.

Tenorio, R. (2009). Brown kids can't be in our club. In W. Au (Ed.), *Rethinking multicultural education. Teaching for racial and cultural justice* (pp. 285–290). Rethinking Schools.

Zentella, A. C. (2005). Premises, promises, and pitfalls of language socialization research in Latino families and communities. In A. C. Zentella (Ed.), *Building on strengths: Language and literacy in Latino families and communities* (pp. 13–30). Teachers College Press.

Picture Books

Alessandri, A. (2021). *Isabel and her colores go to school* (C. Dawson, Illus.). Sleeping Bear Press.

Lachtman, O. D. (1995). *Pepita talks twice/pepita habla dos veces* (A. P. Delange, Illus.). Arte Público Press.

Laínez, R. C. (2019). *My shoes and I: Crossing three borders/mis zápatos y yo: Cruzando tres fronteras* (F. V. Broeck, Illus.). Arte Público Press.

Morales, Y. (2018). *Dreamers* (Y. Morales, Illus.). Neal Porter Books.

Morales, Y. (2021). *Bright star* (Y. Morales, Illus.). Neal Porter Books.

Sotomayor, S. (2019). *Just ask!: Be different, be brave, be you* (R. López, Illus.). Philomel Books.

9

COMBATING ABLEISM WITH CLASSROOM LITERATURE

Emily Poynter and Rachelle S. Savitz

According to the National Center for Education Statistics (2021), 14% of public school enrollees received special education services during the 2019–2020 school year. Of that 14%, 33% had a specific learning disability (SLD), which could be dyslexia, dysgraphia, oral/written language disorder, and related disorders such as ADHD and executive functioning (LDA, 2021). Autistic students made up 11%, and students with hearing impairments and orthopedic impairments made up 1% each of the total number of students served by special education teachers. Of the estimated 50.6 million students enrolled in a public school in the United States, roughly 7 million students with disabilities are actively served by special education and resource teachers (Hanson, 2021). This may not seem like a large number compared to the total number of students in public schools in the United States; yet, most classrooms have students with identified disabilities. Schools must address and incorporate specific accommodations to support student learning, such as preferred seating, extended time, and adaptive technology.

However, these accommodations do not equate to welcoming students into the classroom and having a sense of belonging, which is a needed factor for the success of all students (Gay, 2018; Hattie, 2018; Trauma and Learning Policy Initiative, n.d.). Research has demonstrated that by viewing students through an asset-based approach and incorporating their lived experiences, passions, curiosities, and discovering more about them within authentic learning, students are more likely to be engaged and demonstrate understanding (e.g., Alim & Paris, 2017; Ladson-Billings, 2017; Montgomery, 2001; Muhammad, 2020; Watson et al., 2016). This knowledge leads to questions we ask ourselves. For Emily, her questions relate to how she and her school colleagues are doing this crucial work and what this looks like across classrooms. For Rachelle, questions arise regarding curriculum and materials used with pre-service and practicing teachers when discussing supporting all students.

DOI:10.4324/9781003302216-12

Growing up, people with disabilities surrounded me (Emily). My cousin, Ben, was diagnosed with cerebral palsy and other cognitive impairments due to a lack of oxygen to his brain during birth. Through my interaction with my cousin, I learned how many people believed he could not communicate, but he could—and he did. But Ben talked in his way—through events and characters of a popular TV show. Another pivotal moment for me occurred in second grade when I became good friends with a girl with Down Syndrome. While she received push-out services for support from a special education teacher, she was also in our class throughout the day with an aide. Others questioned her ability to participate in class activities and do the work as "everyone else," often stating that she could not do the work. However, she was part of our classroom community and, more importantly, taught me the necessity to learn about others, including people with disabilities. There is a necessity in classrooms to recognize and appreciate differences and combat stereotypes related to what people, including those with disabilities, "can or cannot do" (Price et al., 2016, p. 33).

In conjunction with the need for educators to develop anti-ableist and inclusive classrooms, there is also a need in education for appropriate and authentic inclusive children's literature to destigmatize disabilities and the implications that accompany them. Creating awareness of disabilities within the classroom walls will assist in developing these types of environments. There are challenges for teachers to overcome when incorporating inclusive teaching and texts in the classroom. These challenges include lack of awareness of and/or knowledge about the types of disabilities represented in their schools or classrooms, inadequate preparation and reference points to strengthen their understanding of current best practices, and operating under the assumption that, unless students specifically inquire, disability does not need addressing in class (Lalvani & Bacon, 2019). Researching and engaging in texts that portray disability appropriately and sharing these texts with students is a logical first step in filling teachers' toolboxes when discussing disability and nurturing an inclusive learning environment. Many children's books feature characters with disabilities, visible and invisible, to promote inclusion, empathy, and respect for all learners.

Therefore, this chapter is a starting point for educators to consider ways to create inclusive classroom spaces that appreciate the uniqueness of all students who walk through the classroom door and determine ways to create learning opportunities for students to learn with and from others. We explore how using children's literature in a classroom invites students to explore stories of students with disabilities, engage in dialogue and inquiry to learn more to investigate impediments and supports in the real world for people of varying disabilities, and invite students to share their experiences and stories. We hope that our examples prompt readers to consider, reflect upon, and examine the texts they use in the classroom and the lessons to determine if we are genuinely welcoming our students with disabilities into our classrooms and if we are promoting space for all students to learn more and investigate others' lives (Pennell et al., 2017; Sims-Bishop, 1990).

What Do We Already Know?

The stance that there is a problem to be fixed as "disabilities are seen as the pre-dicament of the individual in the biological domain (ignoring social or cultural influences)" is a harmful view of students with disabilities (Connor & Ferri, 2005, pp. 109–110). This type of mindset and flawed construct leads to inappropriate assumptions and biases among teachers, peers, and the students with the disability themselves (Bogart & Dunn, 2019). Yet, this is a common stance across all grade lev-els, as observed in our teachers' interactions. Noticeably, while classrooms are becom-ing more inclusive, instruction is not (Wehmeyer et al., 2021). This is problematic as silenced voices mean that children do not see themselves within instruction, often leaving them feeling shame or creating a negative image of themselves (Fisher et al., 2020). As children see inappropriate or harmful images and stories about people with disabilities inside and outside of the classroom, such as through social media (Favazza & Odom, 1997), they are surrounded by this negative perception.

Educators may wonder about ways to be inclusive within practice and peda-gogy to ensure all students in the classroom feel welcomed and that they belong. The good news is that teachers already have the necessary tools and resources! Most elementary classrooms have lots of children's books. Therefore, possibly without even knowing it yet, teachers have the power to share extensively posi-tive images and stories of individuals who have disabilities (Price et al., 2016). Including children's literature in classrooms that promote the strengths of indi-viduals with disabilities will nurture the knowledge needed by non-disabled peers to foster an appreciation for the *students* with the disability (Blaska & Lynch, 1998; Mueller, 2021). We want to do more than simply teach the knowledge of the dis-ability itself, which can undermine the value of the students with the disability.

Children's literature is a concrete stepping stone in teaching non-disabled stu-dents that students with disabilities deserve the same respect and acknowledgment and that their disabilities do not define them as human beings. Instead, their dis-abilities are one piece of the puzzle that makes them unique in their ways, just like their non-disabled peers. But, we must also be careful in choosing books to ensure that depiction is accurate and appropriate to ensure moving past a surface-level understanding. We must also examine potential overgeneralizations, such as all people with cerebral palsy use wheelchairs or that all autistic individuals have behavioral challenges (Dyches et al., 2009; Pennell et al., 2017). We must disrupt naïve misunderstandings, false and inaccurate assumptions, and generali-zations not to create what Adichie (2009) calls "the danger of a single story." All children should be encouraged to read diverse children's literature that portrays characters of all shapes, sizes, and abilities to build appreciation for and a well-rounded understanding of their friends who may have disabilities. Incorporating these materials in classrooms can develop "a literacy learning environment that empowers students and sets them up for the greatest chance for success" (Interna-tional Literacy Association, 2019, p. 2).

Where Do We Go From Here?

At this point, educators may wonder how they can choose high-quality and appropriate children's literature that is inclusive and accurate for individuals with disabilities. Luckily, many children's books feature characters with disabilities, both visible and invisible, to promote inclusion, empathy, and respect while combating the idea of ableism in elementary school classrooms if one knows where to look. For instance, The Schneider Family Book Award, first endowed in 2003, is a platform that not only awards exemplar children's literature, appropriate for children and students from birth to age 18, but that genuinely and accurately portrays people with disabilities. Using the Schneider Family Book Award Manual (2022), teachers can easily access their criteria for evaluating books. Here, they share how the book must portray the character as living with a disability as part of a rich life versus a negative, harmful, or victim-only narrative. Representation is critical in books depicting disability; therefore, it is necessary to avoid stereotypes presented in the story. Another requirement is that the character with the disability should be the focus of the book as either the primary or secondary character rather than a static character. Most importantly, presented information about the disability within the book should be factual and authentic. It should be clear that the author researched the disability and its implications on the character who has the disability without bias or assumption.

Another way to use these criteria is by considering the term "multidimensional" (Kleekamp, 2019). People with disabilities do not carry their disability as their sole identity marker as there are many facets to their identity that influence their daily lives (Kleekamp & Zapata, 2018). Avoiding books that contain "single-story representations" offers readers opportunities to analyze the character from multiple perspectives and lenses and engage in humanizing conversations surrounding characters, and people they know, with disabilities (Bogart & Dunn, 2019, p. 591). When considering the multidimensionality of these characters, it is essential to examine how the story presents the disability. Narrative erasure is the act of keeping the disability omitted until the conclusion of the story to teach the reader that the character with the disability is still similar to their non-disabled and able-minded peers in the story. This erasure reinforces "the traditional ableist binary of sameness/difference that has long served to legitimate structures of exclusion and discrimination" (Aho & Alter, 2018, p. 304). Selecting books for elementary schoolers that resist this type of narrative erasure is crucial in building empathy and battling the social construct of disabilities being burdens or something of which to be ashamed.

Tondreau & Rabinowitz (2021) share various questions to analyze potential books to determine if the story challenges problematic perspectives and negative attitudes toward people with disabilities. Some questions included:

- Does the story's setting inhibit the character?
- Is the character with a disability being taken care of by a non-disabled character?

- Do the emotions of the disabled character depict their feelings about their disability?
- What emotions are conveyed with chosen word choice? What emotions are conveyed based on character depictions?

A final consideration is examining the author and their expertise, such as if the author does not experience first-hand what is being discussed or embedded in this world through familial experiences. Table 9.1 provides already curated literature that meets these criteria.

TABLE 9.1 Examples of Quality Children's Literature Highlighting Disability

Disability	Books Emily has Read and Used in Her Classroom	Recent Schneider Family Book Award Winners	Additional Must-Haves
Autism or Neurodiversity	*Benji, the Bad Day, and Me* by Sally J. Pla	*A Friend for Henry* by Jenn Bailey (2020)	*Here's Hank!* Series by Henry Winkler and Lin Oliver *The Remember Balloons* by Jessie Oliveros (2019 Schneider Honor Book)
Deafness	*Moses Goes to A Concert* by Isaac Millman	*Silent Days, Silent Dreams* by Allan Say (2017)	
Blindness			*My City Speaks* by Darren Lebeuf
Physical Disability	*We're All Wonders* by R.J. Pollacio	*Rescue and Jessica: A Life-Changing Friendship* by Jessica Kensky and Patrick Downes (2019)	*Not So Different: What You Really Want to Ask About Disability* by Shane Burcaw *Itzhak: A Boy Who Loved the Violin* by Tracy Newman (2021 Schneider Honor Book)
Dyslexia	*Thank You, Mr. Falker* by Patricia Pollaco	*I Talk Like a River* by Jordan Scott (2021)	
Speech or Stutter		*A Boy and a Jaguar* by Alan Rabinowitz (2015)	
Multicategory Disability Awareness	*Just Ask!* by Sonia Sotomayor		

What Does This Look Like in a Classroom?

For Emily, when selecting books to expand her inclusive teaching library, she used specific criteria. First, she analyzed the story to ensure that the character with the disability was an integral part of the story, leaning toward books where the protagonist or main character was the person with the disability. This stems from her belief, "Who better to tell their story than the person with the disability themselves?" Second, she evaluated if the information about the disability presented in the book was accurate and did not contain damaging stereotypes, such as people with physical impairments being helpless and relying on people at all times. Finally, she ensures that the main character is in a place of power to challenge situations and narratives within the text and face hardships and challenges. This is important because she wants her students to learn from the characters and problem-solve (Fisher et al., 2020; Rodriguez, 2019).

Ultimately, her goal is that students create their interpretations. At the same time, they read and discuss, and they justify their reactions using textual evidence (Graves et al., 2011), which ensures all perspectives are respected, appreciated, and cherished. Therefore, she includes books about disability in her teaching that display a character's power and resolve when faced with hardship. In conjunction with battling stereotypes and discrimination of those with disabilities in children's literature, including books that highlight the character's talents, uniqueness, and self-worth is critical to challenging ableist beliefs among non-disabled and able-minded readers.

The following are from Emily's classroom and instruction to provide concrete examples of the what, how, and why for readers to consider as action steps within their classrooms. We also include Points to Ponder for each of you to choose a book and try out the activities and planning for your classroom. To start, take a moment to look through some books in your classroom library and use the provided criteria to choose one or two to follow along with us.

Emmanuel's Dream: The True Story of Emmanuel Ofosu Yeboah

Emmanuel's Dream: The True Story of Emmanuel Ofosu Yeboah, a 2016 Schneider Family Book Award winner, written by Laurie Ann Thompson and Sean Qualls, tells the story of a renowned cyclist and how he overcame a weakened right leg to become one of Ghana's most accomplished athletes. Emmanuel and his mother are the focal characters of the book, and Emmanuel's likeness is prominent on each double-page spread. Although the authors describe some of the hardships Emmanuel faced throughout his life, they intentionally highlighted his successes and shared his message: *disability* does not mean *inability*. One person is enough

FIGURE 9.1   Students utilized school and classroom equipment to frame their knowledge about someone with a physical disability before reading.

to change the world (Thompson & Qualls, 2015). This notion is demonstrated by Emmanuel continuing to work with children, both with and without disabilities, in his home country of Ghana after becoming a prominent public figure; he funded scholarships and purchased wheelchairs for disabled citizens of Ghana (Wilkens, 2015). This picture book is an excellent example of one that encompasses the criteria of inclusive children's literature and describes the character's "agency and perseverance in addressing difficult circumstances" (Kleekamp, 2019).

Before reading *Emmanuel's Dream*, kindergarten students voluntarily demonstrated walking and climbing stairs using both legs on the playground (see Figure 9.1). Volunteers were then selected to try the same activities using only one leg. The next activity introduces students to a foot peddler, a way for people to exercise and move their feet while seated. Again, students voluntarily used the foot peddler with both feet and one foot. Students discussed what was easy for them and the challenges they faced during each part of these activities. Students compared their experiences on the playground with using a foot peddler and the differences between two legs versus one. Experiencing these challenges was not framed in a way that people with physical disabilities suffer or cannot move around the playground. Instead, the discussion encouraged students to realize that, while the movement may be different from what they are used to, people with physical disabilities should not be viewed as incapable and with pity. This framing was essential for students to learn the initial background and reading reflection before reading *Emmanuel's Dream*.

Points to Ponder:
- While considering traditional story elements, how might you introduce your story about a character(s) with a disability to students?
- Consider if your beliefs and possible teaching points could be termed "ableist."
- Determine if you need to research the discussed disability and if you have other stories that work well with the one you chose.

Once the book was introduced, students met Emmanuel, the main character, and how he is a bicycle rider from Africa. Students engaged in a close read of the front cover to better understand and investigate Emmanuel on his bicycle with his ride side showing the side with the impaired leg. One student quickly asked how Emmanuel could ride a bike without reaching the pedals on both sides of his bike, as shown on the cover. With conversation quickly moving toward how Emmanuel and others with physical disabilities were able to do amazing things that may have never been considered before, but often with accommodations and extra support.

This understanding supports students in learning the harm caused by people who believed Emmanuel (and others) were "useless, or worse—a curse" (Thompson & Qualls, 2015, p. 3). Students appeared visibly uncomfortable with this phrase as they asked if it was true of people with physical disabilities. They did not understand how Emmanuel did not have value or may be viewed as unimportant simply because he was born with this physical limitation. Students then shared how they have friends and family members with physical disabilities. One student reminded the class of another student who wears a boot to support the proper growth of the bones in his foot, but a follow-up comment was made that the student could still run, play, and interact with his classmates.

As they continued to listen to the story read aloud, students clamored to share how Emmanuel learned unique ways to be himself—and be meaningful. For instance, they were excited when learning how Emmanuel hopped two miles each way to go to school, sharing their disbelief in that long of a walk. Students were also impressed when learning how Emmanuel climbed coconut trees and worked various jobs. When they got to the part about Emmanuel biking almost 400 miles across his country of Ghana, they were astonished and delighted to learn how Emmanuel tackled what others believed to be a curse.

Points to Ponder:
- How could you foster student discussion, critical thinking, and safety in asking questions as they are reading or listening to your story?
- How would you share and connect personal experiences or questions with your students?
- How might you invite students to feel safe enough to ask questions or share their personal experiences?

Students continued sharing their thoughts on why the author wrote this book and why this story is essential to read and learn. Many students shared how people get blamed or judged for things without really knowing anything about the person. They wanted others to understand how Emmanuel may not do things precisely as they, but he learned ways to engage, participate in life, and accomplish many things—making him a significant person.

Students then watched "Emmanuel's Ride—An Inspiring True Story," an interview about his life (Smile TV Group, 2013). Students learned how citizens of his home country did not think his mother should keep a child with a physical disability; however, he stepped up to every challenge he faced, such as working to provide money for his family. Emmanuel reiterated his goal of assisting children with and without disabilities, sharing how he funds student scholarships. The information in the video confirmed what they read and provided more details directly from Emmanuel.

To connect this story to their social and emotional learning objectives, students explored and questioned *why* Emmanuel accomplished the things he did: he worked very hard and learned something he did not know how to do *yet*. Printed on the book's final page is a quote by Yeboah himself that states, "In this world, we are not perfect. We can only do our best" (Thompson & Qualls, 2015, p. 32). This prompted the class to create a list of things they could not do *yet*, such as reading certain books based on complexity, counting to 100 without stopping or scaffolding, riding a bike without training wheels, and cooking a dish new to them like pizza or tacos. Students then discussed how they could accomplish those goals through support, working with others, practice, and being okay, knowing that it will take time. After completing the first list and discussion on ways to gather support and people they could reach out to, the students composed a second list titled "I Can Do Hard Things" using sentence starters such as, "I can . . .", "I will . . .", and "I am going to . . ." (See Figure 9.2). This activity promoted the development of the necessary mindset to believe in their abilities to

FIGURE 9.2 Kindergarten students demonstrated agency after listening to Emmanuel's story to practice goal-setting and self-efficacy.

succeed and accomplish their goals, like Emmanuel. More importantly, students learned the critical skill of agency: to speak up and ask for help and work with other people to pay it forward.

Extension and Community Outreach

Emmanuel's Dream is also a catalyst for authentic thematic learning experiences in the elementary classroom. This story can be used with primary-aged students to encourage goal-setting. Students can cut out a shirt and design it with their motto or what is important for them to share with the world. This connects with how Emmanuel creates his shirt to say, *The Pozo, "the disabled person."* This is his way of saying that having a disability does not mean he is not capable of greatness and that having a disability does not mean "inability." Students can then write things they learn and hope to accomplish on the shirt (Orr, n.d.). Teachers can meet with students in one-on-one conferences to discuss student-identified short-term goals and steps needed to meet them. For instance, they may address specific resources they need to succeed or solve ideas to meet a tough challenge they face.

Literacy-specific activities could have students document Emmanuel's character traits while analyzing his behaviors and actions throughout his life. These character traits can be compared and contrasted with characters in other books. To create a more inclusive school community, students in the upper elementary grades can conduct research into current bills and laws passed to support children and adults with disabilities in schools and workplaces and school policies and practices. Students can then consider ways to address needed changes, such as including desks that work better for people of varying physical disabilities.

Points to Ponder:
- What ways could you extend students' learning based on your story?
- Could students participate in social justice or service-learning projects to communicate information about the disability portrayed in your story?

Conclusion

Ableism perpetuates negative assumptions, stereotypes, and biases about people with disabilities (Lalvani & Bacon, 2019; Villines, 2021). Numerous factors influence various types of ableism at the institutional, interpersonal, and internal levels (Villines, 2021) (see Table 9.2 for additional resources). Without analysis and reflections of mindsets as educators, this may inadvertently lead to ableist views within classroom instruction and materials. It is vital that teachers, and others who spend ample time in educational settings, acquire the knowledge that will assist them in creating inclusive learning environments. Information and training that include "knowledge of disability and legislation, strategies, interpersonal

TABLE 9.2 Where Can I Find More Information About Ableism and Including Diverse Texts in My Teaching?

Resource	Description
Villines, Z. (2021). What is ableism, and what is its impact? *Medical News Today*. Retrieved from www. medicalnewstoday.c om/articles/ ableism#:~:text=Wha t%20is%20 ableism%3F,others'%2 0perceive%20 to%20be%20disabl ed.	This article in *Medical News Today* defines ableism and highlights and describes the various types of ableism. Information about how ableism influences the healthcare of people with disabilities is included and with the physical, social, and emotional impacts of ableism.
Kids Voting Ohio (2022). Anti-ableism in classrooms. Retrieved from www. kidsvotingohio.org/a nti-ableism-in-classrooms#:~:text =In%20 summary%2C%20to%20 create%20 anti,in%20decision%2 Dmaking%20 processes%20espec ially.	This post describes how to promote an anti-ableist classroom through culturally responsive teaching. Included are questions educators can reflect upon "when establishing anti-ableist pedagogies in [their] assessment process."
Lalvani, P. & Bacon, J.K. (2019). Rethinking "we are all special": Anti-ableist curricula in early childhood classrooms. *Exceptional Children*, 1–14.	This publication in *Teaching Young Children* outlines the importance of diversity and inclusivity in the classroom. The authors describe strategies that can be used in the classroom to engage in anti-ableist teaching and learning centered around four major goals based on a framework for anti-bias education.
The Nora Project https://thenoraproject.ngo/	The Nora Project's mission statement states, "we're on a mission to promote disability inclusion by empowering educators and engaging students and communities." Resources for teachers, including sample lessons and activities, are available to encourage the understanding that disability is a part of diversity.
Ladau, E. (2021). *Demystifying disability: What to know, what to say, and how to be an ally*. Ten Speed Press.	Written by a disability rights activist, this book provides a guide to becoming "an ally to the disability community." It provides information about appropriate language and practices to be anti-ableist and promote inclusivity.

communication skills, curriculum development, and differentiation" (Forlin, 2012, p. 86) would allow teachers to promote an anti-ableist classroom. This information will also encourage teachers to analyze, select, and acquire appropriate resources, such as high-quality texts that include characters and accurate information about disabilities. These are logical steps to take when implementing and teaching with diverse, inclusive texts.

We have formed meaningful and essential relationships with people with disabilities prompting us to believe that it is up to us to disrupt, confront, challenge, and unlearn harmful and inaccurate perceptions. While this is only one example from Emily's classroom, we encourage readers to evaluate the books used throughout the school year and the stories offered to students as independent reads. These examples demonstrate how young students can connect and question what they are told to better understand the realities faced among people with disabilities. All classrooms should be safe spaces that praise, acknowledge, and incorporate diversity within instruction and learning. Literature provides a way for students to relate, connect with, and take their learning from inside to outside the classroom. Fostering these types of relationships with texts and others supports students' development of empathetic thinking and inclusive action (Tondreau & Rabinowitz, 2021). Gaining and understanding new perspectives and points of view promotes challenging and dismantling ableist views and ideals in the classroom.

References

Adichie, C. N. (2009, July). *The danger of a single story* [Video file]. www.ted.com/talks/chimamanda_adichie_the_danger_of_a_single_story/up-next?l anguage=en

Aho, T., & Alter, G. (2018). "Just like me, just like you": Narrative erasure as disability normalization in children's picture books. *Journal of Literary & Cultural Disability Studies, 12*(3), 303–319.

Alim, H. S., & Paris, D. (2017). What is culturally sustaining pedagogy and why does it matter? In D. Paris & H. S. Alim (Eds.), *Culturally sustaining pedagogies: Teaching and learning for justice in a changing world* (pp. 1–21). Teachers College Press.

American Library Association. (2022, January). *Schneider family book award manual.* www.ala.org/awardsgrants/sites/ala.org.awardsgrants/files/content/Revised%20Sc hneider%20Family%20Book%20Award%20Manual%202022.pdf

Blaska, J. K., & Lynch, E. C. (1998). Is everyone included? Using children's literature to facilitate the understanding of disabilities. *Young Children, 53*(2), 36–38.

Bogart, K. R., & Dunn, D. S. (2019). Ableism special issue introduction. *Journal of Social Issues, 75*(3), 650–664.

Connor, D. J., & Ferri, B. A. (2005). Integration and inclusion: A troubling nexus: Race, disability, and special education. *The Journal of African American History, 90*(1/2), 107–127.

Dyches, T. T., Prater, M. A., & Leininger, M. (2009). Juvenile literature and the portrayal of developmental disabilities. *Education and Training in Developmental Disabilities, 44*(3), 304–317.

Favazza, P. C., & Odom, S. L. (1997). Promoting positive attitudes of kindergarten-age children toward people with disabilities. *Exceptional children, 63*(3), 405–418.

Fisher, D., Frey, N., & Savitz, R. S. (2020). *Teaching hope and resilience for students experiencing trauma: Creating safe and nurturing classrooms for learning.* Teachers College Press.

Forlin, C. (2012). Diversity and its challenges for teachers. In *Future Directions for Inclusive Teacher Education*, 83–92.

Gay, G. (2018). *Culturally responsive teaching: Theory, research, and practice* (3rd ed.). Teachers College Press.

Graves, M., Juel, C., Graves, B., & Dewitz, P. (2011). *Teaching reading in the 21st century: Motivation for all learners* (5th ed.). Pearson.

Hanson, M. (2021). *K-12 school enrollment and population statistics.* educationdata.org/k12-enrollment-statistics.

Hattie, J. (2018). *Visible learning plus: 250+ influences on student achievement.* us.corwin.com/sites/default/files/250_influences_10.1.2018.pdf

International Literacy Association. (2019). *Right to supportive learning environments and high-quality resources* [Research Brief]. Authors.

Kleekamp, M. (2019, May 28). *How to critically select children's books with representations of disability experiences.* blog.leeandlow.com/2019/05/28/how-to-critically-select-childrens-books-with-representations-of-disability-experiences/

Kleekamp, M. C., & Zapata, A. (2018). Interrogating depictions of disability in children's picturebooks. *The Reading Teacher, 72*(5), 589–597.

Ladson-Billings, G. (2017). "Makes me wanna holler": Refuting the "culture of poverty" discourse in urban schooling. *The Annals of the American Academy of Political and Social Science, 673*(1), 80–90.

Lalvani, P., & Bacon, J. K. (2019). Rethinking "we are all special": Anti-ableist curricula in early childhood classrooms. *Young Exceptional Children, 22*(2), 87–100.

LDA: Learning Disabilities Association of America. (2021). *Types of learning disabilities.* https://ldaamerica.org/types-of-learning-disabilities/

Montgomery, W. (2001). Creating culturally responsive, inclusive classrooms. *Teaching Exceptional Children, 33*(4), 4–9.

Mueller, C. O. (2021). "I didn't know people with disabilities could grow up to be adults": Disability history, curriculum, and identity in special education. *Teacher Education and Special Education, 44*(3), 189–205.

Muhammad, G. E. (2020). *Cultivated genius: An equity framework for culturally and historically responsive literacy.* Scholastic.

National Center for Education Statistics. (2021). *Students with disabilities.* nces.ed.gov/programs/coe/indicator/cgg

Orr, R. (n.d.). *Social emotional learning: Social skills lesson plan.* education.byu.edu/sites/default/files/buildingsocialskills/emmanuels-dream-converted.pdf

Pennell, A. E., Wollak, B., & Koppenhaver, D. A. (2017). Respectful representations of disability in picture books. *The Reading Teacher, 71*(4), 411–419.

Price, C. L., Ostrosky, M. M., & Santos, R. M. (2016). Reflecting on books that include characters with disabilities. *YC Young Children, 71*(2), 30–37.

Rodriguez, R. J. (2019). *Teaching culturally sustaining and inclusive young adult literature: Critical perspectives and conversations.* Routledge.

Sims-Bishop, R. (1990). Mirrors, windows, and sliding glass doors. *Perspectives, 6*(3), ix–xi.

Smile TV Group. (2013, December 12). *Emmanuel's ride: An inspiring true story* [Video]. YouTube. www.youtube.com/watch?v=BHUDh82sZYs

Tondreau, A., & Rabinowitz, B. (2021). Analyzing representations of individuals with disabilities in picture books. *The Reading Teacher, 75*(1), 61–71.

Trauma and Learning Policy Initiative. (n.d.). *Helping traumatized children learn: Frequently asked questions about trauma-sensitive schools.* traumasensitiveschools.org/frequently-asked-questions/

Villines, Z. (2021). What is ableism, and what is its impact? *Medical News Today.* www.medicalnewstoday.com/articles/ableism#:~:text=What%20is%20ableism%3 F,others%20perceive%20to%20be%20disabled

Watson, W., Sealey-Ruiz, Y., Jackson, I. (2016). Daring to care: The role of culturally relevant care in mentoring Black and Latino male high school students. *Race, Ethnicity, and Education, 19*(5), 980–1002.

Wehmeyer, M. L., Shogren, K. A., & Kurth, J. (2021). The state of inclusion with students with intellectual and developmental disabilities in the United States. *Journal of Policy and Practice in Intellectual Disabilities, 18*(1), 36–43.

Wilkens, J. (2015, October 24). A new ride for Emmanuel Yeboah. *The San Diego Union-Tribune.* www.sandiegouniontribune.com/lifestyle/people/sdut-emmanuel-y eboah-ghana-2015oct24-story.html

Literature Cited

Thompson, L. A., & Qualls, S. (2015). *Emmanuel's dream: The true story of Emmanuel Ofosu Yeboah.* Schwartz & Wade Books.

10

ENGAGING DYNAMIC DISCUSSIONS THROUGH STORYTELLING

K. N., H. S., Amanda Carter, and Nayelee Villanueva

Introduction

The challenge of preparing and supporting teachers to work with diverse teaching populations, particularly queer individuals and family structures, is felt worldwide. Historically, countries outside the United States have presented a more inclusive stance on queer curriculum. For example, Toronto, Canada; Australia; and South Africa, while somewhat different in their approach, have made space for the possibility of explicitly addressing homophobia and heterosexism in the K–12 curricula (Butler et al., 2003; Chetty, 2005; Kumashiro et al., 2004; Morgan, 2005; Sykes & Goldstein, 2004). Conversely, in the United States, the National Council for Accreditation of Teacher Education (NCATE) removed explicit discussion of sexual orientation and social justice from its teacher education standards (Powers, 2006). Additionally, and most recently, discussion of sexual orientation or gender identity is prohibited in various states, including Florida's 2022 passing of its Parental Rights and Education Act (Florida Legislative Assembly, 2022).

While policies and accreditation regarding inclusive curricula may differ worldwide, a breadth of research has shown that many teachers enter schools misinformed and ill-prepared to support queer students (Butler et al., 2003; Ferfolja & Robinson, 2004; Mathison, 1998; Sears, 1992; Sumara, 2007; Taylor, 2004) and queer communities. Specifically, "by most counts, U.S. teachers in K-12 settings are woefully ill-prepared to teach LGBTQ and non-gender conforming youth and work against heterosexism and homophobia in schools" (Clark, 2009, p. 711). Furthermore, the pre-service teachers who participated in Clark's study indicated that "despite being personally anti-homophobic, students still felt pressure or expressed the desire to be neutral and apolitical as teachers" (p. 711). The participants expressed that doing *this work* would be too harmful to them professionally.

DOI:10.4324/9781003302216-13

The goal of this chapter is to offer a framework that embraces the sentiments of the pre-service teacher, novice teacher, or veteran teacher—the teacher who understands the importance of an inclusive curriculum and is hesitant to implement the curriculum, no matter the justification. This chapter is also intended for all educators: teacher educators, teacher leaders—any level of teacher. Because at all stages of our personal and professional development, there is a need for learning and unlearning in a supportive environment that encourages us to become even better educators. This chapter explains a professional development opportunity with teachers. It includes the success story of one teacher participant who chose to implement a lesson using the picture book *Prince and Knight: Tale of the Shadow King* (2018), a queer-friendly fairy tale by Daniel Haack and illustrated by Stevie Lewis. This chapter aims to share the conceptual framework that guided the professional development, details the vision and organization of the professional development itself and presents the implementation of a lesson plan created during the professional development.

Conceptual Framework

Sims Bishop's (1990) conceptual framework of mirrors, windows, and sliding glass doors is foundational when justifying the need for diverse texts, particularly in an elementary setting. Sims Bishop explains that when readers see themselves or some part of their identity reflected in the text, they may experience the literature as a mirror. Other times, readers encounter texts as windows, a reading phenomenon that enables them to investigate the life of someone different from them. An opportunity for a sliding glass door occurs when the reader has the chance to learn about someone different from them and essentially steps into this other world through the text.

As Sims Bishop (1990) points out and as illustrated in Figure 10.1, white readers encounter numerous texts that act as a mirror but have limited opportunities to read about others through a window or sliding glass door experience.

Conversely, non-white readers frequently experience reading as a window or sliding glass door and rarely as a mirror. The lack of opportunity to see themselves in texts can be harmful at various stages of life; it may be incredibly demoralizing to young children learning to read. Imagine never having a chance to see yourself, your family, or your community positively portrayed in texts. If one cannot see themselves represented in the texts, the purpose of reading could become disjointed, especially at an age where making personal connections to texts is the general hook into the reading experience.

Windows, Mirrors, Sliding Glass Doors, and Queer Communities

While the attempt to diversify children's literature has slightly improved over the past few years, most of this diversification has been in relation to race, ethnicity,

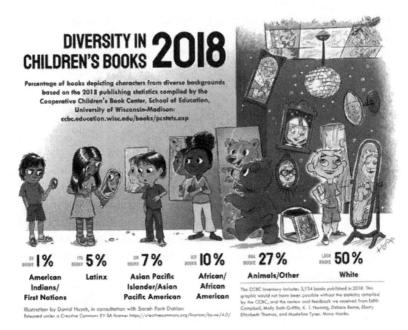

FIGURE 10.1 Huyck & Dahlen's Infographic of Diversity of Children's Books 2018
Sources: https://socialjusticebooks.org/diversity-graphic/

and language experiences. A frequent oversight in this work is the inclusion of texts representing diverse families, specifically those who identify as members of queer communities. Our definition of *queer* is rooted in the work of Quinn and Meiners (2016). Like their work, we use the word queer in multiple ways in this chapter:

> As an adjective and noun that refers to all sexualities and gender identities outside and challenging normative, binary categories, to this end, we include Q for queer with LGBT and use the term queer as a replacement for the letters. We invoke queer as a verb, a stance that assumes and honors human complexities and demands action toward ending oppressive social systems that limit our gendered, sexual, and creative lives.
>
> *(Quinn & Meiners, 2016, p. 29)*

Many school leaders and educators name student parents as the reason they chose not to include queer texts when in reality, the traditional family has become the minority familial situation in the United States (Butler-Wall et al., 2016). In other words, when educators share texts that include a mom and dad who identify as female and male and are married, the text represents the least common familial circumstance. Thus, most students will not experience this text as a mirror. For this reason, educational leaders need to advocate for texts that intentionally name diverse family situations, allow students' lived experiences to be brought to light, create space for sex and gender positive associations and potential conversations, and decenter traditionally dominant heterosexual relationships as gender norms. Additionally, it is important to recognize that it is the educator's responsibility to include diverse texts knowing the consequences that may result. Following other research in this field, it is essential to consider the positive and possible adverse outcomes that may ensue by including this inclusive literature. Sometimes difficult choices are necessary to live one's beliefs, values, and morals in a shared learning space.

Justification for Including Queer Texts

While it is often common to consider the negative *what-ifs* when contemplating whether to use queer-inclusive literature, it is also essential to consider the positive *what-ifs* when debating how this literature aligns with classroom morale. What if the inclusion of a queer-inclusive text is the first time one of your students sees their family represented in a book? What if the inclusion of a queer-inclusive text motivates a non-reader to engage with texts because they can see themselves represented? What if the inclusion of a queer-inclusive text provides a window experience for a student, and this is the first time they feel comfortable asking questions about families or identities that are different than their own? The *what-if* game can sometimes limit our desire to do things differently, but with a slight change in the perspective of *what-ifs*, the justification for queer inclusive texts becomes quite apparent.

While some students may not be able to connect with queer texts in a personal manner, they deserve the chance to read such literature and experience it as a window or sliding glass door. Learning how our identities and interests are alike and different from others is an opportunity to understand ourselves and others in our community better. When we learn about differences, we have a chance to understand various worldly perspectives better. This learning can be done without ever telling the child *what* to think but rather *how* to think. *How* to encourage children to be inquisitive about the world in which they live *and how* to ask questions about people who are different from them. *How* children can work toward a place of mutual understanding with others. *How* to nurture indifference between and among individuals and families. These skills benefit our community because when young children recognize how they are alike and different from others, they can also practice having meaningful, productive experiences together.

Educators have an opportunity to transform teaching and learning. They must give themselves permission to build creative learning experiences that intentionally highlight multiple perspectives, lived experiences, and student identities. The rest of this chapter presents a professional development opportunity for teachers; start Engaging Dymamic Discussions (EDD) which was created to support using diverse children's literature to foster inclusive curricula. While the focus of EDD was not just about the inclusion of queer literature, the discussion and creation of queer-inclusive lesson plans were the most "taboo" during this professional development.

What Is EDD?

Many individuals in educational systems promote culturally responsive pedagogy while simultaneously requiring teachers to use a curriculum that does not reflect these ideas. Orchard Area School District (OASD) had nearly one decade of experience engaging in racial equity work, and their leadership team included a district equity and diversity department. From an outside perspective, it seemed like most employees had similar beliefs about diversity; however, when educators worked to create inclusive resources, they were often met with resistance from those with power in the district. Educators who chose to be more inclusive in their practice were often referred to as "going rogue."

This conflict in ideology and practice led to the creation and implementation of EDD—a three-day professional development experience facilitated by two teacher leaders who were part of the Equity and Diversity Department team. This project was funded by the Equity and Diversity Department within OASD. Each participant was paid their contractual rate for 18 hours of collaboration and participation. Additionally, a set of 10 new books was purchased for each educator.

The overarching goal of EDD was to provide a platform for educators to process, plan, practice, and dream. The purpose of EDD was to inspire and encourage participants to think differently about schools and how perceived barriers often provide justification to live within a flawed and harmful system instead of actively inviting change into practice. Therefore, EDD was organized to create an environment for growth, connection, and an individualized, emerging pathway toward an inclusive curriculum.

Outcomes of EDD Professional Development:

- Engage in authentic identity development activities where educators unpack the ways in which their identities impact the way they teach
- Engage in meaningful dialogue with colleagues focused on teaching philosophies and how they are working toward transformative change both in their personal and professional lives
- Build a community and create an environment of support where educators could lean on one another through the process
- Examine the current literacy curriculum, content, and materials (including books) provided to students in the district
- Identify culturally, linguistically, and racially diverse read aloud books for primary and intermediate grade levels

- Decenter dominant identities and center marginalized, invisible, and silenced identities
- Respond to potential harm, triggers of trauma, and other forms of disengagement commonly seen in classroom environments
- Create learning experiences for students that consistently reflect identity, community, inclusion, and representation

When EDD was created, the facilitators aimed for the time and space to be clearly different from other professional development that incorporated curriculum discussion and lesson plan writing. Before it was time to register for summer professional development opportunities, specific educators and staff members were intentionally recruited based on their shared desire to create an inclusive curriculum. There were nearly 40 educators from 17 elementary schools who registered for EDD. Because the sessions took place in the summer after school had ended, the facilitators chose a Tuesday, Wednesday, and Thursday time slot from 9 am to 3 pm. EDD took place in an elementary school, selected because of its fearless leader who consistently modeled the importance of relationship, community, and belonging at school. The building chosen provided a physical environment where folks could show up authentically and with vulnerability, without fear or judgment. The details of the experience provide insight into how the facilitators were able to build space for meaningful work to happen. It was an environment where educators felt a sense of acknowledgment, belonging, and love to become part of a larger collective that could spark a movement toward transformative change in the district.

The structure of Day 1, Day 2, and Day 3 were similar but incorporated different activities. During the morning of each day, the group participated in community-building exercises that focused on both personal and professional identity. The activities had two objectives: to have fun, share laughs, and simply "be" as we began building our community, and to take a deep, critical dive into who we were as educators and how our lived experiences affected the way we showed up as educators. During the afternoons, participants organized themselves into smaller groups, and we began to work as a collective. The goal of the first afternoon was to choose 10 books for reading aloud in literacy lessons. During the second and third afternoons of the training, educators chose one of the books to write a learning experience or lesson plan. Learning plans should reflect community, creativity, and identity while simultaneously addressing grade-level appropriate skills and standards.

At the end of Day 3, all participants shared their work with the large group. As the community reviewed and reflected on the completed work, there was a feeling of revelation—a sense of how seamless it was to bridge our efforts for an inclusive curriculum with state standards and age-appropriate skills. It became apparent that we, educators, are the ones who police ourselves. **Educators** make intentional choices about which perspectives and stories to showcase in the learning environment and which to leave absent, silenced, or hidden. **Educators** can create change in classrooms alongside brilliant students, families, and community members. **Educators** can be the agents for justice and change; sometimes, all they need is a pathway and a supportive environment of like-minded colleagues.

Planning and Implementing an EDD Lesson Plan

Because of the meticulously planned environment and experience, EDD participants felt more comfortable creating inclusive units and lesson plans that interrupted racist beliefs and discourses. Yet some participants were still hesitant or opposed to including children's literature that interrupted heterosexist and homophobic beliefs and discourses. On the third day of EDD, facilitators introduced *two inclusive texts. The first text selected, Sparkle Boy* (2017), is a picture book that addresses gender norms and expression by Lesléa Newman and illustrated by Maria Mola, and *the second text, Prince and Knight: Tale of the Shadow King* (2018), is a queer-friendly fairy tale by Daniel Haack and illustrated by Stevie Lewis. There was heated debate among participants regarding how and if the texts should be used in elementary classrooms. The facilitators leaned into this discussion and participated in the conversation while also naming and identifying some of the non-inclusive ideas and assumptions shared in the space. There was recognition by both facilitators that without a devoted time to discuss the process and rationale of including texts that interrupt heterosexist and homophobic discourses could cause more harm than good to hesitant teachers and their students.

The facilitators realized that teaching *for* social justice by asking others to share a commitment to teaching against heterosexism and homophobia is imposing an act of assimilation or sameness (Clark, 2009). This tension cannot be ignored as we develop an inclusive curriculum. Simply stated, it was not the right time, nor was there enough time for some individuals to reflect on their beliefs to not include queer literature while lesson planning. With that said, some participants prioritized the inclusion of one or both picture books in their lesson planning.

Implementation of an EDD Lesson Plan

The Courageous Conversations Compass (Singleton, 2015), which was reviewed and discussed during EDD while processing *Prince and Knight*, seemed to be a way to promote a conversation that raised all voices. The Compass is a tool that contains four quadrants: believing, thinking, feeling, and acting; it enables users to recognize and locate the source of their and others' feelings and actions. A version created by an (OASD) employee made the compass student-friendly. OASD uses the Benchmarks curriculum to teach reading, yet educators are free to use whatever read aloud books they choose for the benchmark goal. A teacher participant in EDD developed a lesson plan for first grade in which *Prince and Knight* fit perfectly with the benchmark goal: "I can make inferences in order to make predictions." Preparation included critical conversations with students, teachers, and equity specialists about implicit biases regarding queer communities.

This first-grade lesson began with a brainstorm using a circle map about princes, in which student responses were recorded:

- "Princes marry princesses."
- "Princes have swords."
- "Princes do things for people in the kingdom."

The lesson continued with an introduction to the Making Inferences anchor chart, as shown in Figure 10.2, and the multi-flow thinking map, as shown in Figure 10.3.

While using the making inference chart, the story was paused in three spots to allow students' inferences to be recorded on the multi-flow map. The first text clue, "go with parents to find a bride," led to the inferences "not getting married

FIGURE 10.2 Making Inferences

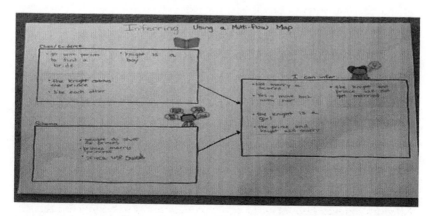

FIGURE 10.3 Multiflow Map

because he is scared" and "yes getting married and moving back with the princess he picks." The next text clue, "the knight catches the prince, and they like each other," led to the inferences "the knight is a girl" and "the prince and knight will get married." The final text clue, "the knight is a boy," led to the inference that "the knight and the prince will not get married."

When the book concluded, students learned the male prince married the male knight. Some students were visibly uncomfortable. Some students smiled at the ending. One student shouted, "What?!? That's gross! Boys can't marry boys!" Another student argued that they could, and she shared, "My uncle is gay, and he married a man. And they love each other very much."

At this point, the conversation paused to address heterosexist and homophobic discourses. For example, the teacher asked, "If a mom said eating broccoli was gross and refused to cook it for her son, was it okay for her son, who loves broccoli, to still eat it?" This became a teachable moment, and a class discussion on whether broccoli was a yummy food began. Students generally agreed that people should be able to choose what food they want to eat. They were asked if there was a different way to disagree about broccoli, and they thought it was more considerate to encourage someone to say, "no thank you" or "broccoli is not a food for me." It was agreed using the word "gross" hurt some students' feelings. Students were then asked if it was okay to say "gross" about two men kissing or if it would be more considerate to say, "no thank you" or "kissing someone is not okay for me." It was agreed that there are more thoughtful ways to respond than saying "gross." Part of the class discussion clarified that the law says men can marry men and women can marry women just as men and women can get married— just as there are many ways to be a family, there are many ways to be in a relationship.

As a post-reading and discussion activity, students completed the Courageous Conversation Compass. Students were asked to move to one of the spaces that reflected their thinking:

The Believing sentence stems:

•   Something I care about is _____.
•   Something I believe is important is ___.

The Thinking sentence stems:

•   I am thinking ___ because___.
•   A question I have is ___.

The Acting sentence stems:

•   I am planning ___ because ___.
•   I am going to ___.

The Feeling sentence stems:

- I am feeling ___ because ___.
- I am in the ___zone because ___.

The teacher encouraged students to share their ideas with other students in their group, and the educator monitored the conversations as students used the sentence stems to share. Students who went to the Feeling quadrant shared:

- "I'm happy they got married."
- "I'm happy they got married because they love each other."
- "It's not okay for me that the boys married each other."
- Students who went to Acting shared:
- "Not for me. I would not marry a man."
- "I would cheer at their wedding."
- "They fought the dragon. I would go to the wedding because they did something for us, we should do something for them."
- "I would say no thank you and not go to the wedding."
- "I would be glad to go."

Students who went to Thinking shared:

- "I think it is okay because it's okay with his parents. It's okay with me."
- "Boys and girls can marry whoever they want."
- "The prince can marry who he wants, and he wants the knight because the knight caught him."

There were no students in the Believing Quadrant.

Students were brought back together when the small group conversations concluded for a final whole-class discussion. The responses from the small group conversations were shared, and then students were asked how they thought someone should respond when someone else had a different opinion. As a class, they agreed it is okay for people to have different thoughts and feelings and to do different things. It was agreed people still needed to show kindness to people even when they think, feel, and do things differently. Together, the class made a list of things they could say and do if someone wanted to honor differences. When asked about the prince and the knight's wedding, students agreed each person could decide for themselves whether to go. The important thing was to respond politely and say "yes please" or "no thanks" to the wedding invitation.

Students were then given a survey to see if they liked the book and would want to read it again. On a fist to five rating, fist indicating no and five indicating yes, students showed between three and five fingers. As a result of the courageous conversations, the initial resistance diminished. It seemed no one was left feeling right or wrong because of their beliefs, and no one was forced to change their beliefs. Together, the class worked through the emotional discomfort to develop more empathy and build a foundation of understanding for non-heteronormative relationships.

Critical Considerations

Implementing a curriculum that includes students who identify as queer and/ or come from queer families requires considering some critical considerations, especially if there are concerns about encountering a conflict in ideology versus implementation (as the EDD community did). The first thing is to consider the inherent bias held by an educator. Regardless of personal bias, it must be mandated to provide an inclusive curriculum. All students, including those in the queer communities, deserve their existence and experiences validated. All students are worthy of feeling connected to a safe and healthy school environment. All students benefit from an inclusive curriculum. According to GLSEN (2019), "Inclusive curriculum supports students' abilities to empathize, connect, and collaborate with a diverse group of peers, skills that are of increasing importance in our multicultural, global society" (p. 1). GLSEN also recommends considering the following when developing a queer-inclusive curriculum:

- Be mindful of fragmentation, which occurs when queer themes are only introduced during Pride month or when educators only include lesbians or gay men to the exclusion of bisexual and transgender people, or when lessons fail to represent ethnic, racial, and other forms of diversity that exist among queer individuals.
- Take action to interrupt anti-queer name-calling, bullying, and harassment immediately.
- Advocate for queer curriculum by addressing questions and pushback as a school, led by administrators, at the start of the school year on curriculum or Back to School night.
- Plan for and find opportunities for queer visibility and inclusion across all grade levels and as part of social-emotional learning. (p. 2)

Conclusion

When the *Prince and Knight* was delivered in 2018, many GLSN considerations were not contemplated. At that point in time, the goal had simply been to read a queer book and provide an accompanying lesson that would meet a benchmark standard. And even though these specific considerations were not thought of in advance, many unfolded naturally. Students did have opportunities to experience literature as mirrors and as windows and sliding glass doors. Students did have opportunities to share how they were thinking instead of being told what to think, and anti-queer comments were interrupted.

Given the silence around queer people and issues in school, educators and educational systems must give voice to the queer communities to ensure equity and inclusion for all students, families, and the community. Today, this lesson could be significantly expanded by providing opportunities to interrupt heteronormativity further and affirm gender and sexual diversity. For example, educators could follow up with the reading of *Sparkle Boy* and courageous conversations that support the inclusion of bisexual and transgender people while questioning stereotypes about queer communities. Workshops could be created for educators to better address their implicit personal biases and learn how to work better through the discomfort. Administrators could introduce more school-wide days of action and visibility, such as GLSEN's Ally Week, No Name-Calling Week, and Day of Silence, instead of narrowly focusing on conversations only during Gay History Month or Pride Month.

References

Butler, A. H., Alpasian, A. H., Strümpher, J., & Astbury, G. (2003). Gay and lesbian youth experiences of homophobia in South African secondary education. *Journal of Gay & Lesbian Issues in Education, 1*(2), 3–28.

Butler-Wall, A., Cosier, K., Harper, R. L. S., Sapp, J., Sokolower, J., & Tempel, M. B. (2016). Queering our schools. In A. Butler-Wall, K. Cosier, R. Harper, J. Sapp, J. Sokolower, & M. Bollow Tempel (Eds.), *Rethinking sexism gender, and sexuality* (pp. 22–27). Rethinking Schools.

Chetty, A. (2005, August). The crowing of hens. *Mail and Guardian*. https://mg.co.za/article/2005-08-17-the-crowing-of-hens/

Clark, C. T. (2009). Preparing LGBTQ-allies and combating homophobia in a U.S. teacher education program. *Teaching and Teacher Education, 26*(2010), 704–713.

Ferfolja, R., & Robinson, K. H. (2004). Why anti-homophobia education in teacher education? Perspectives from Australian teacher educators. *Teaching Education, 15*(1), 9–25.

Florida Legislative Assembly. CS/CS/HB 1557. (2022). *Parental Rights in Education*. www.myfloridahouse.gov/Sections/Bills/billsdetail.aspx?BillId=76545#:~:text=P arental%20Rights%20in%20Education%3A%20Requires,upbringing%20%26%20 control%20of%20their%20children%3B

GLSEN. (2019). Developing LGBTQ-inclusive classroom resources. *GLSEN*. www.glsen.org/sites/default/files/2019-11/GLSEN_LGBTQ_Inclusive_Curriculum_Resource_2019_0.pdf

Huyck, D., & Dahlen, S. (2019, June 19). *Diversity in children's books 2018.* sarahpark.com blog. Created in consultation with Edith Campbell, Molly Beth Griffin, K. T. Horning, Debbie Reese, Ebony Elizabeth Thomas, and Madeline Tyner, with statistics compiled by the Cooperative Children's Book Center, School of Education, University of Wisconsin-Madison. https://ccbc.education.wisc.edu/literature-resources/ccbc-diversity-statistics/books-by-about-poc-fnn/; https://readingspark.wordpress.com/2019/06/19/picture-this-diversity-in-childrens-books-2018-infographic/

Kumashiro, K. K., Baber, S. A., Richardson, E., Ricker-Wilson, C., & Pong, P. L. (2004). Preparing teachings for anti-oppressive education: International movements. *Teaching Education*, *15*(3), 257–275.

Mathison, C. (1998). The invisible minority: Preparing teachers to meet the needs of gay and lesbian youth. *Journal of Teacher Education*, *49*(2), 151–155.

Morgan, R. (2005, October). Same-sex relationships are African. *Mail and Guardian*. https://mg.co.za/article/2005-10-12-samesex-relationships-are-african/

Powers, E. (2006). A spirited dispositions debate. *Inside Higher Ed*. www.insidehighered. com/news/2006/06/06/spirited-disposition-debate%20Retrieved%20April%2011

Quinn, T., & Meiners, E. R. (2016). Seneca Falls, Selma, Stonewall: Moving beyond equality. In A. Butler-Wall, K. Cosier, R. Harper, J. Sapp, J. Sokolower, & M. Bollow Tempel (Eds.), *Rethinking sexism gender, and sexuality* (pp. 22–27). Rethinking Schools.

Sears, J. (1992). Educators, homosexuality, and homosexual students: Are personal feelings related to professional beliefs? In K. Harbeck (Ed.), *Coming out of the classroom closet* (pp. 29–81). Haworth.

Sims Bishop, R. S. (1990). Mirrors, windows, and sliding glass doors. *Perspectives*, *6*, ix–xi.

Singleton, G. E. (2015). *Courageous conversations about race: A field guide for achieving equity in schools*. SAGE.

Sumara, D. J. (2007). Small differences matter: Interrupting certainty about identity in teacher education. *Journal of Gay & Lesbian Issues in Education*, *4*(4), 39–58.

Sykes, H., & Goldstein, T. (2004). From performed to performing ethnography: Translating life history research into anti-homophobia curriculum for teacher education program. *Teaching Education*, *4*(1), 41–61.

Taylor, C. (2004). Queering teacher education: Failures of empathy and their uses. *Intercultural Studies: A Forum on Social Change and Cultural Diversity*, *16*(1), 19–31.

Appendix A

Picture Books Named

Haack, D. (2018). *Prince & knight: Tale of the shadow king*. Little Bee Books.

Newman, L. (2017). *Sparkle boy*. Lee & Low Books Inc.

11

CULTIVATING STUDENTS' CIVIC AGENCY THROUGH PARTICIPATION IN A SOCIAL JUSTICE-THEMED BOOK CLUB AS A SUBVERSIVE APPROACH TO CRITICAL LITERACY IN EDUCATION

Elizabeth E. Schucker

> *They sat completely transfixed. Hanging on every word. Empowered, awakened, and eager to participate in leadership roles as change agents.*

My fourth-grade students synthesized and analyzed the criticality of the novel, connecting the plot to their lived experiences. I could see the questions swirling as debates emerged in focus group discussions and within developing podcasting scripts. My students knew that our partnership held a place of importance, their voices integral to class discussions. Renovating my reading and writing standards, we made room for critical literacy, applying real-world significance as our book club became the vehicle for civic transformation. Curiosity led to a guiding question: How does a subversive approach through a social justice-themed book club impact students' willingness and ability to serve as civic change agents?

Our classroom was a community built upon the subversive framework, which supports the rejection of the status quo, critique of mundane nuance, and allows literacy to become the vehicle for student agency, cultivating a greater sense of civic identity and motivation toward transformative change. We circumvented the existing standardized curriculum that uses labels and categories to lead people to adopt the normative way of viewing and seeing things in their culture and community (Arday, 2018). This process allowed us to intertwine reading and writing with deep inquiry and multimodal resources to encourage student voices toward impactful school-wide projects while also employing technology as a media tool for positive influence based on change agency initiatives.

DOI:10.4324/9781003302216-14

Traditional definitions describe the term "subversive" as resistance against oppressive forces that seek to maintain the status quo or do harm through limited one-sided curricula or repressive mindsets (Dyches et al., 2020). Yet, according to Portelli and Eizadirad (2018), subversion does not have to be seen in a negative light. Students' reading and writing practices have the potential to foster "Communication, relationships, self-expression . . . enacting identities that offer them power in their everyday lives" (Portelli & Eizadirad, 2018, p. 186). Therefore, my students and I took on the ability to grow in the partnership model, using our curriculum to evolve our classroom purpose from isolated skill work to an embedded and authentic textual, service-oriented literacy framework.

Subversive approaches to critical literacy challenge students to purposefully self-reflect and critically analyze biases, positionality, empathy, understanding, and awareness by viewing their social world through different lenses. This framework opposes the isolated and separate dominance of the scripted curriculums used in classrooms across the nation, which leave teachers feeling unsupported as they also lack the necessary resources to construct their dynamic curricular lessons (Ladson-Billings, 2017). This mindset stems from Freire's Liberating Education Model (Freire, 1970) and Dewey's Progressive Education theory (Dewey, 1938) set the foundation of this action research. In Freire's Liberating Education Model, teachers view their students as participants; valued for their role in the experience alongside their teacher, not oppressed recipients of collective subjectivities. Dewey's educational theory parallels this sentiment by encouraging a view of students as citizens whose reasoning, reflecting, reimagining, and reconstructing could be applied to their positionalities.

Therefore, subversive pedagogy rejects the "banking concept of education" discussed first by Freire (1970), whereas the teacher is the knowledgeable person who expels expertise to passive students. It dispels the myth that disciplinarity and social justice are isolated, and that education is simply about passing knowledge from teacher to student from a transactional stance. Student positionality and classroom context subvert instruction, uprooting repressive forms of the education canon. Reading and writing are complex work. Dyches et al. (2020) described how subversive approaches using authentic text redefine the intention of literacy, inviting agency-related opportunities. This approach might include or feature the use of authentic projects and instructional contexts (Stedronsky & Turner, 2020); multimodal reading and writing instruction (Leander & Boldt, 2013); service-learning (Wilhelm et al., 2014), or youth participatory action research (Mirra et al., 2016) to promote student inquiry and agency (Fisher et al., 2020), and social justice, such as Responsible Change Agency Projects (Coffey & Fulton, 2020).

Personal Decisions to Be Subversive

In my (Elizabeth's) school, the basal curriculum is the required curriculum and foundation, contributing to delivering skills-based instruction and assessments through a traditional reading and writing curriculum model. Within an intervention period of our fourth-grade English language arts block, students were grouped based on standardized testing and benchmark test scores. While the recommended teacher curriculum included short stories linked with activities to strengthen fluency and comprehension, its "drill the skill" methodology lacked real-world engagement.

I also felt frustrated by the lack of authentic text and instructions that disregarded the readers' lived experiences as useful or helpful for holistic growth. I felt stifled as their teacher as my unresponsive curriculum lacked the framework for agency-based opportunities. I yearned for a greater context, for my students to take what they learned, combine it with their lived experiences and identity, and apply themselves civically to real-world contexts for leadership within their school and community. I desired to see my students come together as an "intellectual community" (Storm, 2020, p. 15), to empower my students' identity and knowledge of their lived experiences, to extend a vision of literacy that was far greater than reading for skills proficiency (Lacy & Kohnen, 2020).

Leveled, disconnected texts coupled with passive skills-based lessons created a detached disengagement in my classroom during this time, both in the students' feelings toward reading and writing and my ability to connect them to their growth in character and their role as civically minded and self-aware citizens (Mirra, 2018). However, I knew I could not stray entirely from using the basal texts as the foundation in my ELA classroom due to several factors. Still, I could maneuver slightly more within my intervention classroom, allowing me to disrupt the existing curricular routine and show the students more than just the limiting support of the narrow scope and sequence of isolated skills-based instruction.

Therefore, while the traditional basal curriculum was used in the other grade-level language arts intervention classrooms, my curriculum, and what I describe in this chapter, shows how I incorporated reading, writing, and speaking and listening standards within my social justice-themed book club lessons while also paving the way for agency-based opportunities. These opportunities were also supported through global competency standards: "global and intercultural competence as a desirable outcome of a 21st century education" (Mansilla & Wilson, 2020). These pillars for global competence invited students to "investigate the world, recognize perspectives, communicate ideas, and take action" (p. 7). The students and I engaged in a partnership, challenged our thinking, and stepped into leadership roles as we learned how diverse characters tackled injustices or inequalities in their school communities, leading to personal discovery and retrospection.

Our book club included a homogeneous group of 13 culturally diverse fourth-grade students (85% Caucasian, 10% Puerto Rican, and 5% African American). One student received special education services, but all were part of a regular education inclusive classroom model. The book club occurred daily for 30 minutes before our regularly scheduled 60-minute English Language Arts (ELA) block. According to state testing scaled scores and benchmark assessments, seven students were reading on or just below grade level, two were reading below level, and three out of the 13 were reading above grade level. Students not participating in this book club worked with other fourth-grade teachers and reading support aids in small homogeneous groups determined by benchmark testing to scaffold based on student needs.

As a white, middle-class educator, I (Elizabeth) continue to research, evaluate, and renovate my curriculum to subvert the existing curriculum, to better engage students in tackling real-world topics. Though my teaching role has shifted from fourth-grade teacher to Gifted teacher (K–12) for the district and fifth-grade Unified Arts teacher, I investigate how my position as a college-educated white and privileged woman informs my beliefs and expectations of diverse student populations. I intend to support students in critical thinking and cultivate awareness of student agency through the subversion of the traditional educational canon. Yet, I remain sensitive to the delicate balance of understanding the district's curricular expectations and principles, subverting to provide critical literacy opportunities to my students, integral to their holistic growth when possible.

A Book Club Approach

Students must engage in a curriculum that encourages and empowers them as members of an intellectual classroom community (Storm, 2020), helping them make sense of society and other world elements through rich educational experiences (Lacy & Kohnen, 2020). As many educators note (e.g., Fisher et al., 2020; Sims Bishop, 1990), including Enriquez and colleagues (Enriquez et al., 2017), children's literature is a powerful way to "show readers what is possible in their lives, their communities, and the world around them" (p. 713). Therefore, eager to invite my students to enter the proverbial conversations with our authors, I focused on an intersection between two novels that illuminated current real-world social justice-themed issues: *Front Desk* (2018) by Kelly Yang and *Wonder* (2012) by R. J. Palacio.

Our year-long book club emphasized my partnership with students during discussions to prompt investigation of personal beliefs and consider real-world issues while actively listening and engaging with their voices. This created space for strengthening teacher-student and peer relationships built upon respect and appreciation for the lived experiences and perspectives, taking on a social justice-themed lens (Fisher et al., 2020; Learning for Justice, 2022, Identity Anchor Standard 3 and Diversity Anchor Standard 8). Dever and colleagues (2005) echoed the cruciality of children learning about social justice when they are young, therefore helping them to build a framework to oppose deep-seated and ingrained harmful or destructive social attitudes.

An "agent" assumes an active role on behalf of others (Moya, 2017). Student agency not only involves effectiveness in one's faction; it includes leadership and empowerment, the certainty that you have what it takes to effect real change. Empowering my students to use their literacy skills as a vehicle for change meant that I engaged in the subversion of the traditional practices in the district. Critical thinking, student and teacher curiosity, close reading, deeper text-to-self connections with the novels based on students' lived experiences and their sense of personal identity, and the creation of an authentic agency-based product allowed students to conceptualize how to oppose the source of injustice that motivated them to engage in the change initiative. ELA skill instruction was interwoven throughout each daily/weekly/monthly subversive opportunity, empowering students to challenge their thoughts and ideas, making connections while creating an intellectual community of learners within our subversive classroom (Storm, 2020).

Employing a Social Justice-Themed Lens Using Subversive ELA Opportunities

Our book club sessions occurred 30 minutes each day and incorporated building background/mini-lesson, reading, writing, and critical discussion. Students established expectations together instead of rules that could create an inadvertent power dynamic. These included ways of communicating and responding to each other's body language and verbal/non-verbal cues. The students also set expectations for each other's interactions, depth and breadth of conversations, and overall quality of work. Increased student ownership of the process equaled a greater motivation for engagement.

As we investigated various forms of social injustice, each book became an opportunity for cultivating awareness and action, allowing students to become agents of change through a product of learning that sought to oppose destructive forces discussed and experienced throughout the texts and perhaps, in their own lives. Table 11.1 identifies the five phases repeatedly used to explore and examine social justice-themed issues, inspired by Stedronsky and Turner's (2020) framework. Each lesson was adjusted to respond to students' questions and related to the novels' topics and themes while addressing all required ELA standards.

TABLE 11.1 Five Phases to Exploring the Books' Social Justice Themes

Phase 1	Thinking critically and asking questions
Phase 2	Igniting curiosity and drilling deeper
Phase 3	Exploring and making connections
Phase 4	Securing a focus and immersing deeply
Phase 5	Creating a product of learning

A Subversive Approach That Explored Discrimination, Classism, and Racism

Our book club started with *Front Desk*, the true story of an immigrant family who encounters many complex societal challenges. This novel presents a strong protagonist with whom students could identify, seeing themselves in her diverse traits as she grapples with many challenging topics, navigating oppressive forces with courage, resilience, and some good friends! Students were invited to learn from a different lens as they explored the characters' development in perseverance and tenacity to improve situations.

During the beginning, students primarily focused on asking questions, building background knowledge, and sharing their lived experiences of discrimination, classism, and racial prejudice. However, students were divided early on whether the main character, Mia, should approach the antagonist character, Mr. Yao, about how he had been prejudiced against the family due to their cultural and racial background. The students could not agree on how they felt about Mia submitting to Mr. Yao's cruel, unjust ways after he cuts Mr. and Mrs. Tang's pay after something goes wrong in the hotel, forcing them to stay in the hotel to work, and denying them access to amenities, such as the hotel pool, making the Tangs appear inferior and subordinate based on their Chinese heritage. The students wondered why Mia was not addressing this issue with Mr. Yao.

I welcomed their text-to-self connections and their critical thinking and curiosity to evaluate what was happening in the story, many using their lived experiences to identify this as prejudice. We defined classism after a few students said that Mr. Yao was wealthy and thought he was better than everyone else, which fueled his discrimination, prompting new exploration and engaging in a debate, the first of many.

After refreshing and setting any necessary new expectations and norms, they were provided sentence stems to support framing their conversation: *My perspective is . . ., I agree because . . ., I do not agree because . . ., To bring up another point . . . I hear you saying that . . ., I'm confused when you say . . ., What is your perspective on . . ., I need more information . . ., Can you elaborate?* Students chose either side A: Yes, Mia should approach Mr. Yao and call out his prejudice and classism *or* side B: No, Mia should not approach Mr. Yao and call out his prejudice and classism. We used a "debate ball" so that the person with the ball had the floor. This cut down the number of interruptions, highlighted the need to respect the speaker with undivided attention, and prompted richer and deeper responses because they were *really* listening to each other and took turns participating in the experience. The goal was to gain awareness of each side's perspective and understand the social justice themes, not to confirm a winner. The students enjoyed this learning so much that they recreated one of their debates calling it, "An Interview with the Characters!"

By moving into something they created, they secured a focus and immersed deeply into their learning as they made choices, and I became the facilitator.

This sent a message to the students that I valued their voices and that this experience belonged to them. The students picked a partner and pretended that they were an antagonist, such as characters like Jason or Mr. Yao, or a protagonist like Mia, or her parents, Mr. and Mrs. Tang. They wrote interview scripts and used their knowledge of the plot to adlib the answers as the interviewee. This subversive activity showcased comprehension and allowed the students to role-play and improvise in the characters' shoes, truly gleaning as much understanding and information as possible while developing a greater awareness of the protagonist characters' oppression and why the antagonists engaged in that behavior.

After this two-day activity, the students took part in another whole-class focus-group discussion. The students acknowledged that the debate had been difficult but enjoyable to step into the characters' perspectives. They shared that it would have been interesting to record themselves and share them with the school for others to see!

Moving into creating a product, we brainstormed ideas to share our thoughts with our school community. Once we had about 10 ideas, we voted, and they decided to create their podcasts, linking the recordings to QR codes that would be hung up around the school hallways, inviting the student body to scan the codes and listen to the students' recorded podcasts that demonstrated how to combat bullying, injustice, and prejudice. For instance, in one podcast, a student shared with her peers and other people at school, "*and you should definitely stand up for the person who is being bullied because you want to be kind and stand up to that cyberbully because they can say so many things that hurt other people's feelings.*" Another student added, "*Something you should remember to do is to be kind and caring and someone who makes others feel happy, supported, and safe.*"

The podcasts aligned with the social justice continuum of change agency. For instance, one student reflected on serving as a personally responsible citizen (Westheimer & Kahne, 2004) when stating, "*My friends stuck up for me, saying that if you don't have anything nice to say, then don't say anything at all!*" Or a segment that demonstrates an agency role after the student considered the deeper meaning behind the problem of WHY people may be hungry and what they could do to help, as noted with this student comment, "*We made food for people in our community, and I think I might be doing things to help more people going forward.*" The scripts for their podcasts incorporated their short stories in a wide range of genres and topics. Each unique podcast script was a reflection and creative application of their identity and lived experiences.

The students and I were eager to continue with our subverted book club opportunities. However, challenges presented themselves. The time constraint of only having 30 minutes made it difficult as rich and vulnerable conversations blossomed. Some students were more open to this type of learning, while others took more time to engage in the discussions. There were times that I questioned if what I was doing was having an impact: were they developing the skills they needed, or just enjoying an engaging book club? However, the partnership and responsive classroom approaches helped the anxieties fade, rich discussions and eagerness for agency flourished, and the impact of this book club became more apparent as we got ready to read *Wonder* (2012).

A Subversive Approach That Explored Prejudice, Intolerance, and Bullying

Wonder (2012) by R. J. Palacio was our second book club, lasting from late January through June. This novel looks at prejudice, intolerance, and bullying regarding individuals with special needs to engage students with discussion and exploration into the everyday struggles students with disabilities face in school and within our classrooms. Students followed the main character's journey as he navigated middle school with a few other characters who grew and evolved together. All the characters resemble the social fabric of a school, challenging students to see through a lens of compassion and acceptance, not only for these novel characters but also for their peers.

Throughout the beginning of the novel, the students struggled to understand how the main character, Auggie, worked with the craniofacial abnormality with the students in his new school. Auggie Pullman's experiences were cruel, highlighting prejudice and intolerance toward a student through excessive bullying among the antagonistic characters. Students took ample time to understand better what this meant for Auggie, asking many questions during focus group conversations and journaling about what it might be like to live with a disability.

Through discussion with the students, they wanted to simulate what it would be like to live with a disability, specifically, being blind. While this was not Auggie's disability, it provided the students with some insight and challenged the perceptions that they needed for further understanding. Therefore, we created a series of tasks, such as navigating through the classroom to your desk, finding your materials, and walking through a crowd of people . . . blindfolded. Once the opportunity was complete, the students gathered in the "book nook," writing in their reflective journals about their experiences. Many students reported that without the help of their friends, they would not have been successful. This later tied back to how Auggie relied on the friendship of Jack and Charlotte to stand up to the extreme bullying that he faced. It is important to note that simulations must be handled with care, lots of dialogue, and the understanding that no one can ever step into someone else's shoes even through this type of simulation.

Immersing even deeper, students were invited to share personal or familial experiences or share about others related to similar physical challenges at the school. I asked the students to "stop and jot" their ideas in their reflective journals. One of the students connected her change agency to a personal connection with a family member who was sometimes bullied for a scar on his chest due to heart surgery. She explained that he continues to suffer jeering and bullying even now, especially when they are at the pool over the summer. During her stop and jot, she wrote, "he is also like Auggie Pullman, and I can't let the same things happen to other people."

Through a focus group discussion with the whole class, the students commented on how they were learning that it isn't only the main character (or main person affected by the injustice) that "grows" through a transformation. Auggie Pullman's sister, Via, and the rest of Auggie's family also journey through their evolution right alongside him. The students tied this back once again to the student sharing about her brother. The connection had now been made on how much she had overcome, navigating the challenge with him. After each sharing, we wrapped up to set an intention and "next steps" as a takeaway from the opportunity, moving toward the agency aspect of this book engagement. The students decided that more needed to be done to support others with a disability.

We engaged with two multimodal sources during the next book club session: a *People* magazine story about a teen who had a craniofacial abnormality, just like Auggie Pullman, and a YouTube video, entitled "I am Auggie Pullman." After reading the first, we discussed the difficulty of living in a way that sets you apart from mainstream society and how it takes support to navigate the challenges of discrimination and oppression based on something you cannot control. After viewing the video, which showcased how people may be different and may struggle, we are all like Auggie Pullman in that we all struggle at times and with various things. Still, we are all essential members of society and offer our gifts and talents to this world.

Students voted on two change agency projects to work on together. The first was a school-wide project called, "Kindness Rocks." The students were inspired by a rock found on our playground painted on it, "Be Kind." The students planned to paint a clutch of river rocks with precepts and positive messages to be placed around our school campus and in their neighborhood. They hoped that when people found their rocks, they would be inspired and empowered to "pass it on" and make their positive impact in their community.

Like activities with *Front Desk*, the intent was student-centered, with me being the "guide on the side." It is important to note that at the onset, the students had a challenging time with the posed questions, specifically regarding the oppressive nature of what was happening in the text. As we engaged with these terms as they came up in the text, students led the conversations, contributing with their own experiences and thoughts. Another limitation was Covid-19 quarantines and shutdowns that fractured relationships when class moved online.

The Value of a Subversive Approach

One of the most memorable transformative moments was after our exceptionally motivating debates; students were sitting at the edge of their seats, anxiously awaiting their turn to speak their truth and share their perspectives and beliefs. There was a "hum" of excitement defined by the engagement in intellectual inspiration. However, at the culmination of the book club session, it was time to transition back to our regular schedule, and it was clear that students did not want to walk away from the subversive approach and engagement found with their book club. They resolved to cooperate as they slowly disengaged, digging out their one-size-fits-all basal textbooks, and complied. I watched in horror as my once "engaged and eager partners" collapsed into morose souls disintegrating at the thought of leaving the real-world opportunity for an isolated skill-based lesson that lacked connection or potential for civic action. At this moment, I realized the depth and breadth of our experience together. My students were using reading and writing for liberation and synthesis.

I argue that for any curricular change to be truly subversive, our students' voices must be empowered for agency. Their motivation for civic involvement is applied to their real-world contexts and applications. A culturally relevant pedagogy that responds to our students' diverse needs has never been more critical (Coffey & Fulton, 2020). However, this also means that OUR voices and positionality must be valued, respected, and accepted, especially if we continue to evolve in our pedagogy with our students in an ever-changing world. Many of us, including myself at times, still feel the tension within our districts when it comes to our desire to change the status quo, as we yearn to engage in complex real-world topics through a responsive curriculum that some may see as rebellious or radical. Our passion and persistence to think fundamentally and critically may be met with resistance and apprehension. However, we must realize the greater context for our actions and assume our roles as innovative educators empowered with fortitude, ingenuity, foresight, and tenacity. We know this to be accurate based on the fundamental knowledge of the criticality and more significant purpose of the changes we make to our educational framework, which are positive and constructive for our partnering students, teachers, and stakeholders. If not us, then who? For it is teachers who are the most significant change agents of all (Dyches et al., 2020).

Teachers must have the autonomy to think critically and evaluate their perspectives as they choose to renovate and subvert the curriculum to support a diverse and responsive classroom community. To have the freedom and support to learn *with* and *from* their students, evaluating and renovating the status quo. After reflecting on all we had gained at the year's culmination, the students and I regarded ourselves as the "Changed Agents." Our reading intervention time had transformed into an empowering experience that allowed us to use reading and writing for a higher calling, a pronounced civic duty, an elevated purpose, and even igniting a motivation for social action and change (Fisher et al., 2020). The critical literacy texts allowed students to investigate significant and vital, and challenging social situations and topics (Mirra, 2018). The teacher and student partnership played a crucial role as the subversive approach circumvented the existing standardized curriculum that uses labels and categories to lead people to adopt the normative way of viewing and seeing things in their culture and community (Arday, 2018). The subversive framework provides the positive outlook and necessary foundation to elevate and transform your existing approaches, inspiring all of us to reimagine our goals, seizing the opportunity where we can, perhaps even evolving with our partnering students as critically conscious civic "changed agents."

References

Arday, J. (2018). Dismantling power and privilege through reflexivity: Negotiating normative Whiteness, the Eurocentric curriculum and racial micro-aggressions within the Academy. *Whiteness and Education, 3*(2), 141–161.

Coffey, H., & Fulton, S. (2020). The responsible change project: Subverting the standardized English language arts curriculum. In J. Dyches, B. Sams, & A. Boyd (Eds.), *Acts of resistance: Subversive teaching in the English language arts classroom* (pp. 110–122). Myers Education Press.

Dever, M. T., Sorenson, B. & Broderick, J. (2005). Using picture books as a vehicle to teach young children about social justice. *Social Studies and the Young Learner, 18*(1), 18–21.

Dewey, J. (1938). *Experience and education.* Macmillan Company.

Dyches, J., Sams, B., & Boyd, A. (Eds.). (2020). *Acts of resistance: Subversive teaching in the English language arts classroom.* Myers Education Press.

Enriquez, G., Clark, S. R., & Della Calce, J. (2017). Using children's literature for dynamic learning frames and growth mindsets. *The Reading Teacher, 70*(6), 711–719.

Fisher, D., Frey, N., & Savitz, R. S. (2020). *Teaching hope and resilience for students experiencing trauma: Creating safe and nurturing classrooms for learning.* Teachers College Press.

Freire, P. (1970). *Pedagogy of the oppressed.* The Continuum International Publishing Group.

Lacy, A., & Kohnen, A. M. (2020). "Why can't they test us on this?" A framework for transforming intensive reading instruction. In J. Dyches, B. Sams, & A. Boyd (Eds.), *Acts of resistance: Subversive teaching in the English language arts classroom* (pp. 184–198). Myers Education Press.

Ladson-Billings, G. (2017). The (R)evolution will not be standardized: Teacher education, hip hop pedagogy, and culturally relevant pedagogy 2.0. In D. Paris & H. S. Alim (Eds.), *Teaching and learning for justice in a changing world* (pp. 141–168). Teachers College Press.

Leander, K., & Boldt, G. (2013). Rereading "a pedagogy of multiliteracies": Bodies, texts, and emergence. *Journal of Literacy Research, 45*(1), 22–46.

Learning for Justice. (2022). *Social justice standards.* https://www.learningforjustice.org/frameworks/social-justice-standards

Mansilla, V. B., & Wilson, D. (2020). What is global competence, and what might it look like in Chinese schools? *Journal of Research in International Education, 19*(1), 3–22.

Mirra, N. (2018). *Educating for empathy: Literacy learning and civic engagement.* Teachers College Press.

Mirra, N., Garcia, A., & Morrell, E. (2016). *Doing youth participatory action research: Transforming inquiry with researchers, educators, and students.* Routledge.

Moya, J. (2017). Examining how youth take on critical civic identities across classroom and youth organized spaces. *Critical Questions in Education (Special Issue), 8*(4), 457–475.

Portelli, J. P., & Eizadirad, A. (2018). Subversion in education: Common misunderstandings and myths. *International Journal of Critical Pedagogy, 9*(1), 54–72.

Sims Bishop, R. (1990). Mirrors, windows, and sliding glass doors. *Perspectives, 6*(3), ix–xi.

Stedronsky, J., & Turner, K. H. (2020). Pushing back against traditional literacy instruction. In J. Dyches, B. Sams, & A. Boyd (Eds.), *Acts of resistance: Subversive teaching in the English language arts classroom* (pp. 51–64). Myers Education Press.

Storm, S. (2020). Black words matter: Bending literary close reading toward justice. In J. Dyches, B. Sams, & A. Boyd (Eds.), *Acts of resistance: Subversive teaching in the English language arts classroom* (pp. 7–21). Myers Education Press.

Westheimer, J., & Kahne, J. (2004). Educating the "good" citizen: Political choices and pedagogical goals. *American Political Science Association, 37*(2), 241–247.

Wilhelm, J. D., Douglas, W., & Fry, S. W. (2014). *The activist learner: Inquiry, literacy, and service to make learning better.* Teachers College Press.

Literature Cited

Palacio, R. J. (2012). *Wonder.* Doubleday.

Yang, K. (2018). *Front desk.* Arthur A. Levine Books/Scholastic.

12

SCATTERING STARS

Graphic Novel Book Studies With Middle Grades Students to Explore Refugee Stories

Rebecca Harper and Alicia Stephenson

The integration of graphic novels has several benefits, and often challenges students to think deeply and critically about the elements of storytelling utilized in the visual narrative. While novels have long offered students an opportunity to tackle difficult topics and issues in a safe space, graphic novels often are appealing to struggling and unmotivated readers due to their inclusion of both words and images as text. Thus, their inclusion in classroom book clubs focusing on the stories of immigrants can offer powerful opportunities for building empathy and compassion for marginalized groups. Freire (1970) argued that dialogue has transformative power for individual identities and identity construction. His premise of hope that "can be carried out in communion with others" (Freire, 1970, p. 91), presupposes that creating this community through dialogue can only occur when students are able to "speak their world" (Freire, 1970 p. 88) and by naming their realities and situation as true participants in the dialogue that can acknowledge and transform their worlds. For some students, their realities may be different from their peers or may include challenges that they find difficult to openly discuss. While numerous titles have been published that address contemporary and social issues, few classrooms utilize them as primary reading sources (see this volume's Introduction, Savitz et al., 2023, p. *xiv* on the beauty of sharing texts). With this in mind, the integration of graphic novels that focus on the stories of immigrants and refugees will be explored in middle grades classrooms. Titles including *When Stars are Scattered, Illegal, American Born Chinese,* and *Refugee* will be integrated into classroom instruction through a book club/literature circle unit with middle grades classroom teachers. This unit will include writing and storytelling engagements, interviews and discussions with immigrants in the community, and virtual visits with authors of the selected works.

DOI:10.4324/9781003302216-15

In today's unique political climate, conversations surrounding immigration can conjure polarizing opinions regarding border control, the establishment of walls between countries, and the detainment of immigrants. Debates surrounding refugee status, asylum, and deportation often focus on the news media and foreign policy (Grande et al., 2019; Mutz, 2018; Newman et al., 2018). Although the first immigrant detainment facility, Ellis Island Immigration Station, was established in 1892, President Donald Trump's 2017 Executive Order on Immigration thrust immigrant detainment facilities and refugee stories into the contemporary spotlight (Diamond & Almasy, 2017; Miranda, 2017; Rogers et al., 2017). This political event, coupled with the demographic shifts in the makeup of communities, families, and schools, has placed immigrant stories and issues at the forefront of humanitarian discussions.

Since 1980, the United States has accepted more than three million refugees into the country for permanent settlement, more than any other country (U.S. Department of State, 2019). In 2017, the number of individuals forcibly displaced from their homes climbed to over 68 million, with over 25 million classified as refugees (United Nations High Commissioner for Refugees, 2022). According to the UNHCR (2022):

> Refugees are people who have fled war, violence, conflict, or persecution and have crossed an international border to find safety in another country. Refugees are unable or unwilling to return to their country of origin due to a well-founded fear of being persecuted for race, religion, nationality, membership in a particular social group, or political opinion.
>
> *(para. 1)*

Although millions of individuals qualify for refugee status, receiving official refugee status is often time-consuming, with some application processing times taking months or years (American Immigration Council, 2022). As a result, individuals are being held in detainment camps or detention facilities while waiting for paperwork to be processed. Of the millions of global refugees, UNICEF (2021) reports almost half are children under 18. Many face limited educational opportunities, impoverished conditions, and separation from extended family members (UNHCR, 2019). Immigration authorities encountered nearly 150,000 unaccompanied minors at the United States/Mexican border in 2021 (Cheatham & Roy, 2021). Many of these unaccompanied minors, several of whom are 15 years of age or younger, face an uncertain future. Some are returned to their countries of origin, while others are held at border facilities where they await decisions on political asylum and the designation of refugee status (Cheatham & Roy, 2021).

Connecting to the Classroom

While the number of refugees has declined, media attention to this humanitarian crisis has served as a reminder of the importance of discussion in the classroom.

For teachers of refugee students, finding ways to support students who may have experienced disruptions in their educational experiences is essential (Dryden-Peterson, 2015; UNHCR, 2019). Although not every school hosts a large population of refugees or immigrants, building spaces for students to discuss the lives of diverse individuals with varying backgrounds is necessary in today's diverse world. Classrooms can often offer adolescents safe spaces to discuss global issues that may be sensitive yet are essential for students to consider as they develop into global citizens (Herrera, 2012). This nurturing classroom environment can allow students to receive timely and vital information while learning about others whose backgrounds and stories may differ from their own. According to Robinson (2017), research indicates the importance of teaching and allowing adolescent students to discuss controversial topics, such as immigration, when given proper background knowledge to support and develop their beliefs and opinions. Students may begin to connect to their own lives and build empathy for individuals who may be experiencing challenges and experiences that vary from their own.

In some cases, middle school students may lack the knowledge or have a limited understanding of people's struggles outside of their social circle, family, or community. This lack of understanding can often make it difficult for middle school students to relate to people's hardships from different areas. Without the background knowledge, they might not fully comprehend the connection to their lives.

We would be remiss if we didn't note that geographical context can significantly impact some educators' implementation of immigration topics in the classroom setting. Additionally, teachers may avoid discussing issues related to immigration due to student and caregiver beliefs and attitudes, mainly when influenced by social media, family beliefs, political rhetoric, and friends. These beliefs are often developed based on misinformation and without a thorough understanding of the stories of those involved. However, navigating the complex narratives of immigrant stories can be challenging when working with middle-grade students.

Using YAL to Connect to the Experiences of Immigrants

For many students, developing an understanding of individual stories unlike their own can be daunting simply due to a lack of exposure and awareness. In some instances, students may be unaware of the rich narratives of experiences that immigrants and individuals with varying backgrounds possess. According to Mabry and Bhavnagri (2012), developing an understanding of different cultures other than a student's own is imperative in a diverse society such as the United States. Teachers can bring these conversations to the classroom by integrating quality young adult literature. Integrating young adult literature, which focuses on immigrant stories, has many benefits for students (Brown, 2010; Christensen, 2000; Cummins, 2013; Hays, 2017). As Galda (1998) reminds us, there is significant value in young adult texts in that they allow young people to reflect on their own lives and experiences, all while taking a peek into the lived experiences of those unlike them. Research conducted by Graff's (2010) study showed the importance for both teachers and students to read and discuss stories of immigrants, to make connections with individuals unlike themselves, and to develop an understanding of the struggles often faced by immigrants. In this setting, Graff noted that the topic of immigration shifted from a political issue to a tumultuous and complex process with a human face, one that participants could now empathize with through their encounters with the texts they read. With this in mind, we, a university professor and middle grades instructional coach, began to plan how we might integrate titles focusing on the immigration experience with a group of middle school students through optional book clubs.

When we began to plan our project, we knew that there were several features and characteristics we wanted our engagement to include. We knew that we wanted to offer students opportunities to discuss the novels and characters through several activities. These included the implementation of discussions, role-play, and journal writing. Mabry and Bhavnagri (2012) found that these literacy activities helped their students understand the perspective of immigrants when they completed a project with similar goals. By integrating diverse young adult literature, such as graphic novels, teachers can introduce the topic and guide conversations to help students develop empathy and understanding for individuals who are different from themselves (Newstreet et al., 2019). We knew these texts needed to be diverse on several levels. For one, we focused on the graphic novel genre, as it is underrepresented in required readings for students. Plus, we knew that evaluating and critiquing the structure and aesthetics of graphic novels could foster visual learning (Eisner, 1998; Fisher & Frey, 2004; McCloud, 1993; Serafini, 2011; Smetana, 2010). Graphic novels, much like comics, can be used to promote critical inquiry, which was another crucial component of this book club (Brenna, 2013; Chun, 2009; Krusemark, 2015; Serafini, 2014). In addition to this diversity in genre, we chose titles that included main characters that possessed different identities than the students we taught. Main characters who looked different and had experiences outside of what our students had were a deliberate focus when we made our text selections.

Our experiences with novels that addressed immigrant stories led us to develop a project that would offer our students a glimpse of the lived experiences of those with stories that might differ from their backgrounds. As we began to plan, Sims Bishop's (1990) notion of texts serving as windows, mirrors, and sliding doors helped us frame the project that we introduced to our middle grades students. We wanted students to have an opportunity to interact and engage with characters whose lives were significantly different than their own. The counternarratives offered in the literature chosen can provide students with a new perspective aside from the often negative image of refugees portrayed in the media (Hope, 2017; Hwang & Hindman, 2014). Luke (2003) argued that taking a critical approach to literacy is about "engaging with texts and discourses as a means for bridging time and space, critically understanding and altering the connections between the local and global, moving between cultures and communities, and developing transnational understandings and collaborations" (p. 22). By utilizing a specific text that profiled the story of an immigrant refugee, we wanted our students to focus on the potential injustices and social issues prevalent in this novel and use these as a potential catalyst for action. We also chose to utilize graphic novels because, although this genre often appeals to striving readers, we believed that combining the words and images would help students develop a more comprehensive understanding of the narrative told in the story. The use of words and texts may interest readers and promote an alternative to traditional novels, which can sometimes prove intimidating for striving readers due to the high concentration of words on the page. However, reading graphic novels can engage students in critical thinking as they read the text and juxtapose the implied meaning of the words in tandem with the corresponding images (Krusemark, 2017; Sun, 2017). Students can see stories from multiple perspectives, graphically and written. By reading graphic novels, some students can better visualize and empathize with the complex social issues the characters face. We believe that using a graphic novel could engage students in critical and transformative dialogue regarding refugees and their stories since literature is a means to connect with students through stories and characters. Further, teachers can approach complex topics using graphic novels without worrying about students' limited vocabulary knowledge. By including the literature with a cast of characters who are immigrants and refugees, students may begin to understand the stories of diverse individuals, and guided conversations about these sensitive issues can start in the classroom.

Ultimately, our hope with reading graphic novel immigrant stories is to help students understand and empathize with immigrants' trials and tribulations when coming to the United States or another host country. Though there are political and social opinions, whether positive or negative, immigrants face many challenges when moving to a new country. Yet these challenges are not their only story. We were hypersensitive to the potential for our students' ideas and beliefs about immigrants and refugees to become one single story. Adichie (2009) suggests that only having a single story or a one-sided perception of a group or event leads to an incomplete one-dimensional account, creating assumptions or conclusions that do not accurately depict reality. We wanted our students to see that refugees and immigrants are not defined by that one identity—that of a refugee or immigrant. We wanted them to understand the intersectionality of their multiple identities and develop a comprehensive understanding of the individual.

The Book Club

Our graphic novel book club was implemented at a rural middle school in south Georgia with a student population of approximately 900 students, with 68% identifying as white, 18% Black, 6% Hispanic, and 5% of two or more races. 35% of the students receive free or reduced lunch. Students were chosen to participate in the graphic novel book club based on teacher recommendations and standardized test scores. Our book club met five times over four weeks during the students' lunch to discuss the first novel. We chose to utilize this format for the book club for several reasons. Many ELA teachers already had their course readings set, so asking them to incorporate a new title into their instruction was not an option. Additionally, immigration was a sensitive topic at this school, so we wanted to ensure administrators, parents, and students knew that participation in the book club was voluntary and not a requirement. This structure helped us to circumvent any potential pushback from stakeholders.

The first novel that students read was the graphic novel *When Stars Are Scattered* (2020) by Victoria Jamieson and Omar Mohamed. *When Stars Are Scattered* describes Omar and his brother Hassan's life in a refugee camp as orphaned boys. Their father was killed in Somalia, and they were separated from their mother. When they arrived in the refugee camp, the boys were given a foster mother, Fatuma, who cared for and loved the two boys. Throughout the novel, readers get a glimpse of day-to-day life in the refugee camp and the struggle for food and water. During the novel, Omar is allowed to attend school, which offers him an education, hope, and the ability to make and achieve his future goals. The novel also describes the interview and waiting process that refugees like Omar and Hassan go through to determine if they will be allowed to resettle in another country.

One of the reasons we chose this novel was that it provided a cross-curricular benefit. Georgia seventh-grade social studies standards (Georgia Department of Education, 2021) include "examining the history, geography, environment, government, and economies of some of the countries in Africa" therefore, students would have a basic understanding of this region of the world, which could be helpful while reading the novel. Students can make connections between content areas and the ability to view the events through a different lens. For example, understanding the government regulations regarding immigration helped students connect with Omar's story and gave background information that addressed the logistics of refugee status and Omar's narrative accounts. Having this baseline knowledge of the government policies aided students in articulating questions while reading.

When we designed this book club, we wanted the students to do more than simply read the book and discuss the overall theme and events. Instead, we wanted them to explore the dynamic and complex political issues surrounding immigration juxtaposed with the narrative element of Omar's lived experience detailed in the novel. Additionally, we also wanted students to have the opportunity to examine and explore the graphic novel genre and discuss how Omar's story played out on the pages utilizing both words and pictorial images. As a result, we developed activities and engagements centered around these primary goals. Book discussions were a natural item for inclusion, but we also connected these discussions with companion texts that addressed contemporary issues in immigration. These included *New York Times* news articles and other sources from multiple news media outlets and various formats, including video clips and political cartoons. These companion texts helped students examine sources that offered information about immigration issues and current events related to Omar's story.

While reading the novel, our discussions continued to focus on the availability of food, resources, and activities available in daily life, as these were some of the main details and themes explored in the novel. During our book club sessions, students discussed the book's overall themes, women's roles in the refugee camp, the challenges of moving to another country, and immigration. As our meetings progressed, we began a deeper dive into the emerging themes. We started to make connections between the characters' experiences and our lives here in the United States, including comparisons between our school experiences and Omar's experiences. Students discussed the lack of school supplies for refugee students and that girls were separated from the boys within the classroom.

Together with students, we developed questions about parts of the novel to discuss with the author during the author chat. Table 12.1 lists these questions.

This running list of questions helped students prepare for their workshop and author talk later in the project. In our later meetings, the group began discussing the treatment of immigrants to the United States. Because we knew several students in our school setting who had moved from other countries, we could draw attention to these experiences and share information about the day-to-day challenges of communicating, driving, eating at restaurants, and shopping. We watched video clip interviews of immigrants from various locations, including the Philippines, Puerto Rico, and Italy. We discussed how their cultures were different and how they have adjusted to life in the United States. These videos of immigrant stories and refugee experiences in camps like those in the novel allowed us to bring up potential challenges that might be new and different for someone relocating to the United States. Having additional examples for students to consider as they began to learn more about what life in a refugee camp was like offered another tangible example that we could connect back to details and material addressed in the novel.

TABLE 12.1 Novel Questions

Opening Questions	Questions After Completing the Book
Why did Hassan not have the opportunity to go to school like Omar?	Why did Hassan only say one word in the entire story?
How did the food line work?	How did the author conduct the research to write this story?
Did people fight while they were waiting for food?	What is Omar doing now?
How did Omar and his brother come to live in the refugee camp?	What current events are related to refugees?

TABLE 12.2 Potential Questions for Book Club

What challenges did Omar and Hassan face in the refugee camp?
How did Omar build relationships with people he met in the refugee camp?
How do the images used in the graphic novel help you connect with the characters in
  the story?
What was daily life for Omar and Hassan like?

At the beginning of our discussions, we were purposeful with the questions we asked, and the discussion prompts we offered students. We wanted the book club participants to avoid generic remarks about immigrant experiences such as descriptions including words such as "bad" and "lonely." As a result, we developed our discussion prompts and nudge questions with specificity and deliberateness of word choice. In many instances, we each drafted possible question that we posed to each other to offer suggestions that would make the question stronger and encourage the students to think deeply about the connections between the characters and their worlds. Table 12.2 is an example of the questions developed.

We also explored the graphic novel genre structure and selection through participation in a graphic novel workshop with Victoria Jamieson, one of the book's authors. Students were able to see early versions of the manuscript during the workshop, including cover variations, photographs that were the basis for the illustrations, and other material used by the author when researching and writing the novel. Jamieson gave the students a drawing lesson, and each student was able to draw and design their character based on a person from the novel. Students were able to ask the author and illustrator specific questions about the graphic novel genre and her process for writing and publishing *When Stars Are Scattered*. She also discussed her time spent with Omar Mohamed to write the book. Jamieson described to the students the challenges and successes that Omar has had since he immigrated to the United States of America. She provided them with an update on Omar as well. Omar's current work at a center that resettles refugees and his non-profit organization, Refugee Strong, which helps students living in refugee camps, offered students a tangible update to the character in the novel. This critical detail served as a reminder and extension of the real story and lived experience of a character we initially learned about in the novel. Jamieson also discussed the current challenges refugees face as they immigrate to the United States and the need for help with housing and functioning in a different society. She offered students suggestions and ideas for getting involved with projects that aid and assist immigrants and provided ideas for developing school-based support groups.

Students Taking Action

As students continued to read the novel, we explored the importance of immigrant narratives and stories in our discussions, which carried over into an interview project with immigrants in and around their school community. Using Omar's story as a frame, students determined the types of questions they might ask to explore immigrants' lived experiences and narratives in their communities. Before locating an individual to interview, the students completed a group interview of one of the employees at the middle school who had recently immigrated to the United States. This collaborative activity helped the students determine which questions were most effective and allowed them to practice. We often referred them back to the video clips and stories of other immigrants that we had used in our book club meetings as frames for developing their questions.

When we decided to incorporate this component into the book club, we were hopeful that our students would be able to learn about a member of their school community who, like Omar, is an immigrant. Using our novel and our other companion texts as sources and frames for our interview, we helped the students create questions to allow their interviewees to focus on some of the same aspects and themes we saw in the book. These aspects and themes included the difficulties immigrants face due to the relocation to a new country with a different culture, language acquisition aspects, and new daily life skills needed, among others. Most of all, we wanted our students to compare these experiences and Omar's in the novel. Part of the culminating project involved interviewing a subject of their choice, so we felt like students would benefit from having ownership of this aspect of the project and would begin to see the connections between individuals in their communities and their own lives.

Creating Constellations

Throughout our book club experience, we saw students begin to identify specific concepts and ideas that emerged through their reading, reflection, discussions, and independent research. Throughout the four weeks spent with the students discussing the book *When Stars Are Scattered* and the challenges that immigrants face as they come to the United States, we became acutely aware of the benefits of incorporating this title in our book club. In many ways, we saw ideas emerge like stars in a night sky as students encountered these new narratives, both in their graphic novel study and in their own lives and worlds. Themes like "equality" begin to shine along with stars emblazoned with "narrative stories," "lived experiences," "culture," "family," and more. As we continued to read, these individual stars began to cluster together, forming connections and constellations, which started new shapes and ideas informing these students' thoughts, ideas, and opinions.

As we wrapped up our initial book study, students began a new related novel, *A Long Walk to Water* (2010), as they continued their deeper dive into immigrant stories. As a result of this novel, students began working with educators to raise money for wells in Sudan. This initiative was spurred by their reading of this second immigrant story. As educators, it is imperative that we strive to help our students acknowledge our diverse world. Additionally, when we lean into complex social issues that define our worlds while using texts to help navigate these social issues, this allows students and teachers to develop a comprehensive understanding of it all.

References

Adichie, C. N. (2009). *The danger of a single story* [Video file]. www.ted.com/talks/chimamanda_ngozi_adichie_the_danger_of_a_single_story?language=en

American Immigration Council. (2022). www.americanimmigrationcouncil.org/

Brenna, B. (2013). How graphic novels support reading comprehension strategy development in children. *Literacy, 47*(2), 88–94.

Brown, J. (2010). *Immigration narratives in young adult literature crossing borders* (Scarecrow studies in young adult literature). Scarecrow Press.

Cheatham, A., & Roy, D. (2021, December 2). U.S detention of child migrants. *Council on Foreign Relations*. Retrieved April 5, 2022, from www.cfr.org/backgrounder/us-detention-child-migrants

Christensen, L. (2000). *Reading, writing, and rising up: Teaching about social justice and the power of the written word.* Rethinking Schools Publication.

Chun, C. W. (2009). Critical literacies and graphic novels for English-language learners: Teaching Maus. *Journal of Adolescent & Adult Literacy, 53*(2), 144–153.

Cummins, A. (2013). Border crossings: Undocumented migration between Mexico and the United States in contemporary young adult literature. *Children's Literature in Education, 44*(1), 57–73. https://doi.org/10.1007/s10583-012-9176-1

Diamond, J., & Almasy, S. (2017, January 30). *Trump's immigration ban sends shockwaves.* www.cnn.com

Dryden-Peterson, S. (2015). *The educational experience of refugee children in countries of first asylum.* Migration Policy Institute.

Eisner, E. W. (1998). *The kind of schools we need: Personal essays.* Heinemann.

Fisher, D., & Frey, N. (2004). Using graphic novels, anime, and the internet in an urban high school. *English Journal, 93*(3), 19–25.

Freire, P. (1970). *Pedagogy of the oppressed.* The Continuum International Publishing Group.

Galda, L. (1998). Mirrors and windows: Reading as transformation. In T. E. Raphael & K. H. Au (Eds.), *Literature-based instruction: Reshaping the curriculum* (pp. 1–11). Christopher-Gordon.

Georgia Department of Education. (2021). *Georgia social studies standards of excellence (GSE).* Author.

Graff, J. M. (2010). Countering narratives: Teachers' discourses about immigrants and their experiences within the realm of children's and young adult literature. *English Teaching: Practice and Critique, 9*(3), 106–131.

Grande, E., Schwarzbözl, T., & Fatke, M. (2019): Politicizing immigration in Western Europe, *Journal of European Public Policy, 26*(10), 1444–1463.

Hays, A. (2017). *From fiction to fact to potential action: Generating prosocial attitudes and behaviors using young adult literature.* Available from ProQuest Dissertations & Theses Global (1897561879).

Herrera, S. (2012). Globalization: Current constraints and promising perspectives. *Journal of Curriculum and Instruction, 6*(1), 1–10

Hope, J. (2017). *Children's literature about refugees: A catalyst in the classroom.* Trentham.

Hwang, S., & Hindman, J. (2014). Strategies for adopting children's: Refugee literature in the multicultural classroom. *Journal of Arts & Humanities, 3*(12), 42–53.

Krusemark, R. (2015). The role of critical thinking in reader perceptions of leadership in comic books. *SANE Journal: Sequential Art Narrative in Education, 2*(1), 1–25.

Krusemark, R. (2017). Comic books in the American college classroom: A study of student critical thinking. *Journal of Graphic Novels and Comics, 8*(1), 59–78. https://doi.org/10.1080/21504857.2016.1233895

Luke, A. (2003). Literacy education for a new ethics of global community. *Language Arts, 81*(1), 20–22.

Mabry, M., & Bhavnagri, N. P. (2012). Perspective taking of immigrant children: Utilizing children's literature and related activities. *Multicultural Education, 19*(3), 48–54.

McCloud, S. (1993). *Understanding comics: The invisible art.* William Morrow.

Miranda, C. P. (2017). Checks, balances, and resistance: The impact of an anti-immigrant federal administration on a school for immigrant teenagers. *Anthropology & Education Quarterly, 48*(4), 376–385.

Mutz, D. (2018, April). *Mass media and American attitudes toward immigration.* Global Shifts Colloquium. https://global.upenn.edu/sites/default/files/Mutz.pdf

Newman, B. J., Shah, S., & Collingwood, L. (2018). Race, place, and building a base: Latino population growth and the nascent Trump campaign for president. *Public Opinion Quarterly, 82*(1), 122–134. https://doi.org/10.1093/poq/nfx039

Newstreet, C., Sarker, A., & Shearer, R. (2019). Teaching empathy: Exploring multiple perspectives to address Islamophobia through children's literature. *The Reading Teacher, 72*(5), 559–568.

Robinson, R. (2017). Implications for middle schools from adolescent brain research. *American Secondary Education, 45*(3), 29–37.

Rogers, J., Franke, M., Yun, J. E., Ishimoto, M., Diera, C., Geller, R., Berryman, A., & Brenes, T. (2017). *Teaching and learning in the age of Trump: Increasing stress and hostility in America's high schools.* UCLA's Institute for Democracy, Education, and Access.

Serafini, F. (2011). Expanding perspectives for comprehending visual images in multimodal texts. *Journal of Adolescent & Adult Literacy, 54*(5), 342–350.

Serafini, F. (2014). *Reading the visual: An introduction to teaching multimodal literacy.* Teachers College Press.

Sims Bishop, R. (1990). Mirrors, windows, and sliding glass doors. *Perspectives: Choosing and Using Books for the Classroom, 6*(3), ix–xi.

Smetana, L. (2010). Graphic novel gurus: Students with learning disabilities enjoying real literature. *The California Reader, 44*(1), 3–14.

Sun, L. (2017). Critical encounters in a middle school English language arts classroom: Using graphic novels to teach critical thinking & reading for peace education. *Multicultural Education, 25*(1), 22–28.

UNESCO, The World Bank, UNICEF. (2021). *Mission: Recovering education in 2021.* www.unicef.org/reports/mission-recovering-education-2021

United Nations High Commissioner for Refugees. (2019). *Stepping up: Refugee education in crisis.* www.unhcr.org/steppingup/

United Nations High Commissioner for Refugees. (2022). *What is a refugee?* www.unhcr.org/en-us/what-is-a-refugee.html

U.S. Department of State. (2019). *Refugee admissions.* Author. www.state.gov/refugee-admissions/

Book Club Resources

Binford, W., & Bochenek, M. (2021). *Hear my voice: Escucha mi voz: The testimonies of children detained at the southern border of the United States.* Workman Publishing Company.

Brown, D. (2021). *The unwanted: Stories of the Syrian refugees.* Clarion Books.

Colfer, E. (2018). *Illegal: A graphic novel.* Sourcebooks Young Readers.

Gratz, A. (2017). *Refugee.* Scholastic Press.

Jamieson, V., Mohamed, O., & Geddy, I. (2020). *When stars are scattered.* Dial Books for Young Readers.

LaMotte, L. (2020). *Measuring up.* HarperAlley.

Park, L. S. (2011). *A long walk to water.* Houghton Mifflin.

AFTERWORD
On Taboos and Teaching Them Anyway

Kimberly N. Parker

As I sit down to write the afterword of this powerful collection, I am grappling with the word "taboo," especially in the context of our current political moment. The world seems to be on fire, for lack of a more apt description. Legislation that portends the end to abortion and the implications of this move on reproductive justice access will be especially felt by Black and Brown folks. Families send their children to school uncertain if they will return, fearful of the possibilities of gun violence, while educators grapple with how to talk to their curious students about anything related to identity or socioemotional learning amidst fear of losing their jobs. I have to pinch myself to be sure I'm not living in some awful dystopian novel. I understand—completely, heartbreakingly, infuriatingly—that this is, indeed, our present reality.

Fortunately, *Teaching Challenged and Challenging Topics in Diverse and Inclusive Literature* offers us community, encouragement, and immediate suggestions for immediate action and resistance.

The authors have taken an expansive view of what taboo could mean. They have also made an important response and provided an urgent rationale about why we need to teach taboos of all kinds right now. I keep thinking that in any other time and place, perhaps these topics would not be taboo; instead, they would simply be ideas, pedagogical practices, stances, that are informed by equity and a commitment to "teach the truth" as the slogan from Rethinking Schools goes. The contents of *Teaching Challenged and Challenging Topics* would simply be an excellent handbook for educators, administrators, and community folks who seek research-based, informed practices that are grounded in a deep care and concern for children—*all* children. Certainly, this book is those things and now— given the mass exit of teachers from classrooms, of reports that decry "learning loss" from the ongoing pandemic, and of many of us who vacillate between feelings of hope and despair—*Teaching Challenged and Challenging Topics* is a beacon.

My Own Teaching of Taboos

Throughout my 20 years of teaching, I realize how I took up my own teaching of taboo topics. Much because I didn't know they *were* taboo. I am a Black woman from the rural American South, who grew up working class before moving to New England, where I have resided for over two decades. When I began teaching, I was driven by a desire to connect my mostly Black and Latinx young people to positive literacy experiences. Given that so many of them carried "reading trauma" (Stivers & Torres, 2020) and had been subject to other forms of "curriculum violence" (Jones, 2020), I had to first understand and accept their histories and work beside them to envision different literacy futures. What that decision required was to embrace and center all those topics and texts that have become considered taboo.

For young people, however—many of whom are just beginning to figure out their identities and possible selves—"inclusively diverse texts" (Turner, 2016) are *integral* for them. A regular refrain I'd hear soon after a school year began went: students had never read texts that were written by authors who shared their backgrounds. Or, they'd never read texts that were not centered in trauma or negativity that did feature a BIPOC (Black, Indigenous, or Person of Color) character. They couldn't quite fathom, even, that these texts existed. As most of my teaching was with sophomores, that meant they'd endured *years* of literacy instruction, reading (or not reading) hundreds of pages of texts that failed to center or acknowledge their experiences.

Teaching everything that was not mandated, then, was a taboo. However, if I wanted to be an effective practitioner, teaching taboo texts was essential, and that is what I did.

My Evolution

I wasn't always so willing to teach taboo texts. As I gained more experience from the daily work of interacting with honest students and colleagues, I was able to question and challenge the many ways I'd come to accept—often without question—taboo topics. I realized that if I wanted to work for liberation and anti-oppression, I had to confront those taboos within myself, too.

I was also confused about the ways taboos took on lives of their own and could limit students' access to texts. I have spent the majority of my career in city schools with Black and Latinx young people. As a novice teacher, I was guided by a strong desire to make sure my students had access to texts (which I narrowly defined by books one could hold in their hands) that represented and extended their interests.

My first principal was a white woman who insisted I teach "classics"; she was supportive of my other aims to create an inclusive literacy culture, but she also wanted me to include *To Kill a Mockingbird* (Lee, 1960) and Shakespeare plays and sonnets. I was a young teacher. I relented. I didn't have the language for countering her insistence with Ebarvia and Torres (2022), my #DisruptTexts co-founders rationale: "But every day in our classrooms, teachers and school leaders are also canon-makers. As those charged with helping to guide all of our students' literacy and literary lives, we can choose to perpetuate a narrow curriculum that limits the voices and experiences of others, or we can expand and deepen our students' experiences to include a more representative curation of literary voices" (p. 3). I was a complicit canon-maker, despite my best intentions otherwise because I hewed closely to what my principal wanted rather than what young people demanded.

In my heart, I knew what my students wanted and needed, but I also needed to keep my job. I aimed for compromise and the balance I struck between those two competing interests made for a tense two years. As a Black woman navigating a white supremacist charter public school space, those decisions and maneuvers were even more complex. That tension was especially marked when discussing my concerns with my white principal who was rooted in a deficit-framework about students. To her, it made sense to provide students all that they were "lacking," and canonical literature was her way to assure those goals were achieved.

All wasn't lost, though. During that time, I also sharpened my abilities to teach subversively. It was possible to teach those canonical requests through a critical literacy lens while also providing increased time for young people to read what they wanted from the classroom library I curated. There, in those less formal spaces and places, I realize now, so many taboo texts were housed. I listened to students' comments about characters in the required texts and went in search of themes that aligned (some better than others) with those comments but featured different genres, characters, and settings. Those selections were much more intentional and attuned to provide accurate representation and inclusive diversity for students.

Once I left that school, I joined school communities that were more aligned with disruption and questioning literacy practices, particularly ones that purport to be about "social justice." In the school where I spent my longest tenure, the district spent a seemingly extraordinary amount of time publicizing its commitment to equity yet fumbled, time and again, when asked about the persistent inaction about long-standing academic disparities between Black, Latinx and white students. I listened to high-achieving Black students tell me how often they had been overlooked or not recommended for Honors or AP classes by their white teachers, and I've written about my direct response to those students and systems (Parker, 2017).

Centering literature and literacy practices that were inclusively diverse, and giving students choices and time to read those texts, was life-changing for all of us. As my teaching repertoire became more culturally responsive as

I responded to my students, I was able to better challenge taboos and beliefs that threatened to silence student voices. Again, I had a white administrator who wanted literacy teaching that aligned to her outdated beliefs of what reading should be: all teacher-directed and little, if any, student input. At that point in my career, though, I had a better response: I had research that supported my decisions, students who were willing to speak up about their own reading development, and test scores that supported my work (because, unfortunately, test scores matter too much, especially when we are talking about BIPOC children).

Students regularly recalled and wrote about texts that resonated with them. Those texts included popular young adult writers Walter Dean Myers, Matt de la Pena, Jacqueline Woodson, Renee Watson, Sharon Flake, and Jason Reynolds and urban literature writers including Eric Jerome Dickey, Omar Tyree, and Donald Goines. Annually, the books written by these authors were ones that I had to replace because students kept them. Any of these writers can be considered taboo: from the content within them (gender and sexuality; violence; self-harm) to the genre ("urban" or "street lit") or even language (i.e., African American Vernacular English usage or profanity). If I had allowed my own hesitancies about these books or their content, or my administrators', I would have prevented young people from opportunities to have positive reading moments. Also, these books that were considered taboo or problematic limited opportunities to confront a range of literary discussions that those texts invited. Because students were invested in the texts, they were much more willing and able to begin and sustain discussions about race, racism, misogyny, linguistic justice, and others.

It can be easy—too easy—to make decisions for young people that we think are in their best interests but are actually about our own discomfort (or even perceived discomfort). We might worry about what parents will say, or what an administrator will document, or what our colleagues will question about our practices. I have had many of those same concerns throughout the years, and have even caved to the demands of systems rather than listening to what my students required and to what, internally, I knew was the right, equitable response. I can understand, even today, how hard it is to decide to take up the taboo conversations, to stock our classroom libraries with taboo texts, and to actively teach the topics these texts introduce. Yet, we must *still* teach these texts and these topics. We must. Especially now.

Teach the Taboo Anyway

I have moved from the daily work of the classroom to one of an administrator of a college access program. I still teach, but now mostly in the summer, mostly high school seniors, and mostly writing. Taboos remain, though. Now, as I work with seniors to craft their personal statements, the taboos are about personal trauma and what kinds of narratives they want to write, how they want to present themselves on paper. Young people are more than their trauma, we all know; but they live in the world, too, and want to gain admission to a college of their choice. They have internalized struggle stories and think that is what college admissions officers want to hear. Is it taboo, they wonder, to tell a different story? One that is also true for them but might not be the one that the person reading the essay might be expecting? The process of reconnecting with their writing voices is similar to the process of reconnecting with texts. It requires acknowledgment of our own biases about these perceived taboos (here, taboos about race, narratives, writing, and college admissions) and then centering the young person who wants to tell a different, true story. This process takes much longer, certainly, but at its conclusion, the writer has remained true to what they want to say and has said it in a way that is satisfactory for them.

If young people can confront taboo topics, then surely we adults can, too. As the fervor against any topic that challenges white people's discomfort intensifies, the educators who believe in equity, antiracism, and liberatory literacy access and practices must intensify our resistance. I know, too, that it can feel impossible at times, especially when current events make it feel like the world is ending nearly every day. I am heartened by a few reminders: first, we are not in this struggle alone. My group texts with other literacy organizers provides a regular source for voicing frustration, small victories, and collective processing. This moment encourages all of us to look around (both physically and virtually) to find and join individuals and groups who are doing similar work. May we also remember the children and young people who are there and mobilizing, too.

We also have educators who have documented their resistance and success teaching taboos. You hold that proof in your hands. As I read and re-read this powerful collection of educator voices that offer us a way forward, I know that there are more of us working toward equity and justice for and with children and young people than detractors might think. I will hold on to the culturally sustaining practices contained in *Teaching Challenged and Challenging Topics* because they are practices that enable us to weather these current storms and provide the respite and encouragement to keep going. And keep going we must.

References

Ebarvia, T., & Torres, J. (2022). *What is a classic? An educators' guide*. Penguin Random House. https://penguinrandomhousesecondaryeducation.com/wpcontent/uploads/2022/05/4879_Classics-Guide_Intro-brochure_04122-2.pdf

Jones, S. P. (2020, Spring). Ending curriculum violence. *Learning for Justice*. www.learningforjustice.org/magazine/spring-2020/ending-curriculum-violence

Parker, K. N. (2017). Reaching the brilliant and the bored: Centering the literacy lives of people of color in our classrooms. *Heinemann*. www.heinemann.com/pd/journal/2017/parker_reaching_brillian and_bored.pdf

Stivers, J., & Torres, J. (2020, June 24). Ridding schools of reading trauma. *American Libraries.* https://americanlibrariesmagazine.org/blogs/the-scoop/116407/

Turner, J. (2016). Tales and testimonies: Viewpoints on diverse literature from Duncan Tonatiuh and Violet J. Harris. *Language Arts, 94*(2), 124–129.

Literature Cited

Lee, H. (1960). *To kill a mockingbird.* JB Lippincott & Company.

CONTRIBUTOR BIOGRAPHIES

Foreword

Stergios Botzakis is Professor of Adolescent Literacy at The University of Tennessee.

Chapter 1: *Un Maravilloso*, Dual-Language Read Aloud: Making Families Visible Through Testimony in the Primary Classroom

Beth A. Buchholz is Associate Professor in the Reading Education and Special Education Department at Appalachian State University.

Jean Carlos Garcia Reyes earned his MA in Reading Education from Appalachian State University and is a second-grade teacher at the Appalachian State University Academy at Middle Fork in Walkertown, NC.

Chapter 2: What Makes You Unique?: Valuing Classroom Diversity Within Writing Instruction

Kate Bentley is a doctoral student at the University of Tennessee.

Amy Broemmel is Associate Professor of Elementary and Literacy Education at the University of Tennessee.

M. Chris Douglass is an elementary school teacher pursuing his doctorate at the University of Tennessee.

Chapter 3: Sliding the Glass Door: Making Time and Space for Difficult Conversations With Youth Through Multivoiced Young Adult Literature

Heather Waymouth is Assistant Professor of Literacy at West Chester University of PA.

Keith Newvine is Assistant Professor of Literacy at the State University of New York College at Cortland (SUNY Cortland).

Sarah Fleming is Visiting Assistant Professor at the State University of New York at Oswego (SUNY Oswego).

Pamela Margolis is a doctoral student at West Chester University of PA.

Sarah Mellon is a graduate student at the State University of New York College at Cortland (SUNY Cortland).

Tina Middaugh is a high school teacher at West Genesee High School in West Genesee Central School District.

Chapter 4: Exploring Gender Identity and Equity Through *Lily and Dunkin*

Jennifer S. Dail is Professor of English Education at Kennesaw State University.

Julie M. Koch is Professor of Counseling Psychology at the University of Iowa.

Shelbie Witte is the Kim and Chuck Watson Chair in Education and Professor of Adolescent Literacy and English Education at Oklahoma State University.

Lauren Vandever is an ELA teacher in Bristow, Oklahoma.

Chapter 5: Remixing for Relevance: Talking Gentrification in Pride

Brooke Bianchi-Pennington is a high school ELA teacher at Hardin Valley Academy.

Arianna Banack is Visiting Professor of English Education at Purdue University.

Chapter 6: Layering Discourse: Encouraging Diverse Perspectives in a High School Literature Class

Renee Stites Kruep is Assistant Teaching Professor at the University of Missouri.

Lauren Popov is a high school English teacher in Illinois.

Chapter 7: Curating Socially Just Classroom Libraries for Middle Grade Readers

Kristie W. Smith is Assistant Professor, Middle Level ELA, at Kennesaw State University.

Erica Adela Warren is a doctoral candidate at Mercer University and an instructional coach in Henry County Public Schools.

Chapter 8: "I Don't Understand, I Don't Speak Spanish": Exploring Linguistic and Cultural Differences Through Picture Books

Julia López-Robertson is Professor of Instruction and Teacher Education at the University of South Carolina.

Maria del Rocio Herron is a pre-Kindergarten teacher at Palmetto Elementary School in Columbia, South Carolina.

Chapter 9: Combating Ableism With Classroom Literature

Emily Poynter recently obtained an MEd in Literacy from Clemson University and is a kindergarten educator for the Greenville County School District in Greenville, SC.

Rachelle S. Savitz is an Associate Professor of Reading/Literacy at East Carolina University.

Chapter 10: Engaging Dynamic Discussions Through Storytelling

K. N. is the Curriculum and Instruction Coordinator in Minneapolis, MN.

H. S. is an assistant principal in Minneapolis, MN.

Amanda Carter is Associate Professor of Elementary Literacy at Nevada State College.

Nayelee Villanueva is Associate Professor of English at the College of Southern Nevada.

Chapter 11: Cultivating Students' Civic Agency Through Participation in a Social Justice-Themed Book Club as a Subversive Approach to Critical Literacy in Education

Elizabeth E. Schucker is a graduate of Kutztown University of Pennsylvania's Transformational Teaching and Learning Education Doctoral program, a K–12

Gifted Teacher and Coordinator for the Schuylkill Valley School District, and an adjunct professor with Kutztown University's Department of Elementary, Middle Level, Library and Technologies Education.

Chapter 12: Scattering Stars: Graphic Novel Book Studies With Middle Grades Students to Explore Refugee Stories

Rebecca Harper is Program Director and Associate Professor in the Department of Advanced Studies and Education at Augusta University.

Alicia Stephenson is a teacher at Hahira Middle School.

Afterword

Kimberly N. Parker is the Director of the Crimson Summer Academy at Harvard University.

ABOUT THE AUTHORS

Dr. Jennifer S. Dail is a professor of English education and site director of the Kennesaw Mountain Writing Project at Kennesaw State University, GA.

Dr. Julie M. Koch is Head of the School of Community Health Sciences, Counseling, and Counseling Psychology and Professor of Counseling and Counseling Psychology at Oklahoma State University, OK.

Dr. Shelbie Witte is the Chuck and Kim Watson Endowed Chair in Adolescent Literacy at Oklahoma State University.

Lauren Vandever is a middle school reading teacher in Bristow, Oklahoma, where she was a finalist for the 2022 Oklahoma Teacher of the Year.

INDEX

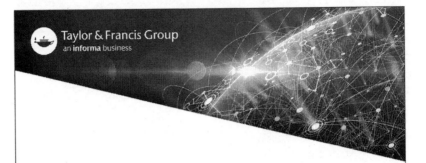